YALE PUBLICATIONS IN RELIGION, 6

David Horne, editor

PUBLISHED UNDER THE DIRECTION OF

THE DIVINITY SCHOOL

LUTHER'S VIEW OF CHURCH HISTORY

By JOHN M. HEADLEY

New Haven and London, Yale University Press, 1963

Designed by Crimilda Pontes,
set in Aldine Bembo type,
and printed in the United States of America by
The Carl Purington Rollins Printing-Office
of the Yale University Press.

Library of Congress catalog card number: 63-7935

Published with assistance from the foundation established
in memory of William McKean Brown.

IN MEMORY OF
MY FATHER AND MOTHER

PREFACE

THE REFORMATION of the Church in the sixteenth century produced a significant readjustment within the traditional medieval, Augustinian view of history. Both the new concept of the Church as the community of believers and the sense of being in the immediate presence and under the direct control of God contributed to the need for a refashioning and a new understanding of the Christian past. Although Martin Luther was not a historian, he was constantly concerned with the past of the Church. As theologian and reformer he found it necessary to understand and to defend the evangelical Church and its previous existence since the Creation. Throughout his life he continued to pass judgment on aspects of the Church's history and to use his historical knowledge as an additional weapon against the Papacy. His writings provide a rich matrix of judgments on the past, historical facts and statements of the nature and major themes of history. The present study attempts to reveal within the total thought of Martin Luther a definite, if implicit, view of Church history.

As a general field of research, Luther's understanding of history has not remained unexplored. Luther's theology of history has been examined,[1] his use of sources and historical judgment analyzed,[2]

1. Hanns Lilje, *Luthers Geschichtsanschauung* (Berlin, 1932).

2. Walther Koehler, *Luther und die Kirchengeschichte nach seinen Schriften, zunächst bis 1521* (Erlangen, 1900).

his factual knowledge of Church history assessed.[3] A varied periodical literature has treated numerous, specific aspects of the problem. Yet the attempt to see the past of the Church as Luther saw it requires a fresh approach to the sources. It demands that Luther's entire knowledge of the Church—its place in the Creation, its past, and the crisis of the Reformation—be seen consistently and comprehensively from his own angle of vision. And since that angle is determined by his theology, history becomes the work of God and must be treated accordingly. Beyond the obvious necessity for the theological basis to this endeavor lie the problems peculiar to Church history itself. The Church in its relation to the world and above all to tradition are integral parts to such a study. Finally, Luther's own experience as a reformer and the context of the sixteenth century work to shape his view of Church history.

Concerning the organization of this study, only the first chapter requires some explanation. To understand Luther's view of Church history, one must first recognize the all-effecting action of God in history, His concealment in the orders of the Creation, and the abiding presence of Christ in time. The point at issue is not the necessity for a theological basis to such a study, it is rather that a statement of Luther's doctrine of God properly precedes his seminal idea of justification. With his peculiar ability to see all events from God's point of view, Luther would not admit the priority of man, least of all himself, in his view of Church history.

As for the problem of interpreting the material, any methodology must take into account the historical development of Luther's thought. In this respect some previous studies have tended to treat the material en bloc and to place an inordinate emphasis upon the early lectures on the Psalms.[4] At this time, however, Luther had not developed his concept of the Church, nor had he broken with Rome and come to his final awareness of himself as a reformer.

3. Ernst Schäfer, *Luther als Kirchenhistoriker* (Gütersloh, 1897).

4. Cf. particularly Erich Seeberg, *Gottfried Arnold: Die Wissenschaft und die Mystik seiner Zeit* (Meerane i Sa., 1923), pp. 431–40.

Two other facts accentuate the danger of basing an interpretation upon the earlier material: first, recent Luther scholarship inclines toward locating in 1518 rather than 1513 the moment of Luther's arrival at an evangelical conception of justification;[5] secondly, his hermeneutics[6] and the distinction between law and gospel[7] are not fully established until his controversy with the Enthusiasts in 1525. A number of factors suggest a date later than 1513 as the turning point in Luther's thought.

These considerations determine the methodology in this study. The works of Luther that have been consulted cover the entire career of the reformer and have not been limited to any one period in his life. They constitute his correspondence, his more important tracts, and especially his exegetical works. Yet in the exposition of Luther's principles of Church history, the material from the early period has not been allowed to have a decisive influence. Furthermore, any historical statement or judgment made in the early period, at least prior to 1518, has been checked against its counterpart in the later period in order to show a change, development, or consistency in a particular position. Therefore, while this investigation takes into account the earlier period, the main emphasis rests on the Luther who has broken with Rome, recognized the threat of the Enthusiasts, and established his mature theology.

Two points need to be made with regard to language. First, the translations from Luther are my own. Second, I have consciously avoided cluttering the text with foreign words and phrases. Only when the meaning has been previously established, or when the

5. Uuras Saarnivaara, *Luther Discovers the Gospel* (St. Louis, 1951); Ernst Bizer, *Fides ex Auditu* (Neukirchen, 1958). Cf. also F. Edward Cranz, *An Essay on the Development of Luther's Thought on Justice, Law, and Society*, Harvard Theological Studies, 19 (Cambridge, Mass., 1959).

6. Gerhard Ebeling, *Evangelische Evangelienauslegung: Eine Untersuchung zu Luthers Hermeneutik* (München, 1942), pp. 87, 348–57.

7. Hayo Gerdes, *Luthers Streit mit den Schwärmern um das rechte Verständnis des Gesetzen Mose* (Göttingen, 1955), pp. 105–06.

sense of the passage benefits from the original, has a Latin or German word been allowed. In the case of such a word as *Regiment* or its plural *Regimente,* the German has been retained, for any devised English equivalent would prove misleading.

"We are like dwarfs on the shoulders of giants." Thus Bernard of Chartres attempted to express the relation of later centuries and of his own age to Greek and Roman origins. The image, which combines a profound sense of indebtedness with the attribute of superior vision, can be applied to the realm of scholarly endeavor, and I appeal to it to express a sincere recognition of my own indebtedness to preceding scholars and teachers. I have tried to give adequate credit to those from whom I have liberally drawn as is evident in the footnotes, but to my adviser and teacher, Roland H. Bainton, I wish to acknowledge a special debt of gratitude for several years of acquaintance, instruction, and aid. In him I found one whose cheerful interest in the reading of the manuscript was only surpassed by the explicitness of his criticism. I have appreciated the support which he has given the work in the many stages through which it has passed.

This study was first presented as a doctoral dissertation in the Department of History, Yale University. Its completion was aided by the grant of a Junior Sterling Fellowship. In this respect, I would like to acknowledge the aid given and interest shown by my readers, F. L. Baumer, E. R. Goodenough, and Hajo Holborn. I also wish to thank the following persons for having read the manuscript in part or in its entirety: Theodore Tappert, George Lindbeck, Jaroslav Pelikan, E. Harris Harbison, Raymond Morris, William Dietel, and Anne Renouf. I am particularly obligated to Schafer Williams for his criticism of certain aspects of the work. And to my friend, Philip Kintner of Trinity College, I owe more than to any other individual for his unstinting efforts in criticizing the manuscript at all stages of its development and for providing invaluable suggestions.

Finally, I welcome the opportunity to express my lasting indebtedness to my former teachers, George F. Thomas and the late T. E. Mommsen, without whose initial direction and stimulation this study would never have been attempted.

J. M. H.

New Haven, Conn.
August 1962

CONTENTS

ABBREVIATIONS

UNLESS OTHERWISE STATED, all references in the text pertain to the tracts and exegetical works of Luther in the Weimar edition (*WA*). For the title and date of composition of each work refer to the register of Luther's works cited in this volume. The first number of any reference indicates the volume and the second number the page. In some special instances, a third number is supplied to designate the line. A slash (/) following a volume number refers to a distinct volume in the edition.

The same system applies to Luther's correspondence (*WBr*) and the German Bible (*WAB*). In the case of the Table Talk (*TR*), the reference is to the number of the item and not the page.

The author's quotations and references to the Bible are from the King James Version.

EDITIONS OF LUTHER'S WORKS

WA *D. Martin Luthers Werke* (Weimar, 1883–)
WAB *Die Deutsche Bibel* (Weimar, 1906–)
WBr *Briefwechsel* (Weimar, 1930–48)
TR *Tischreden* (Weimar, 1912–21)
EA *Dr. Martin Luthers sämmtliche Werke* (Erlangen, 1828–70)
EOL *D. Martini Lutheri Exegetica Opera Latina* (Erlangen, 1829–84)
OVA *D. Martini Lutheri Opera Latina Varii Argumenti* (Erlangen, 1843–72)

OTHER COLLECTIONS

CR *Corpus Reformatorum*, ed. Carolus Gottlieb Bretschneider (Halis Saxonum 1834–60)

MPL Migne, *Patrologiae Cursus Completus, Series Latina* (Paris 1844–1903)

ST *Summa Theologia*, in *Sancti Thomae Aquinatis Opera Omnia* (New York, 1948–50)

PERIODICALS AND GENERAL REFERENCE WORKS

ARG *Archiv für Reformationsgeschichte*

DCT *Dictionnaire de Théologie Catholique*

RE^3 *Realenzyklopädie für protestantische Kirche und Theologie* (in dritter verbesserter und vermehrter Auflage)

RHPR *Revue d'histoire et de philosophie réligieuses*

RSR *Revue de science réligieuse*

ZKG *Zeitschrift für Kirchengeschichte*

ZTK *Zeitschrift für Theologie und Kirche*

1. THE DEFINING OF CHURCH HISTORY

AT ONE MOMENT in the ever-intensifying struggle with Rome, the young reformer Martin Luther reflected upon the forces working in the medieval Church:

> God alone is in this business; we are seized so that I see we are acted upon rather than act. [*WBr* 2:39]

Twenty years later, Luther could look back upon the beginning of that stormy passage which had seen the shattering of Latin Christendom and the re-emergence of Scripture and could assert that everything had happened by divine counsel (*TR* 3944). These two statements, which embrace the core of the great reformer's career, stand together in presenting a single and most fundamental concept in his understanding of history: what takes place in time and what one experiences stem from the activity of God, and in some way man is but the instrument for God's constant and all-embracing activity. In short, history is the work of God.

With his conviction that God is the ground of historical causation, Luther stands within the tradition of Paul and Augustine; only God could be at the root of all temporal events. At the same time the theocentric position separates him from modern historical understanding. This difference is not limited to the problem of causation but appears in its two immediate implications: that every action derived from God gives unity and meaning to history, and, secondly, because man is the instrument of God one is denied the luxury of being a spectator. Man is constantly being acted upon and serves as a cooperator in this action. This unbroken activity of God pushes man into an unbroken cooperation in history. In such a situation there can be no dead history and no flight from history.[1]

In the implications arising from the apparently simple statement of faith that it is God who acts and man who is acted upon, an entire world of historical relations emerges—historical not because they show any chain of causes and events or any development immanent in the human process but because they indicate the way in which God acts in time, how He controls and rules men, and how He reveals to them His purpose.

God and History

In *The Bondage of the Will,* God appears as that Being of supreme majesty and all-embracing powers who is active and working in everything. What man thinks is done contingently is actually done immutably and necessarily according to the will of God, who knows what He wills and wills what He knows (18:615–16). Luther does not hesitate to apply the universal effecting, acting, and working of God to evil. Through His general omnipotence by which He moves and drives everything along, God necessarily moves Satan and the impious. Although He Himself is unable to do evil, He operates in and through evil. If He should stop moving and acting, He would cease to be God and to do good (18:709, 712). This universal activity and omnipotence present one of the central features of Luther's concept of God. It stands in conscious and significant contrast to the inaction of the Aristotelian god (18:706).

1. Hanns Lilje, *Luthers Geschichtsanschauung* (Berlin, 1932), pp. 41–44, 80.

Within the unity of God, Luther makes an important distinction in His nature and activity, which has far-reaching implications for God's treatment of man. There is a revealed or preached God who works for the salvation of sinners; and then there is another God, hidden in majesty, who neither deplores nor removes death but works life, death, and all in all. This God does not define Himself by His word but reserves His will to Himself. The distinction between the preached God and the hidden God is one between the Word of God and God Himself. Although God does and wills a great deal that is not shown to man in the Word, man can only direct himself according to the Word and not according to God's inscrutable will (18:685).

Luther's unwillingness to limit in any essential respect the omnipotence of God leads to the problem of the Creation and the related idea of the absolute and the ordained power of God. His use of these nominalist categories refers not to the distinction between the hidden and the revealed God but rather to the way in which God acts with men. For God with His creation calls man into an historical and not merely a natural existence. If God were to reveal Himself in His majesty and to treat man in this fashion, historical existence would lack all sense of reality; God's direct activity in history would cut the nerve of man and vitiate his significance. Luther says that God does not want to move all things according to His extraordinary or absolute power but through His ordained power, which involves the ministry of angels and of men (43:71). This ordained power includes the Incarnate Son (43:79); it is the Word understood as being the instrument of Creation whereby the various orders and estates are brought into being (17/2:316–17; 31/1:195–96). While God normally chooses to treat man through His ordained power, He can change the law in the case of a special man or hero (43:643). Had He wanted to, He could have saved the human race without Christ, the Word, or baptism (44:95). In these estates and orders that represent the ordained power, God conceals Himself.

Thus by a voluntary self-concealment God preserves His own omnipotence on the one hand and the reality of historical existence on the other. Second only to the recognition of the sole effectiveness of God in history is the idea of the divine concealment for the understanding of history. History involves a self-concealment on God's part. Because His self-concealment is apparent in the ordering of the Creation, the understanding of history ultimately rests upon a faith in this Creation.[2]

With his doctrine of the *Regimente,* Luther represents the nature of Creation and God's action in its orders. That the worldly *Regiment* and the spiritual *Regiment* are both orders of Creation is decisive in determining their constitution and meaning. They are neither metaphysical abstractions nor sociological entities. Although they attain institutional form, the Regimente cannot be identified with institutions. Rather they constitute the two means by which God rules the world. For man they represent the two different ways in which he encounters the divine reality. What Luther wishes to express with the two ideas of *politia* and *religio* are not two mutually exclusive areas of life but the twofold activity of God in the world. In this total conception of the Creation, the separation is not between two different forms of order or between two different conditions within each order but between the orders themselves and God, between creature and Creator. The religious aspect embraces all of reality.[3]

The idea of Creation holds the two Regimente together and permits them to be seen on a religious basis of equal worth. But the most important principle is the separation of the two as they bear upon men.[4] The Regimente are distinguished not as if they were institutions with different functions, but by their differing in structure, means, and ends. The worldly Regiment is a divine order ruled by

2. Ibid., pp. 46–57.

3. Gustaf Törnvall, *Geistliches und weltliches Regiment bei Luther* (München, 1947), pp. 119–28.

4. Ibid., pp. 69–70.

law and reason with its power stretching visibly over the entire world. The spiritual Regiment is ruled by the gospel and cannot be limited to a certain sphere but stretches over the totality of all orders and estates as the direct expression of God the Creator. Here God in His own Regiment works through the preaching office and reminds all the established orders of their appointment by and subjection to the Word. Although it penetrates every aspect of the visible world, this Regiment is invisible—to be heard, not seen. Unlike the worldly Regiment, it extends upward in unbroken continuity toward the invisible Kingdom of God.[5]

While the spiritual Regiment directs men vertically to God that they might be saved and do right, the worldly Regiment as a human realm represses evil and conducts people among themselves so that body, property, wife, and children remain secure. God has made the worldly Regiment subject to reason and law because it has nothing to do with the salvation of souls; therefore, the wisdom of Greek and Roman poets, historians, and jurists can and should be used in promoting order and security. God wants this Regiment to be a symbol of true blessedness and a mask of the heavenly kingdom (51:241–42). On the other hand, the very real presence of Satan makes the Regiment necessary for repressing sin and for restraining the evil tendencies of men. To the wicked and the unbeliever the use of the sword, the hangman, and the jailer makes the worldly Regiment appear a veritable hell. But these requirements should not mislead one to identify this Regiment with the Kingdom of the Devil.[6]

Although the worldly Regiment is a product of the Fall, corrupted by sin, and subsequent to the spiritual Regiment, both are created and ordained by God as His means for acting upon men. Because both have been ordained by God, they remain expressions of divine

5. Ibid., 78–9, 84–6. Cf. *WA* 51:11.

6. *WA* 10/3:175. Cf. Harold Diem, *Luthers Lehre von den zwei Reichen* (München, 1938), pp. 107–08.

good that bear equally upon the total life of man. It is significant that the worldly Regiment is not subordinate to the spiritual, for it has all the blessings of this life to maintain. Yet the spiritual Regiment does enjoy a definite pre-eminence, not simply because of its structure and end but because it is God's own Regiment, in which Christ himself rules.[7] The spiritual and the worldly Regiment stand to each other as the right and left hand of God. They are separated because two different aspects of God's activity occur in them, but they are not opposed to each other. Finally, Luther insists that the Regimente must ever remain separate and distinct; the realm of human reason must be separated as far as possible from the spiritual realm. Consequently the Devil acts on both sides to brew and cook the two together (40/1:293; 51:239).

That Luther should have conceived of God's relation to man in terms of the Regimente is decisive for understanding the roles of each and their relationship. The Regimente make impossible any mystical or spiritualistic flight from the responsibilities of historical existence; within them man lives, led and guided by the leading and guiding activity of God. Man's role in the worldly Regiment is signified by the term *cooperator Dei*. Luther understands by this term not that man shares with God an equal power for action but that man is the instrument of God and responds to His agency (4:61). The point of juncture for the concealed action of God and for the response of man as His instrument lies in the idea of the *larva Dei,* signifying a mask or a veil and at the same time a spiritual presence. In the world that God has created, all creatures and ordinances are designed to be masks of God's presence, but because in this life man cannot encounter God face to face, the mask can never be removed. The Creator is hidden behind the creature as his *larva* or *persona*. Estrangement from God or perversion by the Devil turns the mask into a spiritual presence, so that the *larva* becomes a haunted mask. Only an angry God can be known

7. Törnvall, pp. 69–80. Cf. *WA* 51:258.

behind this twisted mask, and only God's strange work of punishment and wrath can be encountered here.[8]

In the worldly Regiment, God has established the magistrate, the emperor, the king, the prince, the consul, the doctor, the teacher, the student, the mother, the father, the child, and the servant as *personae* or *larvae*. Through these official persons God rules. Although God Himself is no respecter of persons, man must respect them or there will be an end to all order (40/1:174–76). In the spiritual Regiment, where there is but one official person, namely the preacher, the God behind the mask looms even more prominently, so that it can truly be said that here Christ alone works. In His own realm God does not ordain father, emperor, or jailer, but He Himself is the one by whom the gospel is preached to the poor (52:26). This closer identification of God's action with the office needs to be noted. For a preacher may be unbelieving and wicked, yet by his office and as an official person he brings one to faith through Word and sacraments. The office is right and good since it belongs to God, and as in the worldly so in the spiritual Regiment God strives to make His office productive (32:528–30).

The distinction between one's Christian and one's official person does not refer to the actual nature of man, which Luther understands in terms of the Pauline threefold division of body, soul, and spirit (7:550–51). He intends not a division inside of man but one which lies over man and serves to organize his life. The problem is that of man's existence in response to the double activity of God as it is evinced in the Regimente.[9] Each man on earth has two persons—a Christian and a secular person: with the first person he lives free from the obligations of this world and bound to none but God; with his other person he enters into a number of relationships and obligations to his neighbor (32:440). In his Christian *persona* he stands in a realm where God respects no man's person but all are equal before Him. Here through faith he becomes so closely joined

8. T. F. Torrance, *Kingdom and Church* (Fair Lawn, N.J., 1956), pp. 34–35.
9. Törnvall, p. 172.

to Christ that both are as one person, Christ assuming man's sin and man His nature (40/1:285; 12:488). But this exchange of persons does not exhaust the religious relationship; in his secular person man is also related to God. Through the office he becomes an instrument of God, and through the proper exercise of this office in vocation he translates the life of faith derived from the spiritual Regiment into an ethic of love, which works through the various offices and orders of the worldly Regiment.[10]

In his doctrine of vocation, Luther provides the link between the two Regimente and reveals the ground for God's action upon man in history. Vocation is the right care for office, and in the exercise of vocation man becomes a mask of God. In his secular person man is called to a number of offices at the same time; he may be a magistrate, merchant, father, and husband all at once. Each office presents the possibility of a channel of God's love to man. For just as faith constitutes the proper relation of the Christian person to God, so good works and love exercised in vocation define a man's relation to his neighbor. Vocation is ordained not for the person who fulfills the vocation but for the neighbor, and it is here amidst one's neighbors that the *cooperatio* occurs.[11] Yet Luther recognizes that Christians are few and vocation is often not exercised in accordance with faith. The Devil works to pervert vocation and in the consequent struggle between God and the Devil, love born of faith appears as the changeable element in vocation. On the other hand, the divinely ordained offices represent the unchanging element in vocation and act as a barrier against sinful man.[12]

The active presence of the Devil brings these orders of Creation into historical focus within an entirely different set of categories. It has been justly observed that if God directed His action toward a world whose inhabitants were merely ignorant of Him, rather than

10. Gustaf Wingren, *Luther on Vocation,* trans. Carl C. Rasmussen (Philadelphia, 1957), pp. 46–47.

11. Ibid., pp. 11, 29.

12. Ibid., pp. 99–100.

hostile to Him, the divine action would not have the character of government. The existence of the Devil makes impossible a gentle intellectual enlightenment on God's part.[13] God rules man with a left hand and a right hand, through worldly Regiment and spiritual Regiment, law and gospel. But the Devil enters to pervert this order by confusing the distinctions between the Regimente and by violating vocation through a misuse of the proper offices. In the struggle between God and the Devil for the maintaining of the Creation and for the redemption of man, the offices are on God's side, but the persons occupying them can belong to either God or the Devil. According to a man's belief he is related either to God or to the Devil; either God or the Devil rides the will.[14]

The conflict between God and the Devil for man now penetrates to a higher level. In *The Bondage of the Will,* Luther makes a clear statement of one of his basic tenets. On earth, he states, there exist two kingdoms in violent struggle. In the first reigns the Devil as god of this unredeemed age or world. He holds all captive to his will unless released by the spirit of Christ. In the other kingdom rules Christ, who struggles with the Kingdom of the Devil. We are transferred into His kingdom not by our own power but by the grace of God, by which we are liberated from the present age (18:782). These two kingdoms are quite distinct from the two Regimente: the latter refer to the way in which God rules His Creation and acts upon men; the former pertain to the purpose and ends of the divine activity. From the human point of view, however, the two sets of ideas appear to be related: man must live in both Regimente during his earthly life, but according to his affection he belongs to only one kingdom. Luther's understanding of the two kingdoms, therefore, includes his idea of the two Regimente. Both Regimente are to be seen in the perspective of the opposition between good and evil, the pious and the impious; both Regimente transform themselves either by disobedience or presumption into

13. Ibid., p. 79.
14. Ibid., pp. 85; 105–15.

the Kingdom of the Devil.[15] The Kingdom of Christ and the Kingdom of the Devil overarch the two Regimente, and in their struggle they comprise both Regimente, each of which can be transformed into either kingdom.

In order to understand this struggle between the two kingdoms wherein history culminates, it is necessary to recognize first God's control of all historical action and secondly the different way He works in each Regiment of His Creation. Concerning the former, Luther insists upon God's direction of all activity and His lordship of history. Perhaps nothing demonstrates so clearly this divine lordship as Luther's concept of the right time. The idea of the opportune moment (*tempus, occasio, Stündlin*) derives from the *κâιρος* of the New Testament. Luther explains that all human works and endeavors have a certain and definite time of accomplishment which lies beyond human election. God determines when and how an act will occur, and unless the time, the God-fulfilled moment, is present, man effects nothing. Luther specifically rejects any apparently fortuitous circumstance which the philosophers would ascribe to Fate or Fortune. Our works all have their appointed time (20:58–64). The fact that nothing succeeds through its own strength but all must await God's choice of the right moment reinforces Luther's doctrine that one must remain within his vocation, pursuing what is immediately before him and not seeking to accomplish something unusual (20:163). Together with His special times, God also has His special men, the heroes, who will be considered later.[16]

The activity by which God works in His Creation reveals the basic underlying unity of history as well as its diversity. Luther maintains that whether God works in His own realm (*regnum*) or outside it, the manner of His working and the relationship are the same. God does not work in us without us, whether it is done beyond His own realm by His general omnipotence or by the

15. Törnvall, pp. 189, 192.
16. Cf. Wingren, *Luther on Vocation*, pp. 213–28.

special virtue of His Spirit within His own realm (18:754). God's acting in man provides the essential unity. Here Luther's original statement best conveys the idea: *Creatura Deo operanti cooperatur* (18:753:21). Beyond this human cooperation with God's effective activity, there emerges a formidable and significant difference as this activity relates to the two Regimente. For God to work in His own realm by the power of His Spirit and outside this realm by a general omnipotence suggests a distinction between world history and redemptive history. Furthermore, by making this distinction, Luther appears to place the two Regimente in the historical perspective of the divine action.

World history, or that which God works by His general omnipotence, reveals itself as the divine game or masquerade. Here God is ever active in the constant rise and fall of rulers, nations, and kingdoms. Yet if God controls this game and destroys those who are disobedient and presumptuous, He does not act without man. That one ruler should be victorious and supplant another does not mean that he is necessarily right but rather that he is the instrument for the hidden activity of God; world history is not the court of the world.[17] Behind the apparent purposelessness of this external turmoil, God works in a concealed way through His masks to effect judgment on the rebellious and to manifest His power to the faithful.

God's work in the spiritual Regiment is of a different order and requires a consideration of the hidden God from another perspective. In 1525 Luther clearly indicated that within the unity of God there existed a hiddenness behind His revelation. But earlier in the first elaboration of his new theology of the Cross at the Heidelberg disputation he had set forth the paradox of a hiddenness in revelation whereby the hidden God was the revealed God, and only in concealment could there be revelation.

Heidelberg theses nineteen and twenty state that the true theologian seeks to understand God not by speculating on His invisible nature but rather through the Cross and suffering he considers the

17. Heinrich Bornkamm, *Luthers geistige Welt* (Lüneburg, 1947), p. 203.

visible yet back parts of God (*posteriora Dei*) (1:354). While thus asserting a theology of revelation, Luther adds that what is visible of God is, as it were, His back, which includes humanity, infirmity, and foolishness. In short, God reveals Himself in the concealed fashion of the ignominy and abasement of the Cross. The enigma of the Cross indicates on the one hand that for man there is no direct knowledge of God and on the other that God conceals Himself for the sake of His revelation; He wants only to become recognized in the abasement and ignominy of the Cross.[18] Thus by His proper work in this His own Regiment, God works to destroy spiritual pride and to create faith through the suffering and folly of the Cross. As Luther tells us in his *Lectures on Romans,* God does nothing else in the Church but transform our mind. Here the Word as the hidden wisdom of God comes to us daily under forms contrary to our reason—life under death, the kingdom under exile, truth under the form of a lie (56:446, 392). Even if Luther moved beyond this theology of the Cross, the Cross itself persisted as indicative of God's action in time.[19]

Christ's Cross is the most extreme expression of God's concealment and at the same time justifies the entire scheme of concealment. Christ crucified is the central fact and clue to history whereby the hidden revelation has a redemptive significance for all of history. The Cross represents the nature and content of God's revelatory activity in history. He has chosen to approach us indirectly through everything that is opposed to reason and human sense. Only by such a disguise can God's activity in history produce faith. Luther explains that because faith is in things not seen, everything which is believed is hidden. Matters of faith cannot be better hidden than under an aspect contrary to experience, sense, and appearance. Thus when God makes alive, He does it by killing; when He justifies, He does it by accusing; when He exalts to heaven, He does it by

18. Walther von Loewenich, *Luthers Theologia Crucis* (München, 1929), pp. 13–18, 21–25.

19. Cf. Bizer, *Fides ex Auditu* (Neukirchen, 1958), pp. 75, 104.

leading down to hell. Because God's activity cannot be comprehended, room is given for the exercise of faith (18:633).

Redemptive history cannot be understood as a closed district within world history, nor can these two types of history be seen as two parallel strands, for God's revelatory activity is not localized but works in and through every aspect and level of life. The spiritual Regiment, which serves to mediate the revelation of Christ, indicates by its very structure that it is not cut off from the other aspect of God's activity. And the simultaneity of God's twofold action reinforces the impression that there is no area known as world history which remains unaffected by the redemptive purpose. Luther seems to strain beyond the categories of the Regimente in order to represent the unity and meaning of history in terms of God's paradoxical working in all levels of life. Historical existence becomes a gigantic exercise in faith.

In his exegesis of the Magnificat, Luther found an ideal means by which to demonstrate the activity of God in history. For with the Virgin Mary the Holy Spirit teaches that God is the Lord who works to raise up what is lowly and level what is high, to break what is made and mend what is broken (7:546). He is nearest to those who are humble and cast down, and farthest from those who are proud and elated. In elaborating this theme, Luther presents the problem of how to know God from a correct recognition of His works. He has Mary dividing the world into two parts—wisdom, power, and wealth on one side, and mercy, judgment, and righteousness on the other. God is as present in this latter side as He is absent in the former (7:577–78).

In the manner in which God works with each side, Luther makes an important distinction. He uses the biblical term "God's arm" to indicate His own power, which He works without creatures. More precisely, Luther probably intends Christ (cf. 5:477). Here God proceeds secretly, with the result that His activity is only discernible to faith. When He works through the means of creatures, one can see openly where the power or weakness lies. When a prince wins a war, through him has God beaten another prince. Thus God makes and breaks creatures through the use of others. But with His own arm God works otherwise. Luther notes that God only does such work between the two parts of the world—the pious and the wicked. He allows the pious to become powerless and cast down and then, when man's power fails and faith is present and expectant, God's power begins. When the pious seem virtually destroyed, God is most powerfully present, but secretly and hidden. It is not surprising that Luther should here adduce the Cross to confirm his view of God's activity. Christ was powerless on the Cross, yet here He did his greatest work, conquering sin, death, the world, hell, the Devil, and all evil. As for the other part, the wicked, God withdraws His arm and allows them to become great and inflated. Then He punctures them (7:585–86).

How? The question is important, for Luther has stated previously that the action of God's arm applies only in this opposition between the pious and the impious. Luther does not answer the question directly but implies that God's arm is effective with the impious by its absence. For how, he asks, can God better destroy the proud and the wise than by withdrawing His own wisdom and allowing them to become inflated with their own temporal wisdom? They will not prosper forever, because they cannot escape God's arm. We believe that they must fall. Yet where there is no faith, God does not effect such work but allows the matter to go openly through creatures. Here God cannot be recognized as in His own works but achieves His ends through creatures. Luther emphasizes that God does not break the position or office but only its presumptuous holder, for magistracy, Regiment, and power must remain as long as the world exists, but those who bear it unwisely are broken. Thus all histories and experience show how one rich man, prince, or people rises only to go down before another: the Assyrians are followed by the Babylonians, then the Persians, the Greeks, and the Romans. It would seem from this explanation that unbelief and the consequent failure to be obedient to God place one in a realm of inevitable rise and fall whose meaning is only clear to the believer. God allows the disobedient ruler to reach the top and then withdraws His power, letting him collapse of his own accord (7:587–90).

The central significance given to faith on man's part and the emphasis given to God's contrary works, wherein He is far from the proud and near to the unwise, make the *Magnificat* an important statement of Luther's understanding of history. The *Magnificat* indicates a unity to history which transcends all institutions and groups. Because God here works in a hidden and yet revealed fashion within the camps of the pious and the wicked, administering grace and judgment, history becomes for the eyes of faith alone a means of recognizing God through His works. Elsewhere Luther refers to this continual encounter of the believer with God in history as a knowledge of the back parts of God by which man learns of God only through his suffering and apparent rejection (*TR* 5536). But if God in His activity is everywhere evident to the eyes of faith, there is no knowledge of God's presence to the eyes of the world. This faith in God's hidden action, which reaches its supreme expression in Christ, produces an entire historical outlook as well as a division among men.

The Magnificat affords Luther a valuable opportunity to present the two kingdoms with their radical opposition and struggle. Mary's schematization of historical existence into two camps is not something incidental to her view but persists in her presentation of God's works. At the end she distinguishes these same two parts in Israel and makes foremost only that part which serves God and allows Him to effect His own work within. This Israel is God's own dear people, the Christian people (7:595–97). In the *Magnificat* this redemptive history comprehends man's total life within either camp as well as the presence of struggle and the transfer of an occasional soul. Both pious and wicked are the subject of redemptive history. That God acts here without the means of creatures and with His own arm only reflects the fact that the orientation of our life in this world and in the next rests with God's grace. As Luther had said earlier at Leipzig, the work that is accomplished in us by God's operation alone is purer than that which is effected with our co-operation (2:354).

To determine the precise locus of this redemptive history requires a closer definition of the relationship between the kingdoms and the Regimente. The fact that God works in the Kingdom of Christ in a way similar to that in which He works in the spiritual Regiment would seem to identify the two. The possibility of their coincidence exists, since the spiritual Regiment, insofar as it is subject to the Word of God, is also called the Kingdom of Christ and the Church. Yet a clear identification between the two entities appears impossible. It is true that the spiritual Regiment provides the media of grace whereby faith is given and restored, but it is equally true that the pious cannot be identified with all those who serve in the spiritual Regiment. In fact the spiritual Regiment normally remains in the possession of the impious and the Kingdom of Christ's adversaries. Nor is the entire life of the pious comprised in this Regiment. The Devil always works to pervert the spiritual Regiment, and Luther warns that unless the Kingdom of God rules this Regiment, it becomes Satanic and evil (10/3:372).

The impossibility of identifying either kingdom with either of the Regimente demonstrates the fact that the total life of each people, whether the elect or the reprobate, can only be understood within the categories of the two kingdoms. Redemptive history finds its locus in the struggle between two peoples, two kingdoms. But these kingdoms cannot be considered without reference to both Regimente. Thus Luther can observe that this assembled people or Church, which represents the object of God's redemptive activity, exists in the world and is heard through the masks of all the created orders of the Regimente. The Church includes the godly estates but cannot be identified with any of them (*WBr* 9:610; cf. 51:530–31). Finally, in his most explicit effort to relate the Regimente to the kingdoms, Luther explains that the Church as a little band of

Christians collects the pious from the created orders and Regimente. And it is for this persecuted and hidden group that God maintains the world and its estates (31/1:87–89).

With the categories of the two kingdoms, Luther is able to accent the redemptive nature of God's action in time and to emphasize history as an exercise in faith far more effectively than he could with the categories of Creation. Here the issue is the recruiting of a people that transcends all the created orders occupied by both Christians and non-Christians alike. This redemptive activity knows no limits but occurs wherever Christ and that which proclaims Christ are present. Wherever in the world the work of Christ is effective through the instrument of the Word, there world history assumes the character of redemptive history. This Word which proclaims Christ and creates faith drives life beyond its natural and human limits and has well been called the attack of God upon world history.[20] Thus this activity of the Word which works in and through world history and in which God seeks to be recognized in faith produces a redemptive history that is nowhere cut off from the larger stream of history but rather gives unity and meaning to it.

But if the Word as God's instrument provides the core and unity of history, it necessarily produces a division in history. What of world history proper as it appears in the worldly Regiment among peoples that have never heard of the Word? In the history that pertains to the ordering of this life there is to the eyes of reason a chaos of peoples and rulers rising and falling, killing, and being killed—a scene without purpose or meaning. But to the eyes of faith, the power and presence of God are evident. Luther maintains that Providence illuminates even the histories of the Gentiles (44:181). God's judgment is conspicuous in the way that He uses one power as an instrument to destroy another. Luther distinguishes the two aspects of history in the eyes of faith from each other and places

20. Lilje, pp. 114–15.

this total view in opposition to a rational and human outlook upon history.

> Note well that although the history of this people, if it is considered in its appearance, seems similar to Gentile histories—for now they conquer, now they are conquered, now they abound, now they are in need and although miracles are visited frequently—nevertheless God thus conceals Himself so that all seem to be driven by human wisdom and chance. Thus it appeared without doubt to all these impious peoples who build and lay waste as though there were no God in Israel. Indeed the histories of this people must be separated from the histories of all nations as far as heaven is from earth. In the histories of nations one may consider the magnitude or triviality of works. In the other the Word of God must alone be admired and worshiped by whose direction and will all things are conducted and accomplished. . . . Although the deeds of all nations are only the miracles and works of God, nevertheless they have not the testimony of the Word and of the gracious disposition of God. Rather their acts and histories are attestations of wrath—truly terrible indications of the frightful judgment of God. Therefore the histories of all the world have been taken at once as incomparably more worthless than the most worthless story of this people. [14:566–67]

All of history is God's work and God's game; not even redemptive history itself is free from the ludistic activity of God (44:285, 467, 470). But what distinguishes the latter from world history is that its games and miseries are crowned with the Word of God (43:672). The distinction lies between the work of God and the Word of God. In redemptive history alone God's Word illuminates His work. The work of God particularly as evinced in the Incarnation and Atonement is not meaningless, but the Spirit in which these events move is so hidden and opposed to all human thinking that the work of God without the explanatory and revealing force of the Word of God remains fruitless and concealed.[21] The nature of redemptive history rests with the Word of God.

The Doctrine of the Word of God

The doctrine of the Word of God constitutes the core of Luther's theology. It is important for his understanding of the doctrine that he considered the Word not as an abstract, metaphysical principle but as God's eternal announcement of good news. Luther specifically explains the logos of the Johannine Gospel in terms of a copy of the divine heart imparted to man by a direct address. As the spoken Word in Christ this imparting of the divine self creates the world and reaches out to redeem man. With the substitution of religious for philosophical categories Luther elaborates his doctrine of the Word on a thoroughly biblical basis (17/2:314–17). Equally important for an understanding of the distinctive features of his doctrine of the Word is the Word's coming to man through external forms; only in the historical forms of Scripture, the Church, and the sacraments does the Word reveal itself.[22] Because the Word is a unity, its content and its historical forms stand together and need to be examined conjointly.

If Christ is the content of the Word, the activity of the Word and that which gives present reality to Christ is the Holy Spirit. The Spirit activates the motion of faith in man and brings Christ from the dead past into a present, immediate reality. The inner Word is God's own voice by His Spirit. Without this inner Word, the outer Word that appears in Scripture remains a dead letter and has no significance for man's justification. Nevertheless, while the outer

21. Erich Seeberg, *Luthers Theologie in ihren Grundzügen* (Stuttgart, 1950), p. 77. Hereafter cited as *L.T.G.*

22. Heinrich Bornkamm, *Das Wort Gottes bei Luther* (München, 1933), p. 38. Hereafter cited as *Wort.*

Word must wait upon the action of the inner Word of the Spirit for its life, Luther always emphasizes the importance of the external forms through which God reveals Himself and insists that the outer must precede the inner—the outer Word and then the Spirit with the inner Word. [23]

The peculiar richness and complexity of Luther's understanding of the Word resides in its essential character: on the one hand the Word is Spirit because the Word contains and yields the Spirit; on the other hand the Spirit is Word-bound and comes to man through external means.[24] In this type of revelation, Scripture stands as the most significant external means. For in the words of Scripture, Luther found his clue to the nature and activity of a gracious God, and it was his original way of reading Scripture which gave substance and meaning to his doctrine of the Word.

When Luther began his exegesis of the Psalms in 1513, he stood under the influence of the fourfold interpretation of Scripture. Yet in his exposition of the Psalms and in interpreting them all with reference to Christ, he found an inner connection between the literal sense and the spiritual sense, which previously only a few exegetes had occasionally recognized. Guided by the *Quincuplex Psalterium* of Lefèvre d'Étaples, he discovered that the true literal sense is that which agrees with and is revealed by the Holy Spirit. In addition to this inward connection, the literal and the spiritual sense were related in that the former had to do with Christ and the latter with His gospel. This prophetic sense, which went beyond the merely historical events and related all to Christ, was only discernible to one who had the same spirit as that which was in Scripture, for the Spirit only penetrates where it perceives itself in itself. Such a perceptivity is a gift of God in the form of faith and must be exercised affectively. Thus for Luther the spiritual understanding of Scripture

23. Regin Prenter, *Spiritus Creator,* trans. John M. Jensen (Philadelphia, 1953), pp. 102–11.

24. Bornkamm, *Wort,* pp. 9–10.

is not the product of a method of exegesis but the effect of the Holy Spirit through faith.[25]

The exclusively Christocentric exegesis served as the seed for the theology of the Reformation. In his exposition of the Psalms and shortly afterward in Romans, Luther gave particular attention to the tropological or moral sense as that which directly applies to the Christian believer. Proceeding on the assumption that the Bible in its spiritual-literal meaning speaks only of Christ, Luther arrived at his crucial insight that at the same time it speaks in its tropological sense of the believer in Christ. Thus what is true of Christ is true of the Christian.[26] In these first lectures Luther moved toward an exegetical practice and insight that would redefine the role of the Christian believer as well as the nature of the Word.

Despite frequent recourse to the allegorical sense, Luther in his *Lectures on the Psalms* had set forth the canon that the Bible in all its parts has a single meaning. Subsequently, Luther worked out the implications of the true spiritual sense of Scripture and thereby clarified the relation between Word and Scripture. In his first lectures on the Bible, while omitting the anagogical sense, he had recognized the fourfold sense in the Psalms. In the commentary on Galatians of 1519, he consciously attacked the traditional interpretation according to four senses. He asserted that the various senses were supported neither by the authority of Scripture, by the use of the fathers, nor by grammar. Paul had not distinguished allegory and anagogy. Luther opposed Jerome and Origen who accepted the literal sense as figure and story and used allegory for the spiritual or mystical sense; instead the reformer followed Augustine, who

25. Karl Holl, "Luthers Beleutung für den Fortschritt der Auslegungskunst," *Gesammelte Aufsätze zur Kirchengeschichte* (Tübingen, 1932), *1*, 545–48. Hereafter cited as *Ges. Auf.* See also W. Schwarz, *Principles and Problems of Biblical Translation* (Cambridge, Eng. 1955), pp. 172–75; and Gerhard Ebeling, *Evangelische Evangelienauslegung: Eine Untersuchung zu Luthers Hermeneutik* (München, 1942), p. 311. This last work is the best study on the problem. Hereafter cited as *Hermeneutik*.

26. Wilhelm Pauck, ed., *Luther: Lectures on Romans*, Library of Christian Classics, *15* (Philadelphia, 1961), xxxii–xxxiv.

separated letter and spirit not formally but according to content—by which he intended a distinction between a literal and a spiritual understanding. Consequently the law, which according to ordinary standards is never spiritual and always letter, becomes spiritual when considered by the spiritual understanding. The literal only exists when grace is not present. Implicit is the activity of the Spirit in giving spiritual meaning to the literal events of Scripture. Thus while exegesis for the Alexandrian school had been an act of men on the Scripture, exegesis for Luther became an act of Scripture on men.[27] Or, as he stated the idea in another place, the sense of Scripture is to be rendered from it by its own Spirit and not to be brought to the text by our own (7:99).

To the end of his life Luther continued the battle against allegory. But the meaning of this battle cannot be measured in terms of a quantitative diminution in the use of allegory, because Luther established his own rules for allegorical interpretation. Rather it is to be seen as part of a total Christocentric exegesis. In his use of allegory Luther broke with a multiplicity of scopes such as God, Mary, the Church, angels, and virtues in order to concentrate upon a single scope. While the traditional allegory pointed toward historical, visible things, Luther directed it to the reality of faith in Christ.[28] Likewise in all parts of Scripture he found only Christ and claimed that the law and the prophets are not rightly preached unless we find Christ wrapped in them (10/1:81). It is well known that Luther preferred certain books of the Bible and that he found his inner canon in the Gospel of St. John, the Epistles of Paul, and the First Epistle of St. Peter. The magnitude of his exegetical achievement lay, however, not in the fact that he read Scripture with Pauline spectacles but that Christ, rather than the doctrine of justification, was the single scope. Consequently, the unity of Scripture rested neither in a harmonizing of Gospels nor in the play of allegory but on Christ the Word. In recognizing differences in de-

27. Ebeling, *Hermeneutik*, pp. 278–88. *WA* 2:550–52.
28. Ebeling, *Hermeneutik*, pp. 191, 201.

tails, Luther never lost sight of this central agreement among all the books of Scripture. Within the New Testament itself he thought of one gospel, not of four, because he was concerned with the Word and doctrine rather than with works and stories. This outlook enabled him to prefer the Epistle to the Romans to the Gospels proper, because the substance of the Word lay not in a historical report of the outer events of Jesus' life but in the witness of it and what it signified.[29]

Through his reading of Scripture, Luther effected nothing less than a hermeneutical revolution, of which the major implications for the understanding of the Word are intimately related. In the first place, God's revelation of Himself in Scripture assumed a new significance. The belief that the stories of the Bible were of equal worth rested on the unity of Scripture in Christ the Word. Christ is concealed in the Word of Scripture, and this Word is made contemporaneous through the inspiration of the Holy Spirit, the bearer of which is the Word of Scripture. Thus the Word stands in a double relationship to the Spirit: it is activated by the Spirit and it imparts the Spirit. Christ is the subject and content of the Word which the Spirit activates and communicates to man through the medium of the visible Word of Scripture. For Luther the unity of Christ, the Spirit, and the Word in the gospel was evinced in the preached Word of Christ's redeeming work.[30]

Arising from this relationship of Christ with the Word and the Spirit is an insight of supreme significance not only for the theology of the Reformation in respect to its Scholastic past but more particularly for Luther's view of history. This insight is the continuing presence of Christ in time. As a statement of faith it is the necessary implication of Luther's hermeneutics and his understanding of the content and action of the Word. It rests upon the virtually sacramental nature of the Word made visible to faith in Scripture. Luther constantly emphasizes that it is not enough to know the

29. Ibid., pp. 217–19, 271, 366.
30. Ibid., p. 365.

stories relating to Jesus Christ; one must also know their fruit and use. If the story alone is examined, the preaching is useless, for Satan himself can read and understand (17/1:86–87). Luther significantly notes that the Evangelists are silent here and leave one with the story. Nevertheless, the prophets, Peter and Paul, and the Acts of the Apostles are not silent and go beyond what Christ suffered to the reason why He bore His Passion. If we lack this sensitivity to the fruit of the Passion, there is no difference between Christ's death and that of any prophet or martyr. Faith alone given through the Word for the appropriation of the Word enables one to obtain the fruit of the bare history (27:104). And in faith itself Christ is present (40/1:227). The proclamation of Christ does not concern simply a past, historical event but is a gift and a bestowing which endures forever.[31] The story contains its own outgoing contemporaneousness, which is appropriated in faith by the believer.

If Christianity urgently poses the problem of how a person in the present is related to a divine event in the past, then Luther's exegetical method had profound reverberations in the realm of theology and for the nature of the Christian life. Traditional exegesis sought contemporaneousness with the past by imitation and repetition of the past. The piety of monasticism, the late medieval *imitatio Christi*, and the conception of the Mass itself as a bloodless sacrifice manifested this conception of one's relation to the past. In Luther's judgment, Scholastic theology had curtailed the sacramental significance of Christ and had cultivated His exemplary significance. A law book had been made out of the gospel, and the more Christ as content of the announcement of the Church disappeared, the more one sought a repetition of His outer appearance. The revelation of Jesus Christ came to be driven more and more on the surface of the visibility of a story and a work. This exemplary relationship or bond was a legal one between the then and the now, the past event and the present situation. The exemplary meaning not only ended in

31. Philip S. Watson, *Let God Be God!* (London, 1954), p. 151.

placing the history of Christ on the same level as secular history, but tended to replace the Christ as gift with the Christ as example.[32]

This type of exegesis together with its theological implications was entirely antithetical to Luther's understanding of Christian faith. While advocating an imitation of Christ in respect to a man's actions toward his neighbor, Luther never allowed this exemplary Christ to enter the conscience and the domain of the gospel (40/2:42). Only after becoming a gift through faith does Christ become an example (10/1/1:12–14). Since the Christ event cannot be repeated and revelation is a revelation in the past, an imitation which seeks contemporaneousness is impossible, for imitation cannot go beyond the outer appearance of this event. Consequently, one's relation to Christ can only be concealed, never visible, for it is not the work but faith that constitutes contemporaneousness with Christ, because the first attempts the impossible task of copying the example of Christ, while the second appropriates the gift of Christ. The two outlooks are opposed as *exemplum charitatis* to *exemplum fidei*.[33]

By his exegesis Luther expressed the relation between Christ and the mediating Word and the continuing presence of Christ through the Word. Yet this exegetical method was inextricably related to and a result of his spiritual pilgrimage and the discovery of a gracious God. While the religious can never be divorced from the theological in Luther, the present problem does not involve a consideration of the reformer's spiritual progress; rather it concerns how Luther understood through his own struggle the action of the Word as it affects the conscience of the believer. Here in the life of faith the Word as Christ, the Word in Scripture becomes the oral Word, the preached Word, and through the preached Word alone does man encounter God. The impact and operation of this Word on man represents the existential aspect of a reality whose basis is both hermeneutical and existential. For Luther's doctrine of the Word

32. Ebeling, *Hermeneutik*, pp. 233–37, 291–92, 439.

33. Ibid., pp. 237, 442–45.

is derived as much from an experience of faith as it is from a Christocentric exegesis.

From the outset of his university career in his *Lectures on the Psalms*, Luther emphasized the significance of the preached Word and the epistemological distinctiveness of hearing. He felt that the words of Christ are alive and that not on stones and dead books but in living hearts are they intended to be inscribed (3:22–23). He dwelt on the sensuous, living vibrance of the process of speaking and hearing in all its implications. The pen is necessarily empty, but the tongue is solid flesh and full and makes living letters in the heart with words carried to the ear. The law of Moses has been written with human letters by a living tongue for those who read and understand spiritually. Metaphorically speaking, the law is pen or writing and the gospel is tongue. According to whether or not it is spiritually born with the living voice, the law of Moses can become gospel or the gospel can harden into law (3:456–57). Actually the Old Testament is alone Scripture. Luther later explained that the books of Moses and the prophets are also gospel, since they have announced and written of Christ what the apostles later preached. The difference between them, however, is that the Old Testament is written on paper and the New Testament is announced with the living voice. That the New Testament should have later been written down is incidental, for by its nature the gospel is the living preaching of Christ (12:292; 5:537).

Luther's emphasis on the preached Word, which renders all parts of the Bible gospel to those who hear it in faith, manifested itself early in his career and persisted. The nature of the Word of God is to be heard; and unless it is perceived by hearing, it is not perceived at all (4:9). He associates hearing with wisdom that requires faith, while he relates the visual experience to knowledge (4:339). Because God speaks to man, the divine eloquence communicates itself with the living voice rather than in written words (5:379). Later in his life he understood the basic nature of man's relation to God in terms of the receptive, passive act of hearing (40/1:342–43). The

Christian is made not by doing works but by hearing (40/1:345). Gospel and faith belong together.

Through reception of the gospel, man first experiences the reality of the law. In the spiritual cyclone that marked the *Lectures on the Psalms,* Luther devoted considerable attention to accusation of self. The necessity of feeling God's judgment, of being humiliated and humbled, must precede the recognition of God's righteousness in Jesus Christ. Here humility signifies not the virtue of humble obedience but rather the acknowledgment of sin before God. Likewise in his *Lectures on Romans,* Luther asserted that one must be humbled before he can effectively hear the Word of God. In these early lectures justification appears to be a result of humility and the recognition of one's own sin.[34] Later Luther passed beyond this theology of humility to his mature position where faith becomes a faith in God's Word which alone justifies. In this reformulation, law and gospel are clearly distinguished but not separated.[35] They are secured within the dialectical action of the preached Word as it confronts man's conscience with God's judgment and His grace.

In perhaps his most mature work, the *Commentary on Galatians,* Luther gave the clearest explanation of this action of the Word in the life of the believer by his distinction between law and gospel. To Luther, law in itself is always good; only when it enters the conscience and comes to dominate the whole religious life does it assume its pejorative connotation of everything that is opposed to faith. The conscience must be free from the law, but the body must be obedient to it. Often he asserts that the distinction between the two contains the sum of all Christian doctrine, and that the righteousness of the gospel and that of the law cannot be separated far enough. In the worldly Regiment the law is good, for it bridles and coerces the wicked. But this civil coercion, though necessary, does not justify. Luther claims for the law a second proper use which is

34. Gordon Rupp, *The Righteousness of God* (London, 1953), pp. 148–50, 167–68.

35. Uuras Saarnivaara, *Luther Discovers the Gospel* (St. Louis, 1951), p. 117. Bizer, pp. 39, 104, 136–46 passim.

theological, spiritual, and evangelical. Insofar as it increases transgressions and reveals to man his sin, blindness, and just damnation, it becomes an integral part of the gospel. When instructed by the law, a man is terrified and humbled and sees himself as worthy of damnation. Hence the first step is the preaching of repentance and knowledge of oneself. Only then is one ready for the consolation in Christ (40/1:205–24, 479–82). To the degree that the law is understood in the light of the gospel, and not the reverse, the law becomes gospel. In His wrathful love, God crucifies us by His alien work as a preparation for resurrecting us by His proper work (40/3:584–85).

The goal of God's action through the Word as gospel is the creation of faith in the heart of man. Faith is always a gift of God; by distinguishing it from the grace of God from which it follows, Luther could emphasize the alien nature of this righteousness which is completely undeserved and irrespective of merit.[36] On the one hand, faith is related to the Word in whose content it affectively participates by an experience which the Word mediates to the exclusion of all other experience. On the other hand, faith has for its sole object Christ, to whom it is united without being identified and without entirely losing its distinction. Ultimately faith and Christ belong together not as matter to form nor as subject to object but because Christ is present in faith.[37] Faith is a confidence of the heart, a firm assent, "a kind of knowledge or darkness which sees nothing, and yet Christ sits apprehended by faith in this very darkness." It is this confidence in something that we do not see which justifies, because it apprehends and possesses the treasure—the present Christ (40/1:228–29).

Linked with Christ and faith in the drama of salvation is a third factor—acceptation—which serves to remind us of the original meaning of faith alone in Luther's spiritual pilgrimage. Acceptation signifies that our sin is no longer imputed to us. It is covered even

36. Prenter, pp. 35–41.
37. Loewenich, pp. 129–35.

though it still exists in us (40/1:233). We are always just in that by faith we have received God's righteousness as a gift and our sins are no longer imputed. We are always sinners on account of our flesh and we must await completion in another time (2:497). Only by means of faith can man treat with this God who in His majesty brushes aside all the ladders of individual striving and human merit, and through the Word comes to man forgiving his sins and imputing His own righteousness as a gift.

Strands, theological and religious, exegetical and existential, are inextricably bound together in Luther's understanding of the doctrine of the Word. In its unique richness the Word comprises Christ as the content of revelation, with the Holy Spirit, as the means of revelation, who imparts God's redemptive act through Scripture to the believer. It is of paramount significance that Luther understood God in terms of the Word and thus as the God who speaks to man and acts to save him. In his doctrine of the Word of God, ontological and metaphysical categories disappear before religious and historical ones; the deed of God replaces the being of God as the central element in his theology.[38] And through a contemporary proclamation of this Word, God acts within time to collect His people.

The Church

> The gospel, which is the wisdom and power of God, constitutes the Church. [56:165; cf. 4:189]

This statement, made early in Luther's career, announced more than the placing of Scripture over the Church or simply a reaction to the excessive externalization of ecclesiastical life. The statement signified that the real life and the essence of the Church were located beyond itself and that the Church's establishment and existence in

38. Jaroslav Pelikan, *Luther the Expositor* (St. Louis, 1959), pp. 50, 54. Hereafter cited as *Expositor*.

time could be understood only in terms of the Word. Luther even claims that the Church is the virtual creature of the Word; it neither institutes nor ordains but is instituted and ordained—by the Word (6:560–61; cf. 8:419). Its function is that of proclaiming the Word. Luther calls for the Church to be heard, but it is not the Church of the bishops nor of the fathers; it is the Church which has and teaches the Word of God and adds nothing. This Church must alone be heard (*WBr* 2:623).

While he located both the instituting and the function of the Church in the Word, Luther defined it in terms of his doctrine of justification. The Church was the community of believers. The actual words used are important. From his days at Erfurt, the third article of the Apostles' Creed had possessed a peculiar significance for him. Although recognizing its historical basis, he appropriated the ideas of the *communio sanctorum* and the forgiveness of sins and used the article as an authority for religious truth.[39] He preferred the Latin text of the creed to the Greek as a means of avoiding the institutional overtones of *sancta ecclesia. Communio sanctorum* substantiated the priesthood of all believers and confirmed the fact that the Church could not be considered apart from men.[40] Luther found the word *ecclesia* quite unsatisfactory for defining the Church and in a later work he complained because the creed employed such a blind word. He went beyond it to the word's original meaning of an assembled people, a specially called people, a people of God, in order to arrive at his own definition of the Church (50:624–25).

The communion or people which is the Church derives its unity not from itself but from Christ.

39. Walther Koehler, *Luther und die Kirchengeschichte nach seinen Schriften, Zunächst bis 1521* (Erlangen, 1900), pp. 77–78. Hereafter cited as *L. und K.*

40. Ernst Rietschel, "Das Problem des unsichtbar-sichtbaren Kirche bei Luther," *Schriften des Vereins für Reformationsgeschichte, 50* (1932), 9. On the original meaning of *communio sanctorum* and Luther's reinterpretation of it, see A. C. McGiffert, *The Apostles' Creed* (New York, 1902), pp. 24–26, 200–04. For the most complete treatment of the problem, see Paul Althaus, *Communio Sanctorum* (Munich, 1929), pp. 1–22, 27–42.

> Through one faith we adhere to Him and appear as one body with Him and He with us; He, the Head and we the members. [43:582]

Luther made this point particularly clear in his struggle with Alveld, and pursued the implications of Christ as the Head of the Church. In this tract he replaces the misleading word "Church" with that of *Christenheit,* by which he means the assembly of all Christian believers upon the earth (cf. 11:53). In an effort to locate this community beyond particular moments of time and place he quotes the Apostles' Creed and asserts that *Christenheit* is apart from all worldly communities, for it is not physical as the Romanists would have it. Because this assembly is a spiritual community, it cannot have a physical head but must have a spiritual head. The real Church is a spiritual and inner one (6:292–96). Writing at the same time in his *Operations on the Psalms,* Luther defines the Church of Christ as the spiritual collection of the faithful wherever they may be. He warns against romanizing this view and locating the Church in a particular place. Christ and the apostles anticipated the superstition and impiety which would arise from affixing the Church to certain places and thus dragging it from a spiritual gathering into the temporal. Jerusalem was destroyed so that it might not serve as such a place (5:451). Although the Church is scattered physically, it is collected spiritually in Christ (26:506).

Luther's opposition to the Papacy aided the gradual elaboration of a concept of the Church in terms of its essentially invisible nature. But it was his doctrine of justification that actually shaped this understanding of the Church.[41] By the term "invisible" he referred to the nature of the Church itself and not to the number of its members; it signified that which was not sensually perceptible.[42] Its spiritual Head and the distinctive fact of faith made this community a spiritual and invisible one. Luther contended that the holy

41. Cf. Holl, "Die Entstehung von Luthers Kirchenbegriff," *Ges. Auf. 1,* 289.
42. Rietschel, pp. 28–29.

Christian Church is not able to be physically demonstrated but is only able to be believed; the growth of sects and of a righteousness based upon good works derived from this desire to see the Church rather than to believe it (7:685–86). Luther did not neglect, however, the visible aspect of the Church; now through faith itself the invisible Church became visible.

When Luther wrote his *Reply to Ambrosius Catharinus* in the spring of 1521, he was already confronted by Thomas Murner's charge that like Plato with the state he was building a church which was nowhere. In his tract Luther makes clear not only the substantiality of the visible Church but also that the visible and invisible Church are identical and that one cannot exist without the other.

In his central endeavor to identify the Papacy with Antichrist according to the prophecy of Daniel, Luther continued his argument that the Church cannot be confined by place and body. Nevertheless he adds that the Church is not without place and body, although these factors are not the Church nor do they pertain to it (cf. 54:261; 39/2:161). No particular place or person is a necessity for the being of the Church; although it is not able to be without place and persons, these are indifferent and free. Any place suits the Christian, and no place is more necessary than another for the Christian (7:720). He explains that if the Church has the qualities of persons and place, these qualities, however, do not define its nature. Nor do preaching and the proper use of the sacraments in themselves make the Church visible. Here Luther returns to the original nature of the Church—faith. Having established that the word *Petram* in Matthew 16:18 refers to Christ, Luther continues:

> Therefore just as this rock is without sin, invisible, spiritual, and is perceptible by faith alone, in the same way it is necessary that the Church be without sin, invisible, spiritual, and perceptible by faith alone. For it is fitting that the foundation be of the same condition as the building, just as we say—"I

> believe the Holy Catholic Church," for faith is of things not apparent. [7:710–11]

To the believer alone is the Church visible; by faith alone do the signs and means of grace constitute the visible Church.

The circle in which the means of grace are administered is greater than the one in which they are believed. Although the administration of the Word and sacraments belongs to the invisible community of believers, Luther refused to identify the saints and experienced the existing Church as one that included both the wheat and the tares (43:36; 44:23). For a few years subsequent to his return from the Wartburg he entertained the idea of an *ecclesiola,* an inner circle of firm believers.[43] Luther's rejection of the *ecclesiola* placed a limitation on the visibleness of the Church.[44] Ultimately God alone knows the members of His Church. On the other hand, the assurance of one's own membership and of one's fellow members rests upon faith and love respectively. Reacting to the extreme scrupulosity and studied doubt cultivated in the Church of his day, Luther urged that each person should consider himself a saint insofar as he holds with the common faith to God as Creator and Saviour (5:124). On the matter of identifying one's fellow members, Luther would have each person pursue the rule of love. For according to love each ought to consider the other as a saint, but according to faith no saint ought to be distinguished (18:651–52).

The members are as one bread, for they believe that no man lives for himself but that each lives and extends himself toward the other through love (12:488). Thus the Church is not understood as two closed, fixed circles. The centrality of faith and an appreciation of the reality of love give a dynamic quality to the community of believers as a group which is always open and always expanding. The Church is distinguished by invisible believing on one side and

43. Cf. *WA* 19:74–75. Karl Müller, *Luther und Karlstadt* (Tübingen, 1907), pp. 117–23.

44. Rietschel, pp. 34–38, 63.

by visible means of grace accepted in faith on the other.[45] While its true membership is never disclosed to the eyes of men, the Church exists in the eyes of God and through the faith of men.

The Church is no abstraction. Luther's original understanding of the sacraments further substantiates the Church in this life. As divine acts and as the means by which the visible Church becomes real to the believer, the sacraments are of central importance for understanding the Church in its historical reality. Through the concrete exercise of the sacraments and their acceptance by a people in faith, the Church becomes the effective form and subject of redemptive history.

In his conception of a sacrament Luther gave paramount significance to faith and bound the inner Word to the external sign. His departure from the existing Scholastic concept of the sacraments exists not in any difference between a sacramental and a spiritualistic view of religion but in the difference between law and gospel, works and faith. The function of the sacramental Word appears in a new light; it is no longer considered a special Word of consecration but as being identical with the gospel itself. This difference is expressed in the use of the concept *promissio*. In every sacrament there is a divine promise announced through the Word which accompanies the sacrament. The promise is the decisive factor that makes a sacrament valid. Despite its special form, each sacrament is but a deepening of the one sole promise which God has proclaimed repeatedly since the Fall of man. This promise has finally been formulated with specific signs in the testament of Jesus, in the Lord's Supper, and in baptism. With respect to its content the Word of the sacrament both in baptism and in the Lord's Supper is in harmony with the Word that is being preached.[46] Thus for Luther there is actually but one sacrament with three signs. The basic sacrament is Christ Himself.[47]

45. Ibid., p. 75.
46. Prenter, pp. 136–40.
47. *WA* 6:501. Cf. Prenter, p. 157.

Arising from this unity of the sacraments in the Word is a second feature: the sacraments are conceived as being divine acts in the life of believers and attestations of Christ's presence. Luther's basic opposition to the Roman conception of the Mass lay in his dread of understanding the sacrament as a work accomplished by man to obtain God's favor (8:440–45). It is rather man whom God sacrifices in the Mass (6:369). By the sacrament the meaning of a past event streams through time and asserts its continuing presence.

> We believe and it is true that the blood of Christ who now sits in heaven at the right hand of God has been poured out for us at one time and at no other. If one now considers the story whereby he has obtained the forgiveness of sin, so it truly does not occur in the Last Supper but now has occurred and is past. But if one considers the distribution of forgiveness, here there is no time, for it has happened from the beginning of the world as John also says in the Apocalypse that the Lamb of God has been slain from the beginning of the world. [18:205]

The sacrament is no longer a power coming from God to help us to God but a divine act which manifests Christ's presence and confirms the promise which faith retains.[48] Because the sacraments are works of God, their validity is quite irrespective of the piety of the minister through whom God works (6:526). Nevertheless, Luther asserts that where the divine promise is concerned, each must stand for himself; one's own faith is required (6:521). The gap between the validity of the sacraments and the efficacy of the sacraments can only be bridged by the Spirit.

For the believer the activity of God through His sacraments establishes the reality of the visible Church. Wherever the Word is preached and the sacraments administered and received properly, there is the Church. For, in effect, Luther sacramentalizes preaching

48. Prenter, pp. 144, 156.

and makes it the chief sign of the Church from which the other two are derived:

> For the gospel is before bread and baptism the unique, most certain and noblest symbol of the Church, because through the gospel alone is the Church conceived, formed, nourished, generated, instructed, fed, clothed, ornamented, strengthened, armed, preserved—in short the entire life and substance of the Church is in the Word of God. . . . Nor am I speaking about the written but rather the vocal gospel . . . [For] only by the vocal and public voice of the gospel can it be known where is the Church and the mystery of the kingdom of heaven. . . . Thus no one sees the Church, but he believes alone through the sign of the Word which is unable to resound except in the Church through the Holy Spirit. [7:721–22; cf. 12:191]

Luther's accumulating of verbs reflects the preparation of a community in this life from a power beyond itself.

Luther's understanding of the two sacraments demonstrates the unity between internal and external, between the visible and the invisible Church. The Lord's Supper is the sacrament of love, and with its performance and reception in faith the community of all the saints becomes a living reality.[49] Luther considers the breaking of bread to be not alone the body of Christ but also the community of the body of Christ which is one shared and received in common. He opposes those radical reformers who would make this physical community a purely spiritual one. Christ's body can only be shared in a double way—bodily and spiritually. This bodily community is able to be neither visible nor sensible. Yet with the breaking of the bread there must be a genuine and physical being of the body of Christ, although invisible (18:170–72).

After the gospel the most important sacrament is baptism (12:191; 50:630). In attacking the existing view of baptism, Luther says that

49. Althaus, *Communio Sanctorum*, pp. 75–78.

it takes no account of faith or of the promise in the sacrament but fixes man's affection to the external sign. Baptism signifies a death to the world and a resurrection—a constant suffering and continual repentance in this life (6:527, 533, 535). Luther was later compelled to emphasize less the aspect of individual faith and give greater significance to baptism as a divine work and to the authority of a continued practice (26:153, 168). Nevertheless, even at this time prior to his experience with the Anabaptists, he spoke of a vicarious faith—the faith of parents and of the believing Church for the baptised infant whereby the life of the new born is bound to the community of the Church (6:538). As with the sacrament of the Lord's Supper, the symbol gives an eschatological quality to the whole life of the individual by incorporating him into the people of God.[50]

Wherever the three sacraments of the altar, baptism, and the Word are administered properly and received in faith, there is the Church. To these three chief signs Luther occasionally added several more. In his important tract *On Councils and Churches* (1539) he speaks of seven external signs of the Church; he includes therein the use of the keys, the calling and consecration of ministers, prayer, and the bearing of the Cross (50:630–32, 641–43). He represents these signs to be instituted by God and to have a truly common use in the Church. Concerning their institution, he states that God does not want to treat us in His majesty; because of our weakness He must deal with us indirectly in a veiled manner by the instituting of outward Word, sacrament, offices, and signs (50:647). Consequently, in the case of the sacraments, God's action is not impaired by the minister officiating, for the sacrament belongs to the one to whom it is administered and not to the administrant (50:631). Secondly, with respect to their common use, Luther has already made clear how the three sacraments proper mediate the Word that bears on all members of the community. Now he shows that the power of the keys and the calling of ministers belong to the holy

50. Prenter, pp. 147–48.

people collectively (50:632–33). Finally, prayer and the bearing of the Cross are so much a common property of the Church that they distinguish the entire life of the community of believers (50:641–42).

Invisible by its nature yet visible to faith, the Church still lives in the temporal-spatial dimension, although it is not limited to this dimension. If by its nature it transcends the historical, the Church does not escape history. Luther gives complete reality to the Church on earth. The crucial fact which determines this outlook is that the Word attacks men in time and that man's response in faith equally occurs in time. As the fundamental principle of Luther's ecclesiology, faith produces significant implications for the historical reality of the Church. In trying to emphasize the achievement of Luther's relating the invisible to the visible Church, Karl Holl noted the serious difference between a Church based on faith and one based on election. Whereas with Luther the effective Word of God in history builds the Church, with Augustine the Church was bound to an eternal decision concerning election. Augustine's true Church was in itself fully timeless; only through God's yonder will is it called forth and only for Him is it a present entity. Holl charges that this entity is not even a Church, because the decision of election provides no common bond for relating the individuals elected. With the Word, Luther overcomes this incoherence between invisible and visible Church, and through its dynamic activity God continually builds the Church in history.[51] The theology of the Word is a theology of redemption. By effectively smothering the implications of predestination, Luther allowed the redeeming event of Christ to stream outward in time and give historical significance to His Church.

Where the Word of God resounds, there is the people of God; God's Word cannot be present without God's people (50:629). The concept of the Church as the people of God further emphasizes its spatial and temporal condition. Luther cannot conceive of the

51. Holl, "Die Entstehung," *Ges. Auf. 1*, 299.

Church apart from confessing, believing men. The true definition of the Church does not reside in any succession from the apostles but in a people's confessing of Christ through the ages. (39/1:191–92). By the people of God Luther does not intend simply those now existing but includes all the Christian people who will have lived until the end of the world (50:625). While admitting the superior virtues and nobility of the patriarchs, Luther observes that the present Church includes the same people as that to which Moses, Joshua, Elijah, and other saints belonged. As members of the Church all have the same spirit and Word of God and have been the same preachers, servants, and officials of God (51:599).

In his distinction between the Kingdom of Christ and the Kingdom of God, Luther revealed the eschatological definition of this people. The two kingdoms are one by belonging to the spiritual Regiment, and yet they are distinct. One is in heaven, the other on earth; one in seeing, the other in hearing, preaching, and believing (49:573–75). Christ marshals His people not in heaven but on earth and will hand them over to God at the end of time (49:580; cf. 4:406). Writing to Spalatin in 1524, Luther laments the common opinion of the Kingdom of God as meaning simply the future glory; consequently people discount the present inchoate Kingdom of Christ. It is the same kingdom here and in the future—here inchoate, in the future consummated by glory (*WBr* 3:260). And again in the *Commentary on Galatians* he insists that the heavenly Jerusalem is not the Church Triumphant, as the sophists would believe, but the Church Militant. Its conversation in heaven pertains not to a particular place but to the fact that a Christian believes. The true Church is constituted on earth, not in heaven (40/1:662–63).

Eschatology provides the context for the holiness of the Church and in this way defines futher the Church's earthly existence. Like its individual members, who are at once sinners and justified, the Church is holy but at the same time sinful (40/1:197). As the people of faith, its members spend their entire lives in extending themselves toward righteousness by a continual sanctification that is nothing less than a repeated recovery of justification.[52] With a real catholicity Luther claims that the true Church is not so holy and pious as to be without errors. In this world it cannot be perfectly pure and as a living body it must be frequently purged of its excrements by Christ (39/1:145, 165). In its incompleteness and by the character of faith itself, the Church must include many discrepancies and apparent evils.

> For the true Church is that which prays and prays seriously from faith "Forgive us our debts as we forgive our debtors." The Church is that which from day to day advances, that which from day to day "puts on the new man and puts off the old." The Church is that which accepts the first fruits of the spirit, not tithes; and much less does it receive completeness in this life. We are not yet fully divested of the flesh and bare but we are in process of being divested and are moving forward. . . . Thus when you wish to pass judgment concerning the Church it must not[53] be considered simply where no vices and no scandals may be, but rather where there is the pure Word, the pure administration of the sacraments, where there are men loving the Word and confessing the Word before the world.
>
> [40/3:506]

God is the King of that people whose sins are forgiven (39/1:146).

Although holiness and the eschatological definition are important principles, they do not constitute the central feature of the Church in history. Rather it is the fact of being disguised and concealed which distinguishes the entire condition of the Church in time. The Church is hidden—the saints are concealed (18:652). Hiddenness characterizes the total life of man under the Cross: he cannot see

52. Prenter, p. 77. *WA* 56:264.

53. The context makes the *non* of the Erlangen edition preferable to the *nos* of the Weimar edition. Cf. *EOL* of 18:280.

God or comprehend the concealed way that God treats him; he can only apprehend God and submit to His ways in faith. In the same way, hiddenness pertains to the total condition of the Church as the community of believers. The central fact of the Church's existence is its adherence to the Word despite all trials and apparent contradictions. To the eyes of the world the Church remains unrecognized, for God buries His Church under sins and errors and various forms of the Cross (40/2:106). What is pleasing to Christ must be displeasing, deformed, and obscure to the world; externally black, the Church internally is well formed (5:456). The glory and power of Christ's reign are hidden and appear only under the form of ignominy and infirmity, humility and rejection (4:450–51). The hidden Church—not the visible Church nor a militant Church—serves as the proper category for the subject of Luther's view of Church history.

The Crucifixion provides the only clue to the understanding of this reality, for the hidden Church is the Church under Christ and His Cross. Luther explains the seventh sign of the Church as the possession of the Holy Cross by which the Church is outwardly known. He describes this sign in terms of a life of suffering and rejection: the Christian people are the most wretched and the most hated; they must endure all misfortune and persecution, evil and temptation; they must be inwardly sad and cast down, outwardly poor and despised as their Head—Christ. But the Cross comes to signify more than simply suffering; it means an adherence to the Word that entails a denial by the world and a conscious opposition to all the world's values (50:642). And just as the fact of the Cross penetrates every aspect of Luther's theology, in the same way it provides the decisive key to his understanding of the Church's life. The hidden Church conforms to the entirety of the Cross in its suffering, rejection, and condemnation by the world.

Thus the true Church lies hidden, is excommunicated, considered heretical, killed (42:187). Only in such a Church can faith be determinative.

History and Scripture

Luther experienced history as a movement or progression in which God was ever active in using men as His instruments to accomplish His counsels. But Luther also recognized the existence of history as a description of past events. History as a knowledge did not exist apart from history as God's activity in time, for in the first God was the subject and in the second the author or agent of history. The ultimate purpose of recorded history was to bring man to a knowledge of God through His works. This indirect knowledge of God, this knowledge of God's back as it were, expressed the close bond between theology and history both as a knowledge and as a form of moral philosophy. Luther granted to historical knowledge a respectable measure of authority and veracity as well as a considerable utility. Nevertheless these attributes were only possible through the agreement of historical knowledge with Scripture. Recorded history had the core of its knowledge and meaning in Scripture but extended beyond Scripture.

Luther generally uses the term *historia* in its original sense of a narrative or story. Only very seldom does he employ the singular to denote historical knowledge in general (2:289); ordinarily he uses the plural—histories—to convey the idea of the historical knowledge in respect to a people or to some past events. He suggests that these stories and narratives are to be related to a rational type of knowledge. In preparing for the Leipzig debate, he associated histories with rational demonstrations or proofs; they constituted one of the three categories of his argumentation (2:187, 225, 235). Toward the end of his life he again suggested the rational basis of histories. As in all his exegetical works, when he speaks of the historical he means the literal sense of Scripture, the real significance of past events that may be derived from a literal acceptance of the text. In opposing the use of allegory, Luther refers to the concrete narrative as a sort of dialectic which teaches truly and unquestionably. In contradistinction, allegory stands in the capacity of rhetoric; it can ornament history, but it does not have the power of testing or demonstrating (42:173–74).

This implicit rational basis of histories requires some understanding of Luther's conception of *ratio*. In the first place reason has no theological content independent of Scripture. It is a formal method of elucidating logical conclusions from already recognized premises. Luther uses reason only to confirm negative judgments and never to establish statements of faith provided only by Scripture. Consequently, at Leipzig he could group reasons and histories together. They both confirm but do not verify previously established statements. Histories are a knowledge obtained through reason, but like *ratio* itself they derive their content and authority from Scripture.[54]

The nature of history and its expansion as a result of Luther's hermeneutics can be seen in his exegesis of the Garden of Eden in Genesis. He finds the question as to the exact location and existence of Paradise idle unless one realizes that Moses writes about a deed before the Flood and even before sin. We, however, are compelled to speak of things as after the Flood and sin. Luther then states his belief that at the time of Adam there was a place called Eden. The name of this vanished place remained for later generations just as the names of Carthage, Rome, and Athens remain today; but scarcely any vestiges of these republics can be seen. Time and the curse, the rewards of sin, consume all. Before the Flood Eden existed; after the Flood it was destroyed (42:67).

With the Garden of Eden literally accepted, Luther sees Moses' account now in the description of history. God's establishment of the Garden and His placing of man therein are historical in that they should be literally accepted as events which once were and are now past. Luther objects to Origen's allegorizing of the Garden whereby Paradise is heaven, the trees angels, and the rivers wisdom. Origen does not recognize that Moses writes a history about things that

54. Hans Preuss, "Was bedeutet die Formel 'Convictus testimoniis scripturarum aut ratione evidente' in Luthers ungehörnter Antwort zu Worms," *Theologische Studien und Kritiken, 81* (1908), 75–81.

once existed and are now past. Paradise can thus be spoken of as a historical paradise that previously existed. In the same manner we can consider the innocence of man; we can remember this loss with sighs, but restore it in this life we cannot (42:68–69).

It is significant that Luther should develop from Scripture his views of the nature and beginning of historical knowledge. The Bible not only provided him with his view of history but also served as his greatest single source. It is not that he read the Bible with the eyes of a historian; nevertheless, while discovering the Word everywhere present in Scripture, his own exegesis allowed him to perceive history in Scripture. In his effort to discover the Spirit working through the events literally described, he brought the trials and joys of the patriarchs, the sufferings of the prophets, and the struggle of a people into historical reality by a literal acceptance of the text. Although previous exegetes had faithfully employed the literal sense, they had looked for the higher, the spiritual sense elsewhere in allegory, with the result that the events and persons of the Old Testament assumed only a shadowy significance that looked to the Advent of Christ. Luther could recognize events as past events and therefore not recoverable. This past, however, was not a dead past, for its events stood as examples of faith by which one moved from the temporal event to faith in Christ.

The authority and veracity of history as a knowledge derive from its agreement with Scripture. This belief is based on Luther's faith that history itself is God's work; moreover, it drew support from the fact that Luther's historical judgment was religiously bound and guided by his theological assumptions. In the momentous review of medieval authorities and traditions which culminated at Leipzig, Luther manifested many talents of the humanist in detecting the origin of a practice or the location in time of a person, yet his final judgment was based on his theological assumptions and the religious needs of the moment.[55] In his debate with Eck, Luther advanced,

55. Cf. Koehler, *L. und K.*, p. 363 passim.

along with his Scriptural arguments, a historical argument drawn from the fathers, the great Church councils, and the best histories then available to support his contention that the primacy of the Pope was not ordained by divine law but was a result of human law dating only from the last four centuries. When the exegesis of Matthew 16:18 became the central issue of the debate, both contestants appealed to postbiblical history. And despite its formally subordinate position, in the heat of controversy history seemed to move beyond its proper role of illuminating the text of Scripture and threatened to determine the text's meaning.[56]

At the time of the debates, Luther urged with remarkable skill the authority of history insofar as it advanced his scriptural argument and religious assumptions. By noting the historical inaccuracy of a canon attributed to Anacletus, he felt free to deny the authenticity of this controversial canon (2:209). In these instances the authority of history outweighed that of the fathers and popes alike. When Eck used Cyprian as his authority for maintaining that the major part of the clergy could not err, Luther countered the authority of the Church father by pointing to the years that the Arians had ruled in the Church (2:347). Earlier in the debate Luther, in seeking to displace one of Eck's arguments with the authority of history, suggested that the record of events had an objective truth. Eck had protested Luther's use of the historian Platina to counter the assembled authorities of Augustine, Cyprian, and the Roman pontiff for the papal primacy. Luther replied: "I attribute nothing to Platina, but to history which is the mother of truth and which Platina writes" (2:289).

This extreme statement of recorded history's objectivity given in the heat of debate can only be fairly assessed within the context of Luther's belief that history as an action is God's work. In his preface to Galeazzo Capella's *History* in 1538, Luther gave a more mature and balanced consideration of this problem. Here he does not deny

56. Pelikan, *Expositor*, pp. 113–18.

the human element in history as a knowledge, but he struggles to limit the room for human error. Admittedly, it would require a man of unusual integrity to report the truth consistently. Most historians twist their narratives for favor or gain, and the reader must consider whether the author wrote out of favor or disfavor. Thus the authority of histories is diminished and God's work is darkened. The office of the historian is only to be entrusted to those called to it.

> For because histories describe nothing other than God's work —that is grace and wrath—which one must so worthily believe as if they stood in the Bible, they should certainly be written with the greatest diligence, faithfulness, and truth. [50:385]

Released from the pressure of religious debate, Luther can afford to urge a dispassionate and just attitude upon the historian. But the authority and truth of history lie ultimately with the fact that history is God's work and must therefore agree with the Bible and Luther's religious outlook. Histories, Luther states, are nothing other than the announcement, remembrance, and memorial of Godly work and judgment as to how He rules and preserves the world and men (50:384).

From the time of his first efforts to establish the temporal nature of papal claims, Luther continued to emphasize the utility of history. As a part of moral philosophy, history provided a host of examples, and Luther often mentioned the two in the same breath. Histories are valuable, for they teach by example everything which the Word previously communicated through doctrine. One finds there all rights, art, counsel, threats, consolations, teachings, and virtues poured forth as from a living fountain. In being instructed by these histories, those who care little about God may be restrained by fear (50:383–84). Luther understands this moral utility of history as constituting a practical fear of God that falls short of the religious conscience and justification itself. In 1525 Luther wrote that from histories men can order their minds and direct their lives with the fear of God. These histories, which counsel and rule what to seek and what to avoid in this external life, may help men become rational and bring the internal life into conformity (15:45). For the man in high office histories are very useful for ruling and understanding how the world runs and for seeing God's wonder and works (15:52).

The examples afforded by histories provide instruction and guidance. In this instance Luther would appear to approach the historiography of the humanists, whose use of classical examples as models of virtue was intended to have an educative effect upon man. But an analysis of Luther's distinctions in types of examples and his qualified use of the concomitant idea of imitation indicates that his exemplarism was directed more to supporting a religious attitude than to providing moral norms for individual cultivation. The question concerns the examples of men in history and does not pertain to the example of Christ, which stands at the core of the religious life and confronts the troubled conscience as virtual law in the dialectic of law and gospel (cf. 40/2:42–43).

An analysis of the relevant statements in two of his later works reveals an increasing caution toward exemplarism. In the exegesis of Psalm 101 written in 1534–35 he states his theory of the superiorly endowed men. Every people has certain strong men or heroes who are endowed by God with special gifts and who, in appearing to control events within the worldly Regiment, readily offer themselves as examples for imitation. If one is not supposed to learn from and to imitate the good examples of the wise and the great, why are such examples set before us in the worldly Regiment? Luther maintains that of course one should follow good examples in all walks of life. They should not, however, be aped, but imitated according to one's ability and, as Luther would imply, according to what the Holy Spirit allows (51:213). Because the world is a sick thing where, as in a hospital, all is patchwork, man in history must get along as best he can with the help of law and the sayings and examples of heroes until God provides him with another hero or superiorly endowed man who either changes the law or so masters it that life again flourishes in peace (51:214–15).

Once having made this broad statement as to the general application of heroic examples for imitation, Luther tends to focus his attention upon David as the exemplary ruler. He will call upon anyone who is able to be a David and follow his example, but for the most part Luther seeks to present a model ruler to his own prince (51:237). David is an example of how princes and kings are supposed to serve God; he gives himself as an example in the worldly Regiment (51:238). Because he displayed no pride in his office, he serves as an example of modesty to be imitated by those who can. Luther would also include Hercules in this judgment, for both manifest a noble virtue directed by God (51:252, 244). Finally, he will remark that if one is seeking a princely example in the worldly Regiment, Alexander, Philip of Macedon, Augustus, and Trajan offer themselves (51:242). Accordingly, it would appear from these statements that God provides a people with certain gifted men who are to be imitated to some extent by the common man in ordinary life but more particularly by the ruler in his office.

In his initial struggle with the Enthusiasts, Luther recognized the dangers involved in an indiscriminate exemplarism and the need for making some important distinctions (cf. 16:238; *WBr* 5:525). Subsequently, the radical aspects of the Reformation became more pronounced, and at Münster a King David appeared and went down in a sea of blood. With precisely such extravagances in mind Luther clarified his position (43:643). In his last great work, the *Lectures on Genesis,* he had frequent opportunity to treat the matter of exemplarism. It should be noted that when considering the question of the exemplary ruler he does not depart from his former position: he claims that Joseph's act of bringing reverence for the Word into government counsel is an example to be respected (44:408, 658). But more often he is concerned with promoting the common Christian life. In this respect he establishes a definite limit to any general application of heroic examples.

The case that Luther considers is that of Jacob having two wives after the deception concerning Leah. Luther's argument proceeds from the standpoint that some examples are heroic while others are moral, and that the latter type must alone be followed, lest by transgression of the law confusion result. Heroic examples conform to no laws but occur by a special divine inspiration wherein God breaks the law. As they are not to be followed unless they may apply in general to all and conform with common laws, heroic examples have no consequence or value for imitation. The man whom God leads heroically rather than legally is to be admired but not imitated. Jacob here does not act by his own will but is seized by the will of God and forced to do it beyond his own will and opinion (43:640–42). In this way Luther is able to excuse the immoralities of the patriarchs. These divine inspirations imparted to a few special men are in effect the occasional insertion of God's absolute power in the ordained orders of the creation. In his treatment of the problem Luther has constant recourse to the common legal basis provided by God's ordained power.

This limitation to the example of the superiorly endowed men Luther accentuated in the last few years of his life. One hears of Alexander the Great, Scipio, and others and dreams of being equal to them in virtues and in strength and of emulating those who do great things without the Word and invocation. But Luther adds that these virtues and actions are fortuitous gifts scattered indiscriminately on good and bad like the rays of the sun; they are not examples proposed for imitation. The imitation of an Alexander, a Scipio, an Augustus are worth nothing, and although God still produces at will heroes to withstand the pressure of evil men in government, for Luther such examples are not worth one's consideration (44:404–06).

In the realm of the spiritual Regiment, Luther's attitude toward exemplarism is far less ambiguous, for here the problem encounters his doctrine of justification. Any imitation of a saint or great religious figure not only obscures the redemptive action of Christ but leads inevitably to a fatal righteousness from good works. In the case of Daniel, Luther remarks that Christ saved three from the fiery furnace. But on this account the holy life is not to be followed as an example; it should only be praised and extolled as a wonderful sign. For just as God does not want each of us to do a miracle in the fiery furnace, so He does not want to make a Bernard, a Francis, a Benedict, or an Augustine out of each one of us (10/1:606). In the same year, 1522, Luther attacked the authority of the saints which the Roman Church adduced to support its canon of the Mass. He warns us that there is nothing under heaven more dangerous than the deeds of saints unsupported by the testimony of Scripture. The examples of saints are both pernicious and misleading if we seek works rather than faith in them. Their faith not their act is to be imitated (8:449–51). Hebrews 13:7 provides the scriptural text for imitating the faith rather than aping the deeds of the saints (44:676).

This command to consider the faith and not to imitate the deed is of capital significance for understanding Luther's attitude to exemplarism and imitation. In his reading of the events of Scripture as well as the events in the past of the Church, he transmutes what had been examples of works into examples of faith. It is not the external act which is to be repeated, but an inner event which is to be appropriated. The displacement of imitation by faith assigns the significance of an example no longer to a number of good acts but to the support of a religious attitude. If the examples that histories provide do not serve to promote faith and demonstrate God's constant presence and concern for man (43:665), then at least they might inspire a fear of God (15:45). By his treatment of exemplarism Luther desires to limit the imitation and reshape the nature of the consequence. In the spiritual Regiment he emphasizes this imitation of faith as a means of combating the pernicious effects of a righteousness based on good works and the Enthusiasts' appeal to special examples. And in both Regimente he seeks to transmute the imitation of the heroic, the extraordinary, and the great into a praise of God's presence and activity in history (43:391; 44:110, 588); not the unique nor the spectacular but rather the common Christian life is to be promoted. Consequently, Luther's understanding of exemplarism conforms with his theocentric view of history.

Luther sought the aid of histories for more than simply the cultivation of a religious attitude. Specifically, he found support there for his attack upon the Papacy. He continued to lament the lack of good histories and the fragmentary and scattered remains of the past. He felt that this condition had become worse since the time of Eusebius and that in this period Christ had been driven out of the religious life and a new Christ had appeared. Luther urged a historical investigation of the papal tyranny so that faithful and well-preserved histories might warn the pious of subsequent generations (50:3–5). History came to assume an admonitory function in Luther's eyes, and it was not long before he recognized the need to compose and record his own account of previous corruptions and present reforms (30/2:367–68, 390). Certainly in the last part of his life he took an active interest in the printing of documents that notified German posterity of the papal tyranny and warned them to avoid it (50:355, 361). Almost twenty years after the Leipzig debates, Luther could reflect that not being sufficiently versed in histories, he had assaulted the Papacy a priori—from Scripture. Now aware of the agreement between histories and Scripture he took pleasure in attacking the Papacy a posteriori—from histories. He rejoiced that histories supported in specific and individual cases what he had previously learned and taught from Paul and Daniel as to the Papacy's being the Adversary of God (50:5).

In respect to his own dear Germans, Luther urged the necessity of histories. He decried the number of fine events and sayings that had happened in German lands and that had never been written or had failed to be preserved. Thus foreign lands knew nothing about the Germans and quite justly looked upon them as beasts. Luther pointed to the Greeks, Latins, and Hebrews in their diligent and precise recording of themselves for posterity and would have had the Germans emulate them (15:52).

Thus for the two subjects nearest to his affections—the Christian faith and the German people—Luther found that the utility of history surpassed a mere collection of examples. Concerning his Germans he appealed to histories for the recovery of examples but also for filling in a thousand years of the past as a means of giving this people a certain pride, incentive, and self-consciousness. It is true that his later interest in history generally appeared as a search for examples to demonstrate the perversion and corruption wrought by the Papacy. At Leipzig, however, he used his historical knowledge for the more profound purpose of helping to cut through the mass of conflicting authorities in order to prove that the Papacy was not *iure divino* and therefore represented a historical phenomenon.

This auxiliary role of history extended to exegesis, and in the years following the disputation at Leipzig, Luther appealed to the authority of history in order to clarify the significance of a scriptural text. He often allowed extrabiblical history to provide the minor premise of a syllogistic argument. Although he preferred to argue from history rather than from the fathers, he rarely permitted the recorded past to determine the meaning of a text. Only because the Revelation of St. John was an otherwise inexplicable and barren prophecy did he later indulge in a cautious and provisional attempt to establish the text's meaning by comparing its predictions with the subsequent events of history.[57]

With the growth of Luther's interest in history during his later years went an increasing appreciation of the worth of chronology, which he referred to as the light of history (43:138). His *Reckoning of the Years of the World,* intended as a time chart for his own personal use, attests to this respect for chronology. The Bible served as the guide for his chronology, and in the postbiblical period he relied heavily upon Carion's *Chronicle*. In comparing previous

57. *WAB* 7:408. Cf. Pelikan, *Expositor,* pp. 93, 118.

chronicles, he subscribes to Jerome's appreciation of Eusebius' *Chronicle* and announces his dissatisfaction with all the others. Nevertheless, he draws liberally upon contemporary works to aid him in determining this chronology. Concerning a particular discrepancy between a chronology attributed to Megasthenes and that of Scripture, Luther prefers the latter because he believes that in Scripture God speaks, whereas in histories the best men speak; they may be able, diligent, and faithful but they are still mere men (53:24, 27).

Scripture provided Luther with more than a chronology and a canon of authority. In it he found a *sacra historia* which stood apart from all other histories. The nature of this history has already been considered in respect to God's activity in time. Now it must be seen in the perspective of history as a knowledge.

In the exegesis of what appears to be a trivial event in Genesis, Luther asks whether the deeds of the kings of Egypt, Babylon, and Persia are not worthier of relation. No doubt there are more and greater deeds than are described in Genesis, but those ostensible levities surpass all others in consolation and doctrine. What are these gentile histories described by Virgil, Homer, Livy, and others with so many ornate words? They are histories of the Greeks, of Alexander, and of Hannibal.

> But they are abandoned by that magnificence, glory, and crown which is the Word of God and the promise. They lack this diadem. Indeed they are more truly afflictions than histories, for what is history without the Word of God? . . . Although the histories [of God's people] may appear puerile and sordid, nevertheless they have an immense and infinite weight—the Word of God itself. However, the histories of Alexander and Julius Caesar are quite distinguished and certainly brilliant, but they lack the true ornament. Indeed they are like chaff dispersed by the wind and destitute of true weight. They are but the glory of the belly and of the flesh. [43:672]

The Word distinguishes sacra historia from all other histories; profane history knows nothing of the promise—only the deeds and industry of men (42:430).

Sacra historia is present in Scripture but not confined to Scripture. Luther usually applies the term to the Jewish people as it appears in the Old Testament. But because sacra historia signifies the history of a particular people with the Word of God, the implications of the subject extend beyond the written account in the Bible. Luther explains that sacred histories are common to all men having the Word of God and in whom God works with His gracious purpose (43:672). Ultimately this type of history refers to the hidden people of faith in all times and places.

The Word and man's response in faith provide the context necessary for understanding the relationship between sacra historia and Scripture. In the preface to Justus Menius' commentary on the first book of Samuel, Luther rebukes the fathers for having omitted faith, which is the sole virtue that distinguishes sacred histories from profane histories. Under the name of the old they have created new histories that are useless and dead.

> You will see these same stories through the use of faith to be reborn as if by a certain baptism and to be made new for us in our age, yes even to live forever and to serve usefully with splendid and most clear examples of faith for the purpose of edifying, urging, instructing and consoling—in short, for all that Paul attributes to the word of faith. For what is a sacred story but the visible word of faith or work of faith, because it teaches us the same by deed and by work that Scripture otherwise gives by word and by proclamation? [30/3:539–40]

Thus while sacra historia is found in Scripture, it is neither apart from nor identical with the content of Scripture which is the Word. In that it is faith as lived and doctrine as made manifest, it stands as the outer description of that inner gift which is the Word in Scripture. It is important that this type of history provides examples not of deeds but of faith. The word of faith and the work of faith are the responses of believing man to the Word of God and the work of God which are communicated through the spiritual Regiment and operative in God's people. For it is God's Word and work which relate the stories of this people's past with the content of Scripture and with the life of the Church. The God who appears in Scripture as being active through His Word and work in sacred story is the same God who through His Word and work rules the community of believers in history.

Although Luther uses the term sacra historia in both the singular and the plural to connote on the one hand a single design in history and on the other hand a number of stories, a fundamental unity exists. Sacred histories agree and are at one in what drives them and in what they reflect. "In sacred history two things must be seen: faith and unbelief in respect to the Word of God" (13:68:16). And again in the preface to the New Testament of 1522 Luther states that just as the Old Testament is a book which contains the laws and commands of God together with the history of both those who held and those who did not hold to them, so the New Testament is a book which presents the gospel and God's promise together with the history of those who believed and those who did not believe in it (*WAB* 6:2).

Faith and unbelief—these are the great themes of Church history. And at the vortex is the Word, this veritable attack of God upon world history. The Word that constitutes the Church as a community of believers is the same Word that impels this terrible struggle. The arena of its redemptive action is the entire world; the fruit of its redemptive action is the Church—neither physically demonstrable nor triumphant, but crucified, dispossessed, hidden.

2. THE PROBLEM OF TRADITION

A MODERN PHILOSOPHER once characterized Greco-Roman historiography as being substantialistic. Substantialism refers to a metaphysics which identifies real substance with mind or with the objective forms; it implies a theory of knowledge that claims only the unchanging to be knowable. In the understanding of the past, substantialism produces a distinction between act and agent. While history involves only the acts which originate, develop, and terminate in time, the agent from which they flow remains unchanged through the series of its acts. The agent, whether it be an institution, city, or even a body of knowledge, exists as a substantial reality outside any historical process and is unaffected by the accidents of time which may impinge upon it but do not transform it. Since the historian attempts to know the changing and consequently the unknowable, substantialist thinking becomes incompatible with historical thinking.[1]

Substantialism, however, is not limited to Greco-Roman historiography but remains clearly evident during the Middle Ages and into the period of the Reformation. Its persistence in Western

1. R. G. Collingwood, *The Idea of History* (Oxford, 1946), pp. 42–43.

historiography is partly attributable to the enduring influence of Greek metaphysics. The Christian Church imbibed and perpetuated this Platonism. In its own effort to secure the permanence of an authoritative knowledge in time, the Church provided a second reason for the continuance of substantialism. With the concept of tradition, the substantialist attitude underwent both a transformation and a significant restatement in terms of Christian revelation.

Even in its most general sense, the concept of tradition proper has nothing at all to do with a unified historical development nor with any accumulation of practices over a length of time; in fact these ideas tend to disfigure and pervert the concept. The structure of the concept is identical with teaching except that the transmitter must have received the same that he teaches. Nevertheless, tradition is not a learning process, and it signifies no sense of progress, accumulation, or note of personal originality. Tradition as authority denies any critical review, private investigation, or rational verification; consequently, it is opposed to the historical consciousness. The concept involves the necessity for each generation to be reminded of the same unchanged body of knowledge. The binding force and the indispensable core of this body of knowledge exist in its going back in origin to a divine message. On this account, antiquity and more specifically the ancients figure significantly within the concept, for, according to Plato, the ancients stand near the point of origin and have received a message from the divine source.[2] In a similar way for the Christian revelation, the authority of Scripture and sacred letters derives from its proximity and witness to the divine source—Christ.

The mentality which supports such a concept is pre-eminently social. It assumes that men can be trusted and that each generation will hand over to the next the knowledge which it has received. It is quite oblivious to processes in time and it lumps past and present in a single community—a timeless continuum where cause and effect,

2. Joseph Pieper, "The Concept of Tradition," *The Review of Politics, 20* (1958), 475–82.

antecedent and consequence play no part. The authenticity of an idea or an institution demands that it exist through the whole range of time. The condemnation of novelty leveled at an institution or idea signifies that it is cut off from the point of origin, invalid for the life of the community, and as an introduction in time it will perish in time.[3] Yet there exists a fallacy in the traditionalist outlook: the mentality which at first preserved the original tradition eventually perverts it. Since any essential change or innovation is inadmissible, the traditionalist outlook becomes in effect an instrument of present authority; it justifies this authority by assigning antiquity to existing practices no matter how recent in derivation.[4]

At the beginning of the sixteenth century, Latin Christendom was undergoing a re-examination of its past. While the work of the humanists had contributed new sources and a method for the critical examination of texts, a historical outlook upon the past remained in its infancy and the traditionalist mentality prevailed. In the work of Martin Luther one may see the supreme effort of the age to discover the true tradition for the Christian Church. Luther brought to this task a mind which shared many of the principles operative in the substantialistic and traditionalist outlook upon the past, but he uniquely transformed this outlook by his theology of the Word of God.

In the Church of the patriarchs, Luther found the paradigm for all of Church history. This early period of the Church did not provide him with an ideal age in the past to which one must return; rather, by the exposition of its heroes' faith through tribulations and suffering, this period presented most sharply the abiding face (*perpetua facies*) of the Church for all time (42:297). Although Luther inevitably read the past of the Church in the light of contemporary events, this common feature of a traditionalist outlook upon history does not explain his idea of the continuity and the

3. R. R. Palmer, *Catholics and Unbelievers in Eighteenth Century France* (Princeton, 1939), pp. 56–57.

4. Cf. Palmer, p. 58.

permanent pattern of Church history. To understand the nature of this enduring countenance of the Church and the principle of continuity that maintains the Church in time, it is necessary to study first the hidden Church and then Luther's conception of tradition.

The Pattern of Church History

Between 1518 and his departure for Worms in 1521, Luther undertook his second formal treatment of the Psalms. During this period, which possibly comprised the most anxious and crucial years of his life, Luther revealed in the *Operations on the Psalms* the range and direction of his thought. Informative as the work is to an understanding of his spiritual progress, it is equally important in disclosing the genesis of his view of Church history. As he presses forward in his task of exegesis, his dilemma becomes increasingly evident: teaching from the center of the medieval Church, the reformer moves from a hesitant recognition of the Antichrist in the present magnates of the Church to a final outright identification of the Antichrist with the Roman tyranny (cf. 5:336–37, 339–40, 442, 479, 644, 649–50, 653). But far more important than this gradual recognition of the Antichrist in the Church is his attempt to discover the continuing presence of the Church within the ecclesiastical empire which he rejects. In this respect his effort to relate the hiddenness of the Church more directly to the Word prepares for his ultimate understanding of the pattern of Church history.

In attacking the extreme externalization of the Church, Luther begins to define the nature of the hidden Church and its course in time. Birth, place, name, extravagant works, do not mark the Church; only faith, which condemns all names and works, distinguishes the people of God. Having renounced all the external marks and dignities which the world craves, this people must remain separated and hidden on earth, relying on God alone and existing in His sight. The sense of opposition and the nature of the opponent become clearer; there emerges a counter-Church possessing the appearance, power, and above all the name of Christ's Church (5:446–47). In fact this false satanic phenomenon may be called the Church of the name which opposes the Church of the Word (5:515). Luther accuses the present Church of renewing the three presumptions of the Jews who boasted of possessing the blood, the numbers, and finally the glory and name of righteousness and religion. Similarly the present Church boasts of succession in an apostolic race, of numbers, and of the right to establish laws and ceremonies (5:452–53). In contrast, the standard of Christ's kingdom is the Word of the Cross (5:574).

The Word, which distinguishes the hidden Church from its present administration and externalities, also provides the life and continuity of the Church. Always in action, motion, even flight, the preached Word moves men to faith. God's tabernacle, though hidden, resides in the midst of His saints. By being always present God helps the Church (5:505–06). Luther emphasizes the reality of God's presence to the believer. He deplores the fact that people devote excessive attention to the doctrines concerning the past and future actions of God such as the Creation, Incarnation, the Last Judgment, and hell, while remaining insensitive to His present activity which manifests itself through His mercy in the sacraments, His forgiveness, and His grace (5:576). Causes and persons change, but the same Word presides over the Church and engenders the same faith in this hidden house of God (5:581).

The *Operations on the Psalms* does not contain Luther's first treatment of the hidden Church nor does it represent his final exposition of this idea. Nevertheless, the work indicates a decisive development in his use of the idea. The true Church is a hidden one not simply because of its contrast with the externalized Church of Rome but more profoundly because of the nature of faith and of God's revelation in the Word of the Cross. For the Word produces a transvaluation of values, hiding the mystery of God's ways from the wise and the prudent, and making the believer appear impious to the unbeliever (5:523, 657). One should not, however, exaggerate at this stage of Luther's development the struggle between a hidden Church and an apparent Church. He recognized a struggle in Church history but designated it simply as one between the pious and the impious or the obedient and the disobedient (5:313, 327, 514). The subsequent idea of the Church's twofold nature—the hidden and the possessory Church—did not emerge.

Perhaps the complexity of Luther's position to the institutional Church prevented a clearer definition of the hidden Church and its struggle at this time. He never regarded himself as a schismatic and least of all immediately before his encounter with the Emperor at Worms (cf. 2:604–05). In the exegesis of these Psalms he may identify the Roman tyranny with the Antichrist and reject the ecclesiastical system which has arisen, but he never loses his sense of responsibility and obligation to the Church as a single organized community. In deploring the corruptions which the Church suffers and in recalling the Church to her true principles, Luther stands in the midst of this confusion and shares the agony of Christ's body (5:442–43, 574). Neither at this moment nor at any later time in his career does he allow his belief in the hiddenness of the Church to relieve him of his care and responsibility for the institutional aspect of the Church (cf. 50:514).

As the true Church, the hidden Church does not lack organized expression but it is never coterminous and identical with the institutional framework. Luther would appear to be reminding the latter of its essential nature. Faith alone gives unity to the people of God and provides the common study of the Church; anything else is sectarianism (5:662). Yet so grave is the condition of the Church and so real the presence of the Antichrist that Luther despairs of any general reformation (5:345). True, until the end of the world Christ remains in the Church but poured out as water, his bones out of joint, his heart melted, and the gospel of his tongue cleaving to his jaws (5:642). At the end of this exegetical work, Luther gives a final and emphatic definition of the Antichrist in terms of the present Roman tyranny. By means of this eschatological crisis he relates the hiddenness of the Church to its general institutional aspect: the Roman Antichrist persecutes the institutional Church and rears a specious authority which has the name and appearance of Christ and His Church (5:650–53).

In the last years of his life, Luther clearly defined the historical existence of a twofold Church which he had first sketched in the months before Worms. In his *Lectures on Genesis* he established the hiddenness of the Church in the self-concealment of God and elaborated the pattern of Church history according to the experience of the patriarchs. In the exegesis of Genesis 32:32, Luther explains that just as our Head, Christ, is hidden in God, so the hidden Church lies concealed under apparent trifles. Likewise it is fitting for this Church to appear to the world as seditious, erring, heretical —a pool of the worst men who have ever lived. Yet it sustains this opprobrium as a treasure with which God ornaments it in this life. With such an example as the tribulations of the patriarch Jacob, God shows how He exercises the universal Church; here He appears almost as an enemy who would wish to abandon or even to destroy the Church. But to be vexed and ridiculed inwardly even by its own ostensible members is the glory of this community, whose faith is constantly being exercised. But why, Luther again urges, why this contempt, odium, and confusion brought about by the presence of the Church? The answer lies in God's self-concealment. He is hidden and yet not hidden. He is hidden to us and we are hidden to the world because at one with Him. Like His Church, God is revealed and seen in faith, in the Word, and in the sacraments (44:110).

While the hidden nature of the Church arises from Luther's concept of God himself, it is related directly to his own experience and to his understanding of that of the patriarchs. The hiddenness of the Church consists in its standing opposed to the wisdom, power, and wealth of the world; through the proclamation of the Word and its response in faith, this community must suffer persecution rather than receive recognition from the world. Luther pursues this idea of the true Church's hiddenness to its ultimate conclusion in the view that it is hidden not only to secular authorities but even to itself. In his idea of the twofold Church (*duplex Ecclesia*) he seeks to express the profound fact that the true Church is most severely persecuted and mocked not by the authorities of this world nor by external foes but by its own ostensible members who have the name, the office, and all the trappings of the Church without the Word. Through this concept of the twofold Church, the true and the false Church (*Ecclesia vera et hypocritica*), and of their unrelenting struggle, Luther enters upon an explicit consideration of Church history.

The same Word, however, which distinguishes the two Churches and impels their struggle, also sustains the true Church throughout all time. It is therefore necessary to consider momentarily the origins of the Church in time and to relate the factors of division and struggle to that of the factor of permanence. By his literal acceptance of the Garden of Eden, Luther makes Paradise a part of Church history.[5] The seventh day sees the sabbath established for the worship of God, and man thereby directed to a spiritual and higher existence. The real Church begins with God's commanding Adam not to partake of the tree of knowledge. God institutes the Church as a sign to show man that he is distinct from other animate beings (42:60–61, 79). In the state of innocence the tree of knowledge of good and evil was Adam's temple, pulpit, and altar (42:72).

Luther enlarges upon the transcendent beauty, joy, and virtue of existence on the seventh day in a way that serves to emphasize the magnitude of man's sin and the deprivation suffered through the Fall. Significantly, the sin of Eve and the Fall result from unbelief, the source of all sin (42:111, 122). The full depths of man's misery are revealed in the meaning of original sin: human nature has completely fallen and the intellect so darkened that man no longer knows God and His will and no longer perceives His works (42:86).

5. On the theological implications relating to this idea, see Jaroslov Pelikan, "Cosmos and Creation: Science and Theology in Reformation Thought," *Proceedings of the American Philosophical Society, 105* (1961), 464–69.

But in God's consoling of the unhappy pair emerges the permanent element in Church history. For God does not include them in the same condemnation as the serpent and Satan; rather, He revives them by the hope and the promise that the seed of the woman will destroy the head of the serpent. Thus Adam and Eve rejoice in the same hope shared by all believers that sin will be removed, death vanquished, and the lost obedience restored. Through their faith they participate already in this life and righteousness (42:141–47). The Church persists through the hope and the promise of the Christ to come.

Integrally related to this permanent and sustaining factor in Church history is the factor of division and struggle. The Word of God comprises both these activities. Each presents an aspect that suggests its own origin to the Church in history. The patristic heritage similarly reveals this appeal to a double origin. In their recognition of the Church's supra-temporal reality, whose origin was anterior to the Incarnation, the fathers generally recognized Adam rather than Abel as the beginning of the Church. It was Augustine who in his anti-Pelagian writings developed the figure of Abel in the West.[6] Notwithstanding Luther's indebtedness to Augustine in this respect, his doctrine of the Word of God embraces both these activities and posits both points of origin. When Luther wishes to emphasize the continuity of the true Church rather than its suffering, hidden nature, he places its origin with Adam, who has the hope and the promise (42:215, 242–43, 269). But insofar as the history of the Church is a narrative of a dual progeny locked in a terrible conflict which always presents the same essential features, this history begins with Abel and Cain. The blood relationship of the two brothers, yet their radical difference and opposition, signify the apparent bond but violent antagonism between the twin Churches—the true and the false—which Abel and Cain represent

6. Yves Congar, "Ecclesia ab Abel," *Abhandlungen über Theologie und Kirche: Festschrift für Karl Adam,* ed. Marcel Reding (Dusseldorf, 1952), p. 81.

(42:184). Within the context of God's abiding Word there occurs the struggle between faith and unbelief.

With the favor shown by God to Abel's sacrifice, the twofold nature of the Church emerges. Cain's slaying of his brother follows this preference of the second-born to Cain's own primogenitural right. Thus, in the Church of the name and title there is nothing but hypocrisy and external proofs of possession, whereas the true Church is desolate and crucified. Christ considers Abel righteous and makes him the beginning of the generation of the pious; with Cain, on the other hand, begins the Church of the wicked and of those who seek hereditary possession (42:186–87). By its historical appearance, the Church reveals a twofold aspect wherein two posterities stand opposed: one in false magnificence, the other faithful and suffering; one persecuting, the other persecuted (42: 189; 43:159). Cain seeks to be the pope, whereas the true Church is despised in accordance with the figure of Abel, who represents the beginning as well as the image of the hidden Church (42:188).

Beyond the obvious differences there exists a more profound reason for the opposition between the two generations. Luther asserts that from the beginning of the world, God has instituted primogeniture as a law of the greatest significance. Along with the domestic and political rights that adhere to primogeniture, the reformer also recognizes a priestly and spiritual pre-eminence (cf. 43:419, 427, 525). In the case of the holy people, however, experience shows the first-born to have been lacking in the hope of the parents and the second-born therefore to have succeeded to the promise. To account for this apparent perversity, Luther explains that primogeniture produces the pride of rightful possession, whereas God is a God of the humble (42:181). The conflict between Cain and Abel, Ishmael and Isaac, Esau and Jacob reflects this opposition between a reliance on outward possession and a trust in the concealed promise of God.

The struggle between Esau and Jacob in the womb of Rebecca is an important passage for any exegete, but it had been particularly significant to Luther ever since his first years as a lecturer on the Bible (3:243, 274, 323, 454; 4:446). From St. Paul he had learned that there was an Israel after the flesh as well as an Israel after the Spirit and that the heirs of the latter relied only on the election and grace of God, not on any carnal succession (56:394). Thus, the account of Jacob's struggle with his brother not only served to disclose the life and essence of the true Church but it also pointed to the irremovable ground of conflict between the two churches. At the end of his life in the *Lectures on Genesis,* Luther brought to the exegesis of the passage an understanding shaped by the mature theology of the Word and hardened by twenty years of opposition to Rome.

The substance of Luther's argument derives from what he had previously discovered in the cases of Abraham and Isaac and now again finds to be true. The patriarchs do not generate sons of God's kingdom simply by right of the first-born, for primogeniture, though established from the beginning, has been vitiated by the Devil. Beyond creation, the calling (*vocatio*) must be added in order that one belong to the true Church. The first-born is inevitably proud and relies upon what comes from the blood of the parents—wealth, power, the kingdom of the world. But God prefers him who has the calling and who, beyond his first and purely physical birth, is reborn in an act of spiritual regeneration. The perpetual war between those who claim possession by a visible succession and those who have God's Word continues to the end of the world for the glorious title of Church, people of God, kingdom of heaven, life eternal. In the same way, Luther understands his present struggle with a Papacy that seeks to be the people of God. The children collide in the womb; in the world the Church is twofold from the beginning just as the seed is twofold (43:384).

If primogeniture were sufficient, then the Word would be of no use to men. Where there exists only the right of the first-born, there can be only perdition. To be a son of God requires the calling, which is the Word. For Luther, the Jews, the Turks, and especially the pope illustrate this vehement insistence on the claim of first birth. One discovers in such a claim not God's calling and promising but man's working on the basis of his primogeniture. The pope argues that he sits on the seat of St. Peter, but Luther replies that a dog or pig can fulfill the same function. On the other hand, to have the calling or Word and adhere to it beyond any outward succession —this alone constitutes the Church and the sons of God (43:385–87; cf. 53:424–25).

The true Church is hidden not because it is persecuted but because it has the Word, which reveals itself only in terms of opposites. By its very nature the Word creates a community that is unknown and rejected by the world; moreover, it introduces division and strife into any humanly devised order. The Church's sufferings and tribulations are consequences of the fact that it has only the Word and must appear to the world as dispossessed, heretical, and powerless. Therefore, the idea of the hidden Church is intimately related to the double aspect of the Church in which adherence to the Word struggles with possession of the name and the external trappings of authority. In all times, Luther tells us, we are either Jacobites or Esauites. In the presence of the world, the true Christians have not the name of the Church, while Esau remains holy and religious before others and seems to be possessor of the kingdom of heaven (43:418). The distinction between those who hold the title and those who do not thus emerges as an essential feature of the Church during its course in time. To be the Church and to be called the Church are two quite different facts (26:64; cf. 18:650). The dual aspect of the Church reveals itself in the last instance as an opposition between the title and the substance, the appearance and the truth itself (43:428).

This enduring conflict between two peoples presents an essentially Augustinian pattern to Church history. In fact, Luther claimed to be following Augustine and a basic agreement was inevitable.[7] Nevertheless, within the general framework of the two societies and

7. *WA* 42:187. Cf. Pelikan, *Expositor,* p. 96.

their continuing struggle, significant differences appear. For Augustine the two opposing lineages originate and persist more as a result of a previous election than as a consequence of a contemporary act on God's part. Because of the nature of the Word and the hiddenness of the Church, Luther saw the ensuing dualism and struggle as inhering to the Church rather than being imposed from outside. Secondly, Augustine's two cities are distinguished pre-eminently by two different loves. They are not divided by the impact of the Word and according to faith.[8] Furthermore, in contrast to Luther, Augustine states that the Church was not really present with the patriarchs but that they foreshadowed it.[9] Admittedly, Augustine envisaged a theology of history in truly cosmic terms and significantly made the City of God, not the Church, the subject of his work. But this fact does not prevent a tentative comparison between the two princes of Christian thought, for by Luther's time the idea of the Church had practically assumed all the attributes of the Augustinian City of God.[10] Despite the grandeur of Augustine's view, it lacks the coherence, focus, and intensity which Luther achieved through his doctrine of the Word and his definition of the Church as a people of faith.

Luther's understanding of the true Church in history as a hidden one resulted directly from his conviction that the abiding life of the Church lay beyond itself in the Word of God. It signified an explicit rejection of all institutional guarantees for historical continuity and a willingness to face squarely all the tragic discontinuities, the sudden ruptures, and the devastating conflicts which history might bring. In fact, it implied that the pattern of Church history existed not in any orderly succession through a stable hierarchy but appeared as the constant collision of two peoples distinguished by

8. But cf. Heinrich Scholz, *Glaube und Unglaube in der Weltgeschichte* (Leipzig, 1911), passim.

9. Saint Augustine, *The City of God,* trans. Marcus Dods (New York, 1948), XIV, 27, 28; XV, 1, 2.

10. E. Gilson, "Église et cité de Dieu chez Saint Augustin," *Archives d'histoire doctrinale et littéraire du moyen âge, 28* (1953), 15.

their adherence to the Word. Finally, Luther's recognition of the hidden Church involved a complete reformulation of the Christian concept of tradition.

The Reformulation of the Concept of Tradition

Few ideas have had such an importance for the life and history of the Church as the idea of tradition.[11] In its specifically Christian sense the idea comprises the dual problem concerning the content of the authoritative revelation of God and its transmission in time. In Christian thought the term tradition has a definite meaning quite apart from ordinary usage. The word *traditio* and its original Greek equivalent παράδοσις signify both the handing over, delivery, or transmission and that which is transmitted. Consequently a distinction, although not necessarily a separation, exists between tradition as the means of transmitting divine revelation (*traditio activa*) and tradition as the content of this revelation (*traditio passiva*). This double aspect of tradition makes it vital to the Church, for the concept of tradition seeks to understand how the authoritative divine revelation in the past can be transmitted pure and unimpaired to the present. Being both a historical and a charismatic principle, tradition has significant implications for the study of history. According to the way in which it is envisaged, tradition can serve as a mainspring of criticism, growth, or regeneration as well as a source of protection and conservation.[12] The Church's concept of

11. Largely from a theological point of view the problem of tradition has engendered considerable attention in recent years. The most complete bibliography can be found in Kristen Ejner Skysgaard, "Schrift und Tradition," *Kerygma und Dogma, 1* (1955), 161–79. The bibliography does not include the most important, if not unique, historical treatment of the problem in the period of the Reformation: J. N. Bakhuizen van den Brink, "Traditio in de Reformatie en het Katholicisme in de zestiende eeuw," *Mededelingen der Koninklijke Nederlandse Akademie van Wetenschappen* (Amsterdam, 1952), pp. 27–71. Hereafter cited as "Traditio."

12. G. V. Florovsky, "Sobornost: The Catholicity of the Church," *The Church of God: An Anglo-Russian Symposium,* ed. E. L. Mascall (London, 1934), pp. 64–65.

tradition at any one time reflects its understanding of its own source of life, continuity with the past, and movement in time.

To understand Luther's attitude toward tradition and to appreciate its significance for the sixteenth century demand a brief consideration of the development of the idea prior to the Reformation. In the earliest period of the Church, *paradosis* signified what the Lord transmits of Himself through His intermediaries the apostles, who, as eyewitnesses, are bearers of direct revelation. The Risen Christ works in the tradition and is both author and object of the gospel.[13] In the period from the apostolic age to the middle of the second century, the Church recognized the authoritative basis of its doctrine both in Scriptures, which at the time comprised the Old Testament, and in the apostolic testimony expressed in the Church's preaching, liturgy, and catechetical instruction as well as in written documents. During the same period there appeared the idea that the Church's ministers were the divinely authorized custodians of the apostolic teaching. In the following half century the apostolic testimony or tradition came to be regarded as fully canonical and ranked alongside the Old Testament.[14]

In their struggle against the common threat of the Gnostic heresies, Irenaeus and Tertullian gave formal definition to the relation between Scripture and tradition. For both these Christian doctors, Christ in His revelation through the apostles was the ultimate source of Christian doctrine. Both enunciated a concept of tradition in the Church that identified the substance of tradition with the content of Scripture; there were not two distinct sources of authority but a single one—the tradition from the apostles. Without any implied contrast between tradition and Scripture, Tertullian and Irenaeus described the divine revelation as tradition or teaching delivered by the apostles. While each asserted Scripture alone to be normative, both recognized the futility of arguing with

13. Oscar Cullmann, *The Early Church,* trans. A. J. B. Higgins and S. Godman (Philadelphia, 1956), pp. 59–75.

14. J. N. D. Kelly, *Early Christian Doctrines* (New York, 1958), pp. 31–35.

heretics on the basis of Scripture alone. The question arose concerning the interpretation of Scripture and the location of this apostolic testimony or tradition. For Irenaeus the tradition was present in the Church—public, oral, manifest. While he spoke of a canon of the truth, and Tertullian defended a rule of faith, both intended the same reality. As the expression of the Church's oral teaching, the canon or rule represented the distillation and substance of the divine revelation, fluid in its working but fixed in its content. Tertullian claimed to proceed by the rule that the Church transmits from the apostles, the apostles from Christ, and Christ from God.[15] Here *tradere* means to inform divinely, and tradition essentially is the work and activity of Christ.[16] Yet the working of Christ through the Holy Spirit could not prove sufficient for the two great Christian doctors against the heretics. The truth was discoverable in the churches where the bishops as successors of the apostles have conserved and interpreted it through the charism of truth.[17] Here Hegesippus as well as Irenaeus and Tertullian pointed to the great sees founded by apostles and to a legitimate and uninterrupted succession of bishops; the Church's continuous public witness demonstrated the authenticity of the one apostolic and catholic doctrine.[18]

The early Church's conception of tradition as evinced in the writings of these two great opponents of the heretics represents essentially a theological as opposed to an ecclesiastical conception of tradition. The distinctive feature of such a view resides first in the fact that tradition (*traditio*) is not understood in the plural as a number of practices and beliefs but as the divine revelation coming down from the apostles collectively. Such a view does not deny

15. *MPL* 2:50. *In ea regula incedimus quam ecclesia ab apostolis, apostoli a Christo, Christus a Deo tradidit.*

16. J. N. Bakhuizen van den Brink, "La Tradition dans l'église primitive et au XVIe siècle," *RHPR, 36* (1956), 277. Hereafter cited as "La Tradition."

17. Kelly, *Doctrines,* pp. 36–41; Bakhuizen, "La Tradition," pp. 271–81.

18. Einar Molland, "Le Développement de l'idée de succession apolostique," *RHPR, 34* (1954), 19–22.

the inclusion of numerous liturgical and catechetical practices, but these all derive from and express the same content and spirit. The interpretation of Scripture may only proceed according to the rule, which is the single content of Scripture itself. As with the later reformers, the perspicuity of Scripture does not pertain necessarily to every individual passage but to the total intention of Scripture. Secondly, in a theological conception the content of what is transmitted and the agent of transmission coincide in God. In this respect the early Church's rule for interpreting Scripture and what the Reformation was later to maintain did not differ essentially: Scripture should be interpreted according to the tradition of the Church. But this tradition is the immanent content of Scripture which through the Holy Spirit finds its expression in the preaching and confessing Church.[19]

During the third and fourth centuries the Church understood the original tradition from the apostles as being embodied in Scripture and as having a parallel outlet in her general unwritten teaching and liturgical life. While the use of the term "tradition" to describe the latter became increasingly more common, from Clement of Alexandria to Vincent of Lérins, all accepted the scriptural canon as sufficient. In these centuries the entire liturgical apparatus was regarded as part of the apostolic testimony. At the same time that the tradition was becoming broader and more explicit, the Church was being redefined in terms of the bishops; the episcopate emerged as the extension of the apostolate. Although Cyprian insisted upon the equality of all the bishops, the See of Peter possessed a certain pre-eminence. Founded on the martyrdom of the apostles Peter and Paul, the Roman church enjoyed a growing prestige and authority. By the time of St. Jerome, Rome had established its exclusive claim as an apostolic see in the West and was considered to be the guardian and mouthpiece of the apostolic tradition. Finally, formal appeal was increasingly made to the tradition of the fathers; but their

19. Cf. E. Flesseman-Van Leer, *Tradition and Scripture in the Early Church* (Assen, 1954), pp. 194–97.

authority existed only in the fact that they had expounded so faithfully the real intention of Scripture. Thus, if the concept of tradition expanded and became more concrete, the estimate of its position in respect to Scripture remained the same. Throughout the whole period, Scripture and tradition stood as complementary authorities different in the way each transmitted the divine revelation but identical in content.[20]

Two centuries after Tertullian and Irenaeus, the problem of preserving and passing on pure doctrine unchanged had become even more acute. Confronted with a jungle of heresies, the fifth-century father, Vincent of Lérins, betrayed a sense of the Church's growing need for an authoritative interpretation of the tradition; yet at the same time he sought to maintain the tradition in its pristine purity. By his treatment of tradition in its two aspects of authority and the transmission of authority, he brought together the diverse strands in the early Church's conception of tradition. In his *Commonitoria* he frequently distinguishes between the authority of the divine law and the tradition of the Catholic Church. The latter must interpret the divine canon according to the principles of universality, antiquity, and consent; and Vincent went on to explain how the views of past saints and fathers were to be collected and weighed for the interpretation of the canon (*MPL* 50:640; cf. 50:674, 677). Vincent never tires of condemning profane novelties and remains confident that the interpretation exercised by bishops in council could proceed without any embellishment or addition to the original doctrine. His concept of transmission is thoroughly substantialistic. The Church experiences a progress of religion (*profectus Religionis*), which means that each thing grows within itself, whereas change signifies that one thing is transformed into another. Progress is a growth wherein the substance remains unaffected (*MPL* 50:667). That the process of the Church's growth or interpretation of tradition should involve any additions or changes in doctrine would have horrified St. Vincent, and he specifically commends the action

20. Kelly, *Doctrines*, pp. 41–49. Molland, p. 26.

of two Roman bishops for preserving the old doctrine (*MPL* 50: 683–84).

From the early Church, the Middle Ages inherited the view that the reading and interpretation of Scripture can take place only within the Church which Scripture constitutes; Church and Scripture mutally inhere and their authority is mutually inclusive. According to this understanding, the biblical canon might have served as the critical norm for the Church's life and for the interpretation of Scripture. On the other hand, the inherence of the Church in Scripture seemed to justify the attribution of the privileges of Scripture to other writings. Theoretically the canon was closed but through its actual working and inspiration the Church permitted the reception of other scriptures. The most notable instance of this extension of Scripture occurred with the decree attributed to Pope Gelasius (492–96) that accepted as other scriptures a number of councils, all the orthodox fathers, and the decretals.[21] In fact the Middle Ages understood Scripture to comprise the biblical canon along with its interpreters.[22] Once sacred Scripture became sacred doctrine, the critical norm of the original canon disappeared beneath the fusion of authorities that marked a major readjustment of the Christian kerygma to the world.

The fate of Scripture and its relation to tradition are more clearly discernible in considering the practice of the papal monarchy and the nature of medieval theology rather than in studying the contemporary theoretical definitions of the problem. The Gregorian reforms of the eleventh century sought to bring the discipline, life, and organization of Latin Christendom into harmony with the practice of the Roman church and its understanding of antiquity. In the name of antiquity and with the claim of innovating nothing,

21. On the influence of the pseudo-Gelasian *de recipiendis libris et non recipiendis*, see Joseph de Ghellinck, *Le Mouvement théologique du XII siècle* (Bruges, 1948), pp. 21–24; 474–75. On its authenticity, see *DCT, 6,* 1179–80; *RE*^{3}*, 6,* 475.

22. George H. Tavard, *Holy Writ or Holy Church* (London, 1959), pp. 6–8, 15. Cf. Joseph de Ghellinck, "'Pagina' et 'Sacra Pagina,'" *Mélanges Auguste Pelzer* (Louvain, 1947), pp. 23–59.

the Gregorians appealed to the authorities of the fathers and the early Church. Their reforming of the canonical collections cut through the diverse, accumulated customs of local churches and promoted the universal authority of the Roman church.[23] Essential to this formidable achievement was the office of the pope, who supplied the sanction and authenticity for the accumulated authorities supporting the Church. To meet the legal demands of this mighty institution, Scripture continued to be broken up into a number of texts, which served to establish a practice, proclaim the natural law, provide a basis for the authorities, and furnish a divine foundation to the papal hierarchy.[24] The mutual borrowing and interrelations of canon law and theology completed the juridical character of medieval theology.[25]

In the high Middle Ages the reappearance of Aristotle and the amassing of new received texts contributed to a shrinking of the patristic corpus. The ante-Nicene fathers virtually disappeared and the original works of the later fathers fell into disuse.[26] Medieval theologians employed collections of patristic citations as authorities. Argumentation did not appeal directly to the tradition but to an *auctoritas* which affirmed one's adherence to the tradition and substituted for it. Medieval theology did make a formal distinction between the authoritative nature of patristic writings and the opinions of scholastic doctors, but the highest category of authority, known as *authentica,* witnessed an expansion. Despite the Gregorian resort to the literary remains of the early Church, and despite the remarkable care of papal and ecclesiastical archivists for chronology, a historical consciousness was too dim to prevent a process of accumulation behind the apparent harmony. Within the framework

23. Paul Fournier, "Les Collections canoniques romaines de l'époque de Grégoire VII," *Extrait des Mémoires de L'Académie des Inscriptions et Belles-Lettres, 41* (1918), 271–79; 392–93.

24. Gabriel Le Bras, "Les Écritures dans le Décret de Gratien," *Zeitschrift der Savigny-Stiftung für Rechtsgeschichte* (Kanonistische Abteilung), *27* (1938), 74–77.

25. De Ghellinck, *Le Mouvement,* passim.

26. Ibid., pp. 233–35; 243–44.

of scholastic conciliation and exegesis there was no perspective on the past which could allow a theory of development or a defining of the tradition.[27]

Before the thirteenth century had ended, the awareness of other sources of authority helped to justify a tradition whose original features were being obliterated in the broader context of the *auctoritates*. The existence of postapostolic revelations represents one of these new sources. Although the idea was not explicitly articulated until the following century,[28] in its practical workings it had already presented an obvious threat to the original tradition of the apostles.[29] Closely associated with the notion of postapostolic revelations was that of a supplementary oral or unwritten tradition, which now threatened to become a second new source of authority. This idea was not entirely absent in the early Church and had some currency in the Middle Ages.[30] Gratian cites an important text from St. Basil's *On the Holy Spirit* that claims a mystical and secret tradition coming down from the fathers.[31] Toward the end of the thirteenth century, St. Thomas recognized the existence of such a tradition but did not define its nature. He asserted that the apostles had delivered certain things that must be preserved which were not left in scriptures but in the care (*observatio*) of the Church through the succession of the faithful (*ST* III, q. 25, a.3). All things were not de-

27. Joseph de Ghellinck, "Patristique et argument de tradition au bas moyen âge," *Aus der Geisteswelt des Mittelalters: Studien und Texte Martin Grabmann . . . gewidmet* (Münster, 1935), *1*, 403–26. Hereafter cited as "Patristique." M. D. Chenu, " 'Authentica' et 'Magistralia': Deux lieux théologiques au XIIe–XIIIe siècle," *Divus Thomas: Commentarium de philosophia et theologia*, Piacenza, 3e série, *2* (1925), 257–85.

28. Tavard, pp. 34–37.

29. De Ghellinck, "Patristique." Joseph de Ghellinck, "Pour l'Histoire du mot 'revelare,' " *RSR, 6* (1916), 151–57.

30. August Deneffe, *Der Traditionsbegriff* (Münster, 1931), p. 47. Cf. Tavard, pp. 27; 56–58.

31. Dist. 11, c.5. All citations from the Decretum refer to the Emil Friedberg edition of the *Corpus Juris Canonici* (Leipzig, 1922), Vol. 1. On the importance of Basil's text at the Council of Trent, see R. J. Geiselmann, "Das Konzil von Trent über das Verhältnis der Heiligen Schrift und des nicht geschriebenen Traditionen," *Die Mündliche Überlieferung*, ed. Michael Schmaus (Munich, 1957), p. 140.

livered in scriptures; because of their familiarity with the Holy Spirit, the apostles had transmitted certain things—especially those concerning the divine worship.[32] Moreover, in seeking support for a particular observance in the Mass, St. Thomas referred to the last verse of the Gospel of St. John as the scriptural basis for a tradition existing outside of Scripture and claiming apostolic origin (*ST* III, q. 83, a.4).

In his effort to discover an authoritative guide for the preservation of the original tradition, Vincent of Lérins had looked to the faith of the entire Church, to the fathers, and finally to the general councils; he had referred to the pope only as guardian of the deposit. Yet it was with the pope and with the magisterium of the Church that another type of tradition would be elaborated. Although a theoretical definition of papal authority in matters of interpretation had to wait until the nineteenth century, from a very early date the bishop of Rome exercised the power in practice together with an appellate jurisdiction, and in subsequent centuries this magisterium of the Church permitted the theological and scriptural substance of the original tradition to be heavily overlaid with juridical and cultic ordinances.[33] Where the evangelists had left gaps, the Roman pontiff could now introduce new laws.[34] Furthermore, by commingling and equating the authority of Scripture with the authority of papal decretals, canon law served to obscure the classic features of tradition and to merge it in a mass of other authorities.[35]

Medieval theology remained innocent of any redefinition of tradition in respect to the magisterium of the Church. St. Thomas himself claimed for the pontiff only the authority of determining matters of faith by means of making the creed more explicit (*ST* II, 2, q.1, a.10), and not until John of Torquemada in the fifteenth

32. *ST* III, q. 64, a.2. Cf. Bakhuizen, "Traditio," p. 43.

33. Cf. Robert M. Grant, *The Bible in the Church* (New York, 1948), p. 96.

34. C. 25, q. 1, c. 6. Cf. Friedrich Kropatscheck, *Das Schriftprinzip der lutherischen Kirche* (Leipzig, 1904), p. 444.

35. Dist. 19, c. 1; Dist. 20, c. 1.

century did there appear an attempt to define in relation to other authorities the Curia's power of judging those things in matters of faith which were not contained in the canon of Scripture.[36] Nevertheless, though the idea of a tradition existing apart from Scripture and growing out of the magisterium of the Church produced no definition, the reality of such a tradition at the end of the Middle Ages provided the authority for a multitude of practices, beliefs, and obligations.

These three general sources of authority, which had diverged from the original understanding of the tradition and had rendered it almost unrecognizable, became matters of scholastic inquiry and discussion at the end of the Middle Ages.[37] The idea of postapostolic revelations, the existence of an oral tradition, and the theological aggressions of the canonists—all of which had previously been implicit and unexpressed within the medieval Church—now became explicit and conscious problems. All three provided interpretations which worked to justify present authority to the detriment of a past norm. Perhaps the most ominous of the three influences was the pressure supplied by the canonists, who for reasons of power politics made irresponsible theological claims: the living pope loomed to replace both Scripture and its traditional interpretation.[38] By the end of the fifteenth century the increasing disfigurement of the tradition had produced the supreme crisis of the Christian Church.

Luther's principal work can only be appreciated in the context of this increasing obscurity of the original tradition amidst a labyrinth of rival authorities; for, insofar as a historical movement can be judged at its core by its original intention and impulse, rather than from the periphery by its results and the influence of contemporaneous movements, the Reformation had nothing at all to do with economic and political pressures, with moral corruption, or

36. Deneffe, pp. 73–79.
37. Tavard, chaps. 3 and 4.
38. Ibid., pp. 38–39.

even with the need to articulate lay religion. In the light of its initiator's life and actions, the Reformation sought to recover and to re-establish the authority of the original tradition in the Church. The task required the destruction of that fortress of interlocking, rival, and conflicting authorities made viable by the established Church. The way had been partially prepared by the humanists, but the real thrust had to come from within the Church itself. The breakthrough occurred at Leipzig. In those vitally significant debates which initiated the Reformation and transformed Latin Christendom, Luther endeavored laboriously, at times unsuccessfully but always decisively, to disassociate and to exalt the authority of Scripture from competing authorities and to gain that perspective on the past which had been absent for a thousand years. Leipzig marked the turning point in the course of the West's attitude to Christian dogma and scriptural authority. Never again could there be an unconscious possession of tradition. Looking back upon the collapse of this imposing structure of authority, Luther remarked that it was incredible for this Troy, after having remained unconquered so long, ever to have been taken (18:640).

When Luther appeared before Cajetan at Augsburg in 1518, he was nearing the final formulation of his principle of authority.[39] At this time he recognized the tremendous issue involved, and shortly afterward he expressed what was to be the central endeavor of his life—the freeing of the Word of God from the traditions of men. In reporting the events at Augsburg, Luther directed his readers to the source of the controversy. He observes that the canonists granted to the doctors the authority of interpreting Scripture and retained for themselves the power of judgment between conflicting causes. Significantly, he then distinguishes the juridical from the theological competence; in the former much is permitted which in the latter is inadmissible. While the true theologian maintains the integrity of Scripture, the jurists promote their own traditions and even boast that the pope is not able to err and that he stands above Scripture.

39. Cf. Bizer, *Fides ex Auditu*, pp. 104–05.

If this position be admitted, Scripture perishes, as does, in consequence, the Church, and nothing remains but the word of man (2:22).

The significance of Luther's consideration of the papal decretals lay not in any overthrow of canon law or the magisterium of the Roman Church, for such was not his intention at this juncture; it lay in his effort to preserve the integrity of Scripture and to assert its sufficiency as a single ground and source of authority by which conflicting authorities might be measured. In Luther's report of his interview it may be doubted that Cajetan, a distinguished theologian, actually considered the pope to be above Scripture.[40] This idea, however, was entertained by Prierias, the Master of the Sacred Palace, together with some less responsible minds of the period (*OVA* 1:346–47, 367). Luther was therefore responding to an existing danger. Cajetan's distortion of Scripture through the use of *Unigenitus* hardly surprised him, for he was aware of the Roman Curia's presumed power of interpretation resulting from long custom; nevertheless, he deplored the consequence that whatever the Roman Church condemned or recognized, all people must condemn or recognize (2:17). If one was to obey the papal decretals as though they were the voice of St. Peter, this obedience could only pertain to those decretals which were consonant with Scripture and not at variance with previous decrees of the pontiffs (2:10).

The real difference between the position of the medieval Church on the one hand and that of Luther and the Reformation in general on the other did not concern Scripture as the basic source of the knowledge of faith so much as it concerned the problem of the interpretation of Scripture. In his struggle with the Papacy, Luther came to assert the clarity and sufficiency of Scripture, whereby Scripture became its own interpreter, and insofar as Scripture was the Word of God, the Church existed as its creature. The vigor and relevance of his attack brought Catholic champions to the defense

40. *WA* 2:8. Cf. Jean Rivière, "Cajétan défenseur de la Papauté contre Luther," *Revue Thomiste*, 17 (1934–35), 248.

of the Roman position, and in the *Assertio* of Henry VIII an admirable effort was made to redefine the papal attitude to the Church, tradition, and Scripture. Henry claimed for traditions an equal place beside Scripture and maintained that Christ had placed the Church above all the evangelists. While both Henry and Luther agreed that the Church was able to distinguish between the gospel and the words of men, Henry extended this competence to an unfailing ability to distinguish between the true and false sense of Scripture. Consequently, God ruled in things which were not written and the power of interpreting Scripture entered into the complex of traditions and the magisterium of the Church. In short, tradition embraced the Church's knowledge of God's revelation as much in Scripture as in the unwritten traditions, and, moreover, it meant her authority for interpreting Scripture according to its true sense. Henry's formulation marked a milestone not only in that it pointed toward the final Tridentine definition but also because *traditio* now came to replace *auctoritas.* In the ensuing period, the authority of the Church had to be continually related to its understanding of tradition.[41]

The opening created in the fortress of ecclesiastical authority at Augsburg became, after Leipzig, a breach through which Catholics and humanists marched as well as Protestant reformers. The assertion of *sola scriptura* as a critical principle and absolute authority made it impossible to accept indiscriminatingly the complex of authorities upon which the medieval Church had stood; it necessitated a complete reappraisal of the Church's concept of authority. The Council of Trent claimed that the Church exercised authority as legitimately over the active aspect of tradition, which embraced the function of handing down doctrine together with the interpretation of Scripture and all articles of faith, as it did over the passive aspect of tradition (*traditiones passivae*), which included the formulated doctrines, interpretations, and customs themselves. Trent was more concerned with preserving the individual unwritten traditions

41. Bakhuizen, "Traditio," pp. 28, 47–49.

than with the defense of tradition as a function of the Church.[42] It spoke of traditions in the plural and tended to confuse the ecclesiastical with the apostolic traditions. When the council stated that the gospel was contained both in Scripture and in the unwritten traditions, it intended nothing new and understood the formulation as sustaining the concept of St. Vincent. Trent's real innovation, however, existed in the fact that from the stock of ecclesiastical tradition it had exalted certain traditions pertaining to faith and morals, designated them as apostolic, and claimed for them an equal dignity with Scripture.[43]

Any attempt to understand Luther's attitude toward tradition first requires a consideration of the meaning of *sola scriptura* as his principle of authority. In his defense of all the articles, condemned by the papal bull of 1520, Luther distinguished Scripture as a sufficient authority from the complex of existing authorities and in particular from the papal right of legislating. He discovers the original source of perversion in the claim taught by the canons of the pontiffs (*sic*) that Scripture can be properly understood only by a few and must not be interpreted by its own Spirit. Such a principle leads to the burial of Scripture and theology's immersion in the commentaries of men, where the sophists seek not the substance of Scripture but what they may notice in it. To one man alone, the Roman pontiff, surrounded by these most unlearned people, is attributed the right of interpretation. If Scripture is not allowed to be understood according to its own Spirit, much less will Augustine be allowed to be understood according to his own sense. In order to assure that one may understand Augustine correctly, another interpreter is provided and there follows an endless succession of interpreters and conflicting interpretations (7:96).

By asserting the principle that Scripture is its own simplest, most

42. Ibid., pp. 55–56.

43. Pontien Polman, *L'Élément historique dans la controverse religieuse du XVIe siècle* (Gembloux, 1932), pp. 306–07. Hereafter cited as *L'Élément historique*. Geiselmann, pp. 161–67.

certain, and direct interpreter, Luther sought to reverse this process and extract Scripture from the wrappings of commentaries and interpreters. The scriptures can be understood only through the Holy Spirit by whom they were written and this Spirit is nowhere to be found more living and present than in His own sacred writings. This apparent tautology by which the Holy Spirit is both the agent and the content of authority presents a familiar feature of the Word of God. Having disposed of the writings of men, Luther recognizes here the increased dangers of understanding Scripture according to one's own spirit. He urges that only through constant meditation and study of these writings will their Spirit come to expel one's own and establish itself in man. Once made intelligible in this manner, Scripture provides the basis for judging all the writings of men and of the fathers (7:97).

In his aim to restore pure theology, Luther demanded a return to the divine words as first principles in order that human words might be tested by them. He discovers the reverse to have previously been the case; with their glosses, the fathers have made the scriptures more obscure than their own writings by a process of elucidating the known by the unknown. Luther announces his thorough dissatisfaction with the fathers and states that they must be judged by the authority of Scripture. He recognizes the authority of no saint or pope unless it is fortified by Scripture. Although he quotes Hilary and Augustine as well as Scripture itself to support his idea of the supremacy and sufficiency of Scripture, their confirmation only serves to demonstrate the true dimensions of his principle of authority. One does not attain the truth by conjuring many diverse sayings of the fathers and presuming the scriptural meaning from them; rather, by having rendered the intelligence from Scripture through the collation of itself alone, one judges the fathers and accepts what conforms with Scripture (7:98–100). As Luther's principle of authority in matters of faith, *sola scriptura* asserted first the clarity and sufficiency of Scripture in revealing its own meaning, and secondly it signified that the content or meaning of Scripture stood as judge to all other authorities and could accept none which opposed Scripture. To the extent that Scripture is the Word of God, it conforms to the nature of its life and source, the Holy Spirit, in being both the agent and the content of revelation.

Two years later in his treatise *Against King Henry of England,* Luther formally applied this principle of authority within the context of contemporary theological controversy. In opening he declares that he understands his own work and God's action as a desire to have divine letters alone rule and to remove human inventions and traditions from the center of religious life (10/2:182). He consciously sets forth the principal points of doctrine taught in Scripture (10/2:185–86). He accepts no articles of faith outside Scripture and urges a pragmatic attitude toward human customs and authority that do not conflict with Scripture. Human regulations are to be tolerated as a matter of Christian liberty and used, changed, or abolished as circumstances require, but if they are established as necessary articles of faith, they are to be condemned (10/2:191–92).

Luther directs his attack against the source and basis of all Henry VIII's argument—the common agreement of men. If Christian faith has no strength aside from what it derives from length of time and the custom of many men,[44] then it does not differ from that of the Turks or Jews. Neither the traditions of men nor long usage have value in matters of faith, for custom is of uncertain origin, free and mutable, while the Word of the gospel remains certain and immutable. Beyond the Scripture nothing may be established, or if established it must be considered as free and not necessary (10/2: 192–95, 202, 215). Luther ascribes this method of proving traditions by tradition to the Roman Church's assumed right of legislating (*ius leges condendi*). He attributes this assumption of a legislative authority to a deliberate misuse of Augustine's much quoted statement that he would not have believed the gospel had he not been moved by the authority of the Church (cf. *MPL* 42:176). In treating

44. *WA* 10/2:193:1, *nisi longitudinem temporum et multorum hominum usum.*

Augustine's statement, Luther distinguishes between the right of judging and recognizing (*ius judicandi et cognoscendi*) and the arbitrary right to legislate. The former right amounts to a power of discriminating between true and false dogmas. Luther claims that Christ gives this right to every individual Christian and that Augustine speaks here of a judgment and authority of the universal Church scattered throughout the world (10/2:216–17; cf. 2:430–31). On the other hand, the officials of the Church have seized this right that belongs properly to the people of God. They have appropriated it for their exclusive use and have transformed it into an unlimited authority to command and legislate in the life of the Church. In the Council of Nicaea, Luther believes he has discovered the root of this assumed legislative authority and the consequent appeal to the common agreement of men (10/2:217–19).

Luther recognized two opposing conceptions of tradition. The first accepts Scripture alone as canonical and final in the life of the Church. The other claims that Scripture is not sufficient for the life of the Church and that the Holy Spirit has been entrusted to the Church in order that many other necessary laws might be taught. Luther attacks the ostensible scriptural basis for the necessity of more traditions. The favorite papist texts in the Gospel of St. John[45] refer not to something other than what has been given to the apostles (7:642–44; 34/1:372–76). The papists have twisted these texts to mean that the Holy Spirit will not allow them to err and that they can fill the world with their human traditions (17/1:268; 28:50; 7:423, 425, 427; 21:470). Against this misuse of the Johannine texts, Luther presses Colossians 2:8, 16 (7:609, 661). For further support he adduces Acts 15:10 and claims that Paul frequently called his gospel the tradition (39/2:301).

In a remarkable passage, Luther presented his own understanding of that tradition which he assailed.

Not to transpose the boundaries established by one's predeces-

45. John 14:16, 26; 16:12–13; 21:25.

> sors [means] to add nothing to the doctrine handed over by the apostles (*ab Apostolis traditae*) as if there existed better counseling in matters of conscience. This passage the sophists and pontiffs vehemently boast for themselves, while they claim that their own statutes and customs, which the fathers established, must not have their boundaries transposed. By fathers, however, they do not understand the apostles but their own pontiffs and doctors. Thus by an allegorical meaning they stabilize their own fables, not seeing meanwhile how they themselves are the first and only ones . . . to transpose not only the boundaries of faith and of the spirit established by *the* predecessors—the apostles and Christ in the gospel—but even those boundaries established by their own predecessors and by themselves. Their one endeavor is to change laws with laws, accumulate them and, as one says, fasten and unfasten laws at a price, as though legislation were a game of dice, which they play in the consciences of men. Yet they object to others transposing the boundaries which the predecessors have established. [14:690]

The University of Paris' altered attitude toward William of Ockham provided Luther with demonstrable proof of this tradition: truth is made to suit the moment (6:183).

With his principle of *sola scriptura,* Luther certainly did not intend to reject all that the Church had held and used for the past fifteen hundred years, and in his attitude to the dogmas established by the early Church he revealed the more conservative and constructive aspect of his principle of authority. Luther reasserted the Apostles' Creed together with two other formularies that frequently appeared with this creed in psalters made after the ninth century;[46] these were the Athanasian Creed and the Te Deum, to which Luther appended the Nicene Creed (50:263). He found in the concise statements of the Apostles' Creed the perfect expression

46. J. N. D. Kelly, *Early Christian Creeds* (London, 1952), p. 425.

of his own religious understanding of the Christian belief. But he did not consider the creed as a product of a historical period of the Church. In his Catechism he describes it as the very distillation and essence of scriptural belief (30/1:182–83). Similarly in the case of the Nicene Creed, he urged adherence to this creed as the best explanation of the doctrine of the Trinity (30/3:160). Later he showed how the four great councils had established no new articles of faith but merely defended what had been given by the Holy Spirit to the apostles at Pentecost (50:551, 607). When the councils, fathers, and the witness of the Church agreed with his own religious appropriation and understanding of Scripture's content, Luther gladly employed them as support for his position; otherwise he preferred his faith based on Scripture to all these authorities. Because he saw the articles of faith as already existing in Scripture, he could not understand the dogmatic formulations of the early Church as products of a particular period of the Church. In adhering to the ancient creeds, Luther remained quite consistent with his principle of scriptural authority.[47]

In his controversy with the Anabaptists, Luther had to make an apparent concession to the common agreement of men. When confronted with the problem of the authority for infant baptism, Luther admitted that there existed no text in Scripture which would prove this doctrine. Consequently, he had to appeal to the universal witness and practice of the Church through the ages and claimed that the doctrine had been received from the apostles. While this clear appeal to the previous witness of the Church may have gratified his opponents, Luther still maintained the integrity of scriptural authority by demonstrating the positive aspect of this critical principle. For at the very outset of his argument, while admitting that Scripture provided no proof for infant baptism, he claimed nevertheless that nothing existed in Scripture which would contradict such a use of the sacrament (26:166–68). Although Luther was unquestionably embarrassed by the problem and had to allow his argu-

47. Otto Ritschl, *Dogmengeschichte des Protestantismus* (Leipzig, 1908), *1*, 268–75.

ment to rest on what God accomplished in the Church through time, he had not denied *sola scriptura,* which as a critical principle claimed only to reject what was contrary to Scripture. Luther understood himself as following a middle course between the papists, who would retain all practices and customs, and the radicals, who felt compelled to overthrow all papal traditions in order to be pure (40/2:176). By distinguishing the eternal and abiding from the temporal and mutable, Luther sought only to reject those historical accretions—the traditions of men—which opposed the Word of God as the Church's life and source.

The new principle of authority in Scripture now served to shape Luther's understanding of tradition. By the time of his break with Rome Luther had arrived at an implicit conception of tradition that was not unlike the concept held by the early Church. A confusion in vocabulary serves to obscure this fact. The original sense of *traditio* as both the agent and content of divine revelation had become so corrupted through successive generations that by the sixteenth century, Catholics and Protestants alike used the term in the plural to indicate a multitude of customs and ceremonies which may or may not have had their source in a form of divine revelation.[48] Luther's works reflect this change in the meaning of the term. On the other hand, Scripture as the Word of God began to assume the essential features of *traditio* in its original sense and to resume the unity of the apostolic testimony. As a principle of authority Scripture confronted in terms of a critical tension all the extrascriptural beliefs and practices comprised by traditions. By sharpening the critical aspect of Scripture, Luther clarified the real tradition of the Church; by understanding Scripture to comprise and to allow more than simply the Bible, Luther moved to prevent this clarification from causing an impoverishment of the Church's life and a complete rejection of her past.

In the period prior to 1530, Luther generally used the substantive

48. On this point, see Polman, *L'Élément historique,* p. 306; Bakhuizen, "Traditio," pp. 43, 70.

of the term "tradition" in its pejorative sense and retained the verbal form to signify a divine action in the process of revelation. In an interlinear gloss of his first lectures on the Psalms he relates traditions to a decline from the Spirit into the letter (4:128:10). In the same work he consciously opposes the traditions and mandates of men (4:246:3) and accuses the great officials in the Church of exercising human traditions (4:353:15). In his preparation for the Leipzig debates, Luther objected to Leo IV's insinuation that papal decrees and Scripture were of equal authority;[49] the result is a confusion of customs and faith, traditions with the gospel, the word of man with the Word of God (2:199:41). After Leipzig he made the following statement:

> It is certain that it is absolutely not in the power of the Church or of the pope to establish articles of faith or even laws of customs or of good works, because these have all been delivered in sacred letters (*quod haec omnia in sacris literis sint tradita*). . . . It is fitting in making clear the articles of faith that this function may not become associated with those who are versed in human traditions, laws, and opinions. . . . [Their] fatuous trust in the presence of the Spirit and their security in pronouncing doctrine must be removed and the function (*res*) must be conducted with fear and with mature consideration of sacred letters. [2:427]

Later in his *Reply to Ambrosius Catharinus* he ascribes papal iniquities and the total fragmentation of the religious life into sects to the traditions of men (7:724–25). In all these statements he conceives traditions as being particular practices and beliefs established by men in the religious life; the German equivalent (*menschen satzunge* or *lere*) confirms this meaning and emphasizes the neglect of the idea's active aspect (cf. 8:453:35 and 553:17; 8:454:17 and 534:6;

49. Cf. Dist. 20, c. 1.

8:475:1 and 560:37). According to their new meanings, Scripture and traditions stand opposed.

He rarely employs the term in the singular and with reference to the divine revelation. Usually the original meaning of tradition persists in the verbal form alone. In *The Babylonian Captivity* he sharply distinguishes what has been divinely handed over in sacred letters[50] from what has been invented in the Church by men. In 1523 he expands his idea:

> If the office of teaching the Word is handed over to someone, at the same time all things which are accomplished by the Word in the Church are handed over (*traduntur*), namely the office of baptising, of consecrating, of binding, of loosing, of praying, and of judging. Yet the office of preaching the gospel is the highest of them all and truly apostolic because it provides the basis for all other offices. [12:191]

Luther implies that the scriptural and the apostolic are one and that the Word of God contains and transmits all the offices of the Church.

No less a person than Philip Melanchthon compelled Luther to present explicitly his understanding of traditions and their relation to the authority of Scripture. Writing from the Diet of Augsburg, Melanchthon complained that nothing had plagued him more in the negotiations than the question of customs or traditions. While admitting that traditions were traps for consciences, he suggested that if made by pious opinion they must necessarily be maintained for the sake of the law of power, not for the sake of the cult itself. He proceeded then to submit to Luther five causes of traditions and inquired whether in the last three instances the traditions that had been allowed must be preserved on account of authority and whether they oblige consciences (*WBr* 5:475–77).

Luther proved somewhat slow in meeting the problem, but he

50. *WA* 6:553:18, *quae divinitus in sacris literis tradita sunt.*

was quick to shift the discussion from final to essential causes or from purposes and ends of traditions to their sources. He was thus able to introduce his distinction between the political and spiritual authority and to assert that a bishop as bishop has no power to impose any tradition or ceremony on his church unless by consent of the congregation (*WBr* 5:492–95). Shortly afterward he referred his colleague to a recent work in which Luther claimed that all the articles of faith were in Scripture and that Scripture stood over the Church in the capacity of a judicial and higher authority (*WBr* 5: 502; cf. 30/2:420). This reply left Melanchthon unsatisfied, for he indicated his discomfiture at the abrupt shift to essential causes and pressed the question whether a particular observance such as one chosen by St. Bernard should be considered as a work or as part of the service of worship (*WBr* 5:508).

In the two letters which followed within a day of each other, Luther presented his position. In the first letter he rejected the observance of Bernard as a work or exercise. There is but one worship of God, and it is not of Bernard but of God alone. For man to teach how God is to be worshiped can only be a work. With the efficient cause lacking, the final cause can only be chimerical (*WBr* 5:523–24). Luther now emphasized the disagreement between Melanchthon's final causes and his own efficient causes of traditions. One can boast of piety, discipline, and works but God requires only His mandate. If the efficient cause is removed, none of the abominations of Antichrist is able to be resisted, for who is to judge, who is to define? Luther then proceeded to find all of Melanchthon's final causes impossible.

> For if I might inquire what are these pious or permitted observances, necessarily established by traditions (*per traditiones statuenda*), you will say—the Eucharist, the ordering of religious life, etc. But these have long been established by the divine Word (*verbo divino sunt statuta*). For God prescribes the praying, preaching, giving thanks, disciplining the flesh, instructing the

> people and boys. Give to me therefore some other work subject to traditions. Will you give purgatory, pilgrimages, brotherhoods, the cult of saints? These indeed are beyond the Word of God and at the same time also impious. Thus when there is no work that tradition is able to decree anew, it follows that a tradition may seize upon a work previously commanded by God and gradually assume the category of substance, because afterward it may solemnize as they say and clothe with quantity, quality, location, time, and what have you, so that giving thanks is a work of tradition—nay, rather not of tradition but of the divine command. It is done truly of tradition as long as one may say repeatedly—at this hour, at this place, by this voice, with such a pause, with this vestment, with this gesture we wish to do it. But God has wanted these predicates of accidents to be free and truly accidents—by no means truly the substance. [*WBr* 5:525–26]

Confronted by the abiding divine revelation, traditions appear as mere historical accretions to be judged and accepted or rejected according to whether they agree with the Word of God through which the efficient Cause is accomplished; the Word exercises the function of judge (*judex*) and determiner (*definitor*) (*WBr* 5:527, 525). In the task of providing the articles of faith and their transmission the Word of God stands as both the agent and the content of revelation.

The writings from the latter half of Luther's life indicate no departure from the formulation given at the Coburg in 1530. Although the terminology at times proves misleading, the basic relation remains between the accidental and historical nature of traditions and the eternal articles of faith contained and delivered by the Word. To the end of his life Luther pressed his relentless attack upon the traditions of men, by which he meant more specifically those human legislative enactments which had invaded the religious life through the assumed magisterial and judicial authority of the Papacy (8: 453:35; 42:634:27, 652:4). If Luther or perhaps his Melanchthonian editors can employ the singular in respect to a particular idea or practice which derives from the tradition of the patriarchs, these statements do not endanger the position of the Word of God as the deliverer of the content of faith (42:94:39, 218:22, 263:25; 43:200: 14, 305:6).

His later statements become especially valuable in revealing his position on the active aspect of the divine revelation and the question of transmission. Here the concern is less with the body of articles of faith contained by the Word and more with their actual delivery. In the *Lectures on Genesis* he states,

> With the beginning of the reborn gospel, Müntzer, Carlstadt, and the Sacramentarians arose and, having abandoned the gospel borne by the Holy Spirit from heaven (*tradito per spiritum sanctum de coelo*), they followed their own special illuminations. . . . [Likewise the pontiffs] have imagined that not everything necessary to our salvation had been handed over by Christ and the apostles (*per Christum et Apostolos tradita esse*) but that many oracles have been reserved to the bishops and to themselves and these must repeatedly be set forth more clearly to the Church. [43:225]

Luther not only rejects explicitly any second form of delivered revelation but he also unites Christ and the apostles together with the Holy Spirit in a common act of delivery. Luther states that the Word as the content of revelation is divinely delivered to us (43: 674:34) and that the Holy Spirit delivers what must be taught in the Church (43:671:36). While he can continue to refer to the content of revelation as being handed over by Christ and the apostles (43:668:42), the ultimate and specific agent of revelation remains the Holy Spirit.

> Although He has ascended to heaven and no longer preaches personally or physically on earth, still He has not stopped speaking through the apostles and their successors; nor will He stop extending His gospel farther and farther and working powerfully in it by means of the Holy Spirit. [41:196]

All Luther's statements about the content and delivery of the divine revelation are directed toward a single concept—the Word of God. Only the Word of God possesses this double function of comprising the gospel and articles of faith and communicating them to the Church. In the Word of God the two aspects of what had once been tradition come together again in a single source of revelation. Beyond this authority are the practices, customs, and laws of men that are to be judged and to be disposed of according to the Word.

Luther's reformulation of the concept of tradition in terms of the Word signified an achievement of the greatest importance for the relation of divine revelation to the life of the Church. If in his opposition to Rome, Luther emphasized Scripture as being over rather than in the Church, he never lost sight of the fact that the total working of Scripture was inseparable from the Church. Yet in theory at least, Scripture, which was the pre-eminent external form of the Word, became its own interpreter and stood as judge and determinant of all human institutions within the Church. The absolute authority of Scripture removed a legislative and judicial authority from the heart of the Church's life.

> For what is the law of the Church? It is the Word believed through the Spirit for eternal life and delivered by God (*a Deo traditum*). [*WBr* 5:530]

From this understanding of absolute authority as being transcendental and self-transmitting, there emerged a new concept of the Church's continuity and movement in time.

The Word in Church History

In his first lectures on the Psalms, when confronted with the fact of the proud seducing the simple in the Church, Luther addressed himself to the problem of the Church's progress in time:

> For this was and is particularly unavoidable at the time of the Pharisees and [now] with the heretics when many good men are seduced, who previously served and feared God in simplicity. But then with truth having been raised and revealed, which before had been hidden, just as always from the beginning truth has been revealed more and more to which the earlier people were not held explicitly and just as always newly revealed truth raises up its attackers and defenders, thus, I say, these simple people are in danger. For the proud with power, boasting, and pomp resist and impugn the truth, because their own long-accustomed way and ignorance are more pleasing to them than the new truth, just as the Jews hold now as before to their own letter. . . . [The faithful] have known, that is, they have wanted to know and with works they have shown themselves to have known, adhering in the fullness of faith to Your testimonies, although they may not yet see the substance of the testimonies. Thus it is certainly done constantly today in the article concerning the conception of the blessed Virgin, likewise with the Bohemians as regards the sacraments and the primacy of the Roman Church. For they boast about their ancient ways, and because they observe these things from former times or rather pretend to have observed them, soon they resist with the gravest contention the highest source (*caput*) for divulging truth. In the same way it is done in many other questions, whence arise opinions and Scholastic sects. All these people do not know that truth moves from clarity to clarity, yet in the same form. Indeed they resist it and along with the Jews they do not want to be extended toward the future—

> most foolish ones. . . . Therefore, what is first always stands as letter to that which is to be and what is to be stands as spirit to the earlier thing in its forward quest. Thus he who does not want to advance toward the future reality wishes to persist in the letter like the Jews. [4:345]

In his first exegetical work, Luther emphasized the antithesis between the Old and the New Testament more sharply than former exegetes had done.[51] Because he had not yet attained his insight into the law, he repeatedly opposed the two, contrasting wrath to grace, law to gospel, letter to spirit. He conceives the two basic categories of letter and spirit in the Pauline sense of opposing ways of understanding existence and comes close to associating the Jews with the outlook of the world and the Christians with a mind that has been clarified by God. Luther here attempts to understand within the categories of letter and spirit the movement or development of the Church, which he relates to the magisterium of the Church and its power of elucidating the divine deposit. The movement from letter to spirit derives from his understanding of man's own spiritual life which is always in motion—partly acquired, partly to be acquired—a progress that is nothing other than an ever-new beginning (4:350, 362). This movement, which involves more a continual struggle for faith than a development or improvement, he now relates to the Church and the process of revelation:

> [The Psalmist] seeks for intellect as against letter because intellect is spirit. But along with the passage of times letter and spirit have arisen, for what to earlier people then sufficed as intellect now to us is letter. As I have said before, the letter is now more subtly with us than it once was and this on account of the forward movement of time. For, as I have said, with everything that advances what is left behind is to it letter and

51. Gerhard Ebeling, "Die Anfänge von Luthers Hermeneutik," *ZTK, 48* (1951), p. 211.

> what it extends itself toward is to it spirit, because always that which is possessed is letter to that which must be acquired, as we have said concerning motion. Therefore the article of the Trinity, plainly expressed at the time of the Arians, was spirit and given to a few; now, however revealed, it is letter unless we can bring to it something else, namely a living faith toward it. Therefore intellect must always be prayed for lest we harden in the dead letter. . . . Thus if the flourishing of grass is compared to us, it is not fitting for us to languish but always to flourish, always to go from strength to strength, from clarity to clarity, from faith to faith. . . . It is correctly said that the intellect of Scripture always advances and has no end. . . . Others, however . . . love God's law in the letter and not in the spirit because they do not want it nor do they want to advance with it but to stand on the initial step. . . . For they do not want, as I have said, to be directed, but only to be ruled, not led further but to remain in the present, as the Jews particularly have done. [4:365–66]

Here Luther conceived the life and movement of the Church in terms of the individual Christian's effort to recover and deepen his faith. In his effort to understand the position of the law and the impact of Christ as the transformation of the Old Testament into the New Testament, Luther extends the process of an implicit revelation's becoming explicit into the period after Christ, and he involves the movement of the Church with the further elucidation of the divine deposit. This involvement of the individual's struggle to rejuvenate his faith with the process of revelation and inevitably with the magisterial function of the Church is not to be understood as Luther's final position on the matter of the Church's continuity and movement in time.[52] The development of his hermeneutics, a new appreciation of the law and gospel, and the attainment of his

52. Cf. Koehler, *L. und K.*, pp. 171–72.

belief in the sufficiency and clarity of Scripture lead to the displacement of the progressive dialectical opposition between letter and spirit and the rejection of the view that revelation is ever being made more explicit in the centuries after Christ. Through 1517 there lingers the idea that the new excites pride, suspicion, and contention and that the martyrs and teachers of the Church suffered because they seemed to be despisers of the old and had advanced without the counsel of the old (*WBr* 1:122). By 1518, however, the designation of newness is avoided and Luther's theology claims to be the old one; the Scholastics and commentators are the innovators (1:379; *WBr* 1:185; *OVA* 7:489). Any sense of an increasing clarity in the deposit of revelation collapses with the development of his principle of the sufficiency of Scripture and is specifically rejected afterward (23:67; 34/1:372–76).

In the same exegetical work, Luther expressed another view of the Church's progress and its relation to the divine authoritative revelation. Here he places the emphasis on the permanent, transcendental source of revelation rather than on the response of the faithful to this revelation. By an interesting reinterpretation of an anology employed by Innocent III, Luther identifies Christ with the sun and the Church with the moon:

> The Church is always born and always changed in the succession of the faithful. Now this and now that is the Church, yet always the same. This truth is signified by the changes of the moon which the prophet, recognizing, understood and now declares: God did not similarly constitute the sun, for it does not change but is always the same, illuminating nevertheless always another moon. Thus are read in creatures the Passion and Resurrection of Christ and the succession of the Church. [4:169]

Luther observes furthermore that although the moon undergoes twelve or thirteen changes during the year, it is still the same moon:

> It is said to be formed more than the sun is through the vicissitudes of time. Thus the militant Church is one from the beginning of the world; one generation passes, another comes, one after the other the Church succeeds in the same Church. And Christ, the sun, while remaining always the same, has nevertheless died—not indeed another Christ followed by another succession—just as the same sun sets and rises always with its full light. [4:188]

The analogy retained its vigor and underwent elaboration in Luther's subsequent thinking. In preparation for the Leipzig debates he expressly opposed the papal interpretation and again presented the sun as Christ and the moon as the Church (2:224). In his last great work, the *Lectures on Genesis,* he repeated the analogy with the Church being illuminated by the grace of Christ (42:371). The analogy proved effective, for it expressed on the one hand the abiding, transcendent revelation supplied by Scripture and on the other the dependence of the Church's life upon this revelation which may be darkened but never extinguished. For the flourishing of the Church depends upon the flourishing of the Word, and anything that should obscure the sun of Scripture will affect the life of the Church (5:131; cf. 10/1/2:118). Speaking of the proceedings at Augsburg in 1518, Luther complained that with their decretals the canonists had distorted and obscured the true sense of Scripture as a cloud which covers so as to conceal the brightest sun (2:18). One must remain within the sun of Scripture and allow its heat to dispel the clouds which are its dark passages (8:239). Later he employed the image of the clouds to describe the effect of the radicals upon Scripture (26:174). And at the end of his life he altered the analogy for the purpose of describing the new appearance of the reformed Church: it shone like the sun after emerging from behind a cloud, and yet like the sun it had always been the same Church.[53]

53. *WA* 51:486. On the currency of this last image in late medieval preaching, see G. R. Owst, *Literature and Pulpit in Medieval England* (New York, 1961), pp. 190–92.

Translated into theological terms, the analogy refers to a new conception of tradition in its fullest and truest sense. The continuity as well as the life of the Church lie in the Word of God. The Church is divinely sustained, and while it may be more flourishing at one time than at another, it always presents the same countenance and remains essentially unchanged. For the content of revelation remains eternally the same and acts to preserve the true Church from the corrupting and disintegrating forces of time:

> For just as all things are broken [by time], it is impossible for the Church of any one time to preserve that inner form of all times, if the Church is sought beyond the articles of faith. For it was, is, and will be necessary for times to be changed with those things which are subjected to time—namely, places and persons. Truly, the Church within the articles of faith has one simple, perpetual form through all ages. . . . In all other things there is the shadow of vicissitude and change. For God alone, who is the head of the Church, there is no change. Now His Word which remains eternal is in the Church; this makes the Church always the same just as He Himself is the same. . . . Beyond Scripture or the Word of God the Church is not able to retain its resemblance through time. [*WBr* 8:344–45]

The Word of God alone preserves and maintains the Church from one moment to the next.

Luther understands the historical problem of continuity in time under the aspect of a succession which exists beyond the sudden ruptures and catastrophes of history. In combating the Romanist position that the Church's continuity lies with an uninterrupted chain or succession of bishops coming down from the apostles, Luther claims that the succession is supposed to stand with the gospel because the faithful are bound to the gospel, not to the officials who teach the gospel. In the same sense bishops are identified by evangelical purity, not by a formal succession. Bound to the ministry of the Word, the Church is not preserved in time by bishops. Rather the gospel must be the succession.[54]

This removal of the Church's continuity from the historical level to the transcendental level in the Word cannot be overemphasized, for it springs naturally from Luther's doctrine of the Word of God and distinguishes his outlook on Church history from that of his contemporaries. The prevalent idea of the *testes veritatis* provided the more radical groups of the Reformation with tangible proof of their unbroken descent from the true Church of the apostolic age: a line of witnesses whose moral purity was sealed by suffering and martyrdom attested to the true Church's continuity. The idea found champions not only among Protestant martyrologists but in the camp of Lutheran orthodoxy itself. Flacius Illyricus espoused the idea of a line of doctors in order to demonstrate the continuity of the hidden Church; these doctors provided external proof for an unbroken succession of doctrine and perpetual opposition to the Papacy.[55] Melanchthon himself entertained the idea and even included Christ in a continuous line which led from Noah, John the Baptist, and the apostles down to Luther.[56]

Not only did Luther avoid constructing a chain of witnesses, but the whole idea was quite antithetical to his understanding of the relation between the Church and the Word.[57] The source and continuity of the Church exist in the Word of God. Only in the period prior to Christ does Luther recognize for the Church an external succession of men who are distinguished not so much by their moral virtue and martyrdom as by having been entrusted with God's promise:

54. *WA* 39/2:176–77, 180–82. *Evangelium sol dye successio sein.*

55. Günter Moldaenke, *Matthias Flacius Illyricus* (Stuttgart, 1936), p. 320. Polman, *L'Élément historique,* pp. 185–86.

56. Peter Meinhold, *Die Genesisvorlesung Luthers und ihre Herausgeber, Forschungen zur Kirchen-und Geistesgeschichte* (Stuttgart, 1936), p. 50. Hereafter cited as *Die Genesisvorlesung*. Cf. *CR* 11:727.

57. Cf. Seeberg, *L.T.G.*, pp. 161–67.

> The patriarchs had carnal succession just as even afterward in the law carnal succession was in the priesthood. But in the New Testament there is no such carnal succession. Because Christ did not beget carnal children, thus the Church wandering in respect to place and persons is only there where the Word is. [42:424]

In a rather unreliable passage which appears in the *Table Talk,* Luther also adumbrates a line of witnesses which runs from Adam to himself as the Jeremiah and which includes Christ and the Nicene Council. Yet in contrast with Melanchthon, Luther understands them not as constituting a continuous succession but as serving to demonstrate how God preserves His Church (*TR* 5242). Luther again reminds us that in the Church bishops are not made by any external succession; the Lord alone is the bishop sustaining bishops and at times giving the faithful an Augustine or a Hus, an Ambrose or a Jerome (53:74).

Luther's tendency to discover in the history of the Church men whose beliefs were consonant with his own should not be confused with an effort to establish the continuity of the Church in a line of such witnesses. This effort to associate Bernard, Hus, the conciliarists, and other ostensible pre-reformers with the evangelical cause derived more from a psychological need on Luther's part to demonstrate that he was not alone than from any belief in an unbroken chain of witnesses. In describing his discovery of the works of the Dutch nominalist, Wessel Gansfort, he compared his prior feeling of isolation and ineffectiveness to that of the prophet Elijah before God appeared to him in the cave; the encounter with Wessel's doctrine like Elijah's knowledge of the seven thousand righteous persons gave Luther the same sense that he was not alone and that his work had a concrete meaning (10/2:316–17). The hitherto undiscovered saints and doctors who reappear with the restoration of the gospel gave Luther great confidence (26:124). This tendency to adopt earlier doctors as evangelical witnesses pertains to his struggle for faith and relates only obliquely to his view of Church history.

By claiming that the continuity of the Church lay in God's hands, Luther did not mean to imply that the Church existed somewhere in the clouds. Because the Word is never without some response in the world, the Church has very definite external manifestation in the form of true believers on this earth. Although he may find the Church conserved at a single moment in one person such as Paul at the Council of Jerusalem or Hus at Constance, he never denies it a concrete, material reality (40/1:203; 44:774). Nor is the Church deprived of external succession in an organized ministry:

> Christ commands the apostles [that His Word is to be heard]. The apostles give it to their successors, the bishops and preachers, and these to the entire world. Thus are the apostles and preachers nothing but conduits whereby Christ leads and guides His gospel from the Father to us.[58]

In this sense Luther can consider himself as participating in the process of transmission (43:463:3).

Yet despite all these indications of an objective continuity, Luther recognizes the possibilities of apostasy and rebellion and does not allow his judgment to be determined by the facts of an external succession and the existence of some believers. He rests his conviction in the Church's continuity on his faith, not on any historical knowledge of witnesses. When repeatedly confronted with an especially dark period in the Church's history which seems to deny the existence of a true Church, Luther does not scramble for witnesses but calmly repeats the Apostles' Creed: "I believe in a holy Christian Church, the Communion of Saints . . ." (26:168; 50:593). As an article of faith it states that there is always a Church, always a group of believers, although they cannot be specified.

58. *WA* 45:521. Cf. Rupp, *The Righteousness of God,* p. 339.

Faith makes the Church visible; the Word maintains it at any one moment in time. This theological conception of continuity, in which God constantly acts to preserve His people, does not allow for any idea of the Church's development according to some immanent power; at the same time it seriously restricts the significance of the Church's transmission through men. The Church is not constantly shaped and determined from the horizontal development on the level of history but is constantly being restored by God from above. God's bond with time is not limited to the event of Christ fifteen hundred years ago, but includes the effects of the ever-active Word. The fact that God transmits the promise through the instrumentality of men does not disguise the divine agency. In his ordained office of minister or preacher man serves as a channel for the divine action and remains *cooperator Dei*.

The continuity of the divine purpose and the apparent discontinuities of historical existence arise from the nature and activity of God's Word. As the instrument of revelation the Word not only presents to man God's enduring promise despite human unfaithfulness but also through its very revelation under the aspect of contraries it introduces a division within history. This division in response to the divine promise assumes the form of two generations which God bears through history. The generation of believers constitutes those who are exercised in faith and recognize their preservation and continuity in God's Word. In this sense the Church in history moves from faith to faith. The other generation, which God in His wrath bears in a reprobate sense, are those who through pride, ingratitude, and unbelief have rejected the abiding promise of the Word and have devised their own preservation and continuity (3:566; 40/1:245).

> A great doctrine and consolation are proposed to us in this fact when we trace both churches from these virtual fountains and we observe how God always governed each with marvelous counsel so that the true Church was in one time better, at

> another time worse, yet always essentially the same, and the hypocritical and possessing church had the glory in the presence of the world and crucified the true Church pleasing to God. [42:187]

The continuing presence and countenance of the Church attest to the continuity of the divine action through the Word.

Luther's assurance of the continuity of the divine purpose gave him the courage to break with the historical continuity provided by the medieval Church. His insight into the nature of faith and the hiddenness of God's revelation made him recognize that the abiding nature of the divine purpose reveals itself more in the discontinuities than in the continuities of history. As man's only response to God, faith seeks continuity neither in an institution, a hierarchy, a body of doctrine, nor in any series of spiritual accomplishments, but in the divine promise alone. The signs of the visible Church attest that the continuity of the faith of believers can only be maintained from God's side.[59]

Luther's review of the tradition in the Church proceeded on the firm basis of his principle of scriptural authority. Implicit in his final rupture with Rome was the conviction that the real tradition of the Church lay in God's promise manifested in the Word and not in anything humanly devised. The persisting nature of this revelation in the proclamation of the gospel bore a community of believers down through time and introduced conflict into the world.

59. Daniel Jenkins, *Tradition, Freedom and the Spirit* (Philadelphia, 1952), pp. 88–91.

3. THE PROBLEM OF PERIODIZATION

THROUGHOUT ALL TIME the same Word maintains and preserves the community of believers; throughout all time the same Church responds with the same faith to the vivifying action of the Holy Spirit. The extreme emphasis upon continuity and the fact that the Church remains substantially the same would seem to deny any sense of change or progression and ultimately to exclude any form of periodization. Furthermore, the ever-repeated and ever-new encounter of the believer with the active Christ reduces the significance of any tight periodization of Church history. In this respect it has been noted with considerable justification that the presence of the dramatic, existential element in history prevents Luther from imposing a Procrustean scheme upon the course of Church history.[1] Notwithstanding all these facts, there does exist for Luther a periodization of Church history.

If by His immutable activity in time Christ creates the constant and continuing factor in redemptive history, He also introduces the essential division in the course of Church history. The immense

1. E. Kohlmeyer, "Die Geschichtsbetrachtung Luthers," *ARG, 37* (1940), 160, 168.

significance of Christ's appearance in time early distinguished the Christian view of history from previously existing views. To St. Augustine, the Incarnate Christ represented a unique event that shattered all cyclical views of history and introduced into history a progress.[2] In *The City of God,* Augustine elaborated the momentous implications of this fact in a total view of history. His achievement marked the culmination of the patristic effort to relate the Old Testament to the New Testament—human history with the divine providence. Irenaeus and Chrysostom, Basil and Gregory Nazianzen had already enunciated the idea of the unity of the human race in its temporal development. Similarly these fathers understood the existence of a pedagogical element in the linear course of history by which God educates his people through the means of greater degrees of revelation.[3] Yet it was Augustine who most fully recognized the profound implications of Christ's appearance in time and who most successfully related the pattern of divine interventions to the course of history.[4]

As the recipient of this rich inheritance, Luther was subject to this concept of change in terms of the Incarnation and the increasing clarity of revelation. But these factors, integral to any Christian understanding of history, now had to be adjusted to the permanent activity of the Word in time. To Luther, the Incarnation represented the fulfillment of God's promise to mankind and the final act of the divine revelation in which God discloses the Word to men. The increasing clarity in the announcement of the Word produces the main divisions of Church history. Because periodization is a function of the divine revelation, God again appears as the efficient agent of history and man as his recipient and *cooperator.*

Heretofore the major problem has been that of understanding in

2. *City of God,* XII, 13.

3. Henri de Lubac, *Catholicism,* trans. Lancelot C. Sheppard (New York, 1958), pp. 127–33.

4. Oliver Rousseau, O.S.B., "La Typologie augustinienne de l'Hexaemeron et la théologie du temps," *Festgabe Joseph Lortz,* ed. Erwin Iserloh and Peter Manns (Baden-Baden, 1958), *2,* 47–58.

Church history the permanent elements which derive from the content of revelation. The problem of giving periods to history presents the fact of change and differentiation as a result of the divine elaboration of revelation. The present task is to discover Luther's appropriation of traditional schemes of bestowing periods upon Church history and to understand their applications in terms of his conception of God's revelation in time. Although such a study would seem to pertain more to the history of doctrine than to Church history, the necessary relationship between the life of the Church and the proper use of the Word and sacraments justifies this consideration. But the study of change in Church history must not blind one to the constants in the life of the Church as a community of believers. The signs change, but faith, the Church, and Christ remain.

The First Epoch: the Patriarchs

The millennial typology of the week of Creation provided the most influential scheme for the Christian periodization of history. According to this conception the biblical week served as the basis for eight ages, and each of the six days of Creation prefigured a millennium of history. This idea found its biblical authority in the statement of Psalms 90:4 that a thousand years in the sight of God are as one day; the scheme of periodization entered Judeo-Christian eschatology in a Jewish apocalyptic work, the Slavonic Enoch, and was reiterated in the Second Epistle of Peter (3:8). The Eastern Church interpreted the biblical number seven as a figure of the total time of the world, to which was opposed the eighth and eternal day. On the other hand, the Western Church sought in the biblical week a key to the succession of historical epochs. Millenarianism became a salient feature of primitive Christianity and continued until Augustine rejected it and deferred the historical end to the indefinite future. He envisaged the seventh age not as the millennium but as the sabbath that exists for all blessed souls throughout all six ages, and he had the eighth age begin with the end of the world. Furthermore, Augustine considered the six ages themselves to be of unequal duration. Bede confirmed the replacement of chiliasm by eschatology and helped to establish the Augustinian conception of the six ages as the orthodox version in Christian historiography.[5]

Under the influence of the so-called prophecy of Elias, the millennial typology underwent a refinement. This idea originated in Jewish doctrine about the time of Christ and appeared in the Babylonian Talmud, where it was described as an opinion of the school of Elias. It accepted the scheme of the six millennia but organized them into larger periods: two thousand years before the law; two thousand years under the law; and two thousand years of the Messiah. Paul employed this scheme in his own periodization: before the law, under the law, and under grace; and Augustine himself recognized this triadic pattern. The theory enjoyed considerable popularity and was known, among others, to Bodin.[6] When Johan Carion published his influential *Chronicle* in 1532, he incorporated the prophecy at the beginning of the work as the main periodization of world history.[7]

Luther did not escape the influence of these traditional schemes of giving periods to history. With some validity it has been suggested that Luther was largely indebted to Carion and to the Melanchthonian school for his periodization of history.[8] All known statements made by Luther concerning the main divisions of history postdate the publication of Carion's work. In 1540, in his *Table*

5. Jean Daniélou, "La Typologie millenariste de la semaine dans le christianisme primitif," *Vigiliae Christianae, 2* (1948), 1–16. Wilhelm Levison, "Bede as Historian," *Bede: His Life, Times, and Writings,* ed. A. Hamilton Thompson (Oxford, 1935), pp. 122, 151. Cf. Roderich Schmidt, "Aetates mundi," *ZKG, 67* (1955–56), 288–318.

6. Herbert Grundmann, *Studien über Joachim von Floris* (Leipzig und Berlin, 1927), pp. 88–89. William J. Bouwsma, *Concordia Mundi: The Career and Thought of Guillaume Postel 1510–1581* (Cambridge, Mass., 1957), pp. 282–83. Emil Schürer, *Geschichte des jüdischen Volkes im Zeitalter Jesu Christi* (Leipzig, 1886), *2,* 447.

7. Johan Carion, *Chronica* (Wittenberg, 1532), B1v.

8. Meinhold, *Die Genesisvorlesung,* p. 307.

Talk, he identified a thousand years with one day in God's sight, and in the same year he divided the world's history into six ages whose governors were Adam, Noah, Abraham, David, Christ, and the Pope, respectively (*TR* 5299; 5300). The only work in which Luther applied this scheme was the *Reckoning of the Years of the World* in 1541, but his *Lectures on Genesis* did not contradict this pattern. Unlike Augustine, Luther confined each age to a millennium. But he treated their limits freely and never committed himself to the precise divisions of this periodization; they were the conveniences of chroniclers, not articles of faith (42:649).

While Luther's indebtedness to the Melanchthonian school of historiography cannot be denied, it needs to be qualified. In the first place it is somewhat circumstantial that Luther's statements concerning periodization appear after the publication of Carion's work, because at this time Luther's efforts to provide history with a scheme of periodization conformed with his growing interest in chronology and history toward the end of his life. Secondly, contemporary literature was so thoroughly imbued with these systems of periodization that it is almost impossible to attribute their influence to any one source. While it is true that no formal statement by Luther regarding the three great epochs can be found prior to Carion's work, Luther had long previously appropriated this scheme from its Pauline and biblical source. In 1523 he presented this idea implicitly in respect to the divine elaboration of revelation:

> Previously one revelation always followed upon another. Thus God speaks in Exodus 6: "I have not announced my name Lord to them." For although the patriarchs knew God well, they still at the same time did not have such a public announcement of God as thereafter went forth through Moses and the prophets. But now is no more excellent nor more public proclamation come into the world than that of the gospel. Thus it is the last. All times have run their course but now at the end it is revealed to us. [12:293]

Four years later he remarked that the gospel was also given to Adam, but more clearly to Abraham and finally appeared with an ultimate clarity in Christ (24:252–53; cf. 16:99–100, 596–99). Consequently, prior to Carion's work the three great epochs had become part of Luther's intellectual furniture.

Although the prophecy of Elias appeared at the beginning of the *Reckoning*, in his *Lectures on Genesis* Luther adumbrated a different triadic periodization that placed extreme emphasis upon the Flood as the great division in history. The obscurity of Luther's precise intention in this scheme arises from the several senses of the word *mundus*. Normally the term "world" possesses a spatial connotation or, more frequently, in its Johannine sense it refers to everything that has been disfigured by sin and remains alienated from God (cf. 18:776). In his exegesis of Genesis 5:5 through 6:10, Luther distinguishes in temporal terms three distinct worlds. Within this passage Enoch's transfiguration provides the inspiration for a new scheme. Luther claims that each world must have the hope presented to it of a better life after this life. Therefore Enoch stands to the first and original world as Elias stands to the second world which had the law. Luther continues:

> We in the New Testament are as if (*tanquam*) in the third world (*tertio Mundo*). We have however the illustrious example, Christ himself, our Liberator ascending to heaven with many other saints. For God wanted witnesses of the resurrection of the dead to exist in all ages (*omnibus seculis*). [42:257]

The passage clearly indicates that it is not a question of a Stoic succession of worlds. In the first place Luther uses the term figuratively in a way that suggests a temporal succession within the same world conceived both as a created order and as that which is alienated from God. Secondly, the temporal overtones of *mundus* are confirmed by the equation of the three worlds with the ages. What remains to be discovered is the exact meaning of *mundus* for Luther in this passage.

In order to appreciate Luther's intention it is necessary to observe that he has allowed his knowledge of 2 Peter 2:5 to control his exegesis of the entire passage. The Petrine text, which concerns God's not sparing the original world, is an unusual one, for it represents one of the few cases in the New Testament where a plurality of worlds is suggested. But the term *κόσμος* here has the meaning of mankind.[9] In his own exegesis of this text in 1523 Luther, while distinguishing between a preceding and a new world, gave *welt* the sense of an unregenerate mankind (14:45, 48). In his present use of the Petrine text he specifically refers to this verse (42:251, 264, 269) and continually designates the world before the Flood as *originalis* or *primus*—an appropriate translation of the Petrine *ἀρχαῖος κόσμος* (42:251–78 passim).

The semantics of *κόσμος* helps to elucidate Luther's intent. Already by the time of the Septuagint, the cosmos had come to be considered as the theater of human activity and had assimilated the meanings of the inhabited world and mankind. With the New Testament the idea of cosmos assumed the new sense of mankind, fallen creation, and the theater of redemptive history. God's judgment was upon the world as all mankind, yet it was in this world that the revelation of Christ occurred. Paul identified cosmos with *αἰὼν οὗτος* and in the context of the two opposing aeons God appeared as confronting His cosmos which had been disfigured by sin. This cosmos meant the essence of everything in God's Creation—most specifically mankind—which had fallen and lived under His judgment. As the reconciled world, the Church belonged no longer to this world nor this aeon but partook of the new aeon. For John, also, the world frequently possessed this sense of theater for the drama of salvation. The faithful stood in a double relation to the world: they were in the world but not of the world.[10]

9. Gerhard Kittel, *Theologisches Wörterbuch zum Neuen Testament, 3* (Stuttgart, 1933), 885.

10. Ibid., pp. 889–94.

Only in the light of this special understanding of the Church, the world, and their relationship does it become evident that Luther's conception of three *Mundi* pertains to Church history and not to world history. Here the perspectives are religious and redemptive and relate not to the world as worldly *Regiment,* with its own responsibilities and blessings for this life, but to the world as unregenerate mankind in which the divine revelation operates and to which the Church brings all its energies. In this intimate relationship between Church and world, the Church sustains the world through doctrine and prayer without which the world would perish (43: 664–65; cf. *WBr* 10:5). In the temporal succession of worlds each is distinguished by God's act of destruction and re-creation as well as by that which is redemptively operative in it. Changes in the covenant or form of the promise distinguish one world and its period from another. What occurs in the Church establishes this triadic periodization.

While this scheme pertains to the Church in its broadest effectiveness, Luther uses the same terminology to define more narrowly the fruit of the Church's contact with unredeemed mankind. At the center of this passage from one mankind and its epoch to another, the permanent promise creates a permanent race and a permanent time in the community of believers. Earlier in his first sermons on Genesis in 1523 Luther had observed, according to Stephan Roth's version, that the best human race (*optimus mundus*) existed at that time in the holy family—Adam and Eve (14:179). Fifteen years later Luther again suggested the fundamental conviction that the Church embraces a regenerate people and continues to participate in the new aeon of grace:

> The generation of the just remains forever [*in secula seculorum*]. For all perished with the Flood, nevertheless the generation of the just is preserved as if an eternal world [*tanquam aeternus mundus*]. [42:264]

The term *aeternus mundus* pertains more to Luther's doctrine of justification than to the accepted Aristotelian notions of time and eternity.[11] For Luther, the Christian participates in two times: he carries within himself the time of the law and the time of grace, alternating. Here time is conceived as a total spiritual condition under either law or gospel. Through the time of grace the Christian comes within the orbit of eternity. Through faith in which Christ is present one participates in eternity without being in eternity. While in this life one is subject to the time of the law with all its attendant circumstances (40/1:524–26; cf. 4:51). Now by a curious inversion he employs the term *mundus* to denote that ultimate temporal dimension in which the Church lives. For the Church is the Christian people, and as he had explained twenty years before, it is a spiritual generation of people in which the older members are not supplanted by those following them, but both are gathered together into one generation of people—spiritual yet in the world, eternal yet still mortal (5:671).

With respect to the prophecy of Elias, Luther's extensive use of the Petrine text proves both confusing and suggestive. By bringing the first humanity and its epoch to an end after the first millennium, Luther presents a variation from the conventional triadic periodization. The relation of the second millennium to the three great epochs remains uncertain, because he claims that a new humanity begins with Noah (42:302) as well as another with Abraham at the beginning of the third age (*aetas*) (42:436). While there may be four humanities within the entirety of mankind, the existence of four great epochs appears impossible. In stating that the first world was

11. From Aristotle, Luther recognized the existence of a clock time provided by the motion of the heavens. Here time is a measure of change according to which civil life is ruled (42:32–33). While Luther was also acquainted from his early years with Augustine's idea that time is a stretching out of the human mind, he seems to have derived from Aristotle again his concept of eternity. For in contrast to the mind's awareness of enumeration and succession, with eternity there is no possibility of recognizing individual, measured moments, but everything happens as if at once. Eternity is thus a point, a now—timelessness. Fritz Blanke, "Miszellen zu Luther," *Zeitschrift für systematische Theologie*, 4 (1926), 236–38.

destroyed by the Flood, the second was wasted by various calamities, and the third will be consumed by fire, Luther reasserts the triadic scheme (42:263). According to this pattern the epoch of the second world is thrice as long as the first.

Luther's emphasis upon the crisis of the Flood relates to a different school of thought and does not constitute any deliberate revision of the prophecy of Elias. Within the context of the particular exegetical passage, Luther is more interested in establishing the Flood as the great division in history than he is in presenting an exposition of these epochs. Concerning Noah's obedience to God and his faith in the promised seed, Luther remarks:

> Therefore just as before the Flood the new Church in Paradise begins with Adam and Eve believing in the promise, thus here also the new humanity (*Mundus*) and new Church are raised from the wedlock of Noah, which is as it were (*tanquam*) the nursery of his humanity (*Mundi*), that will last up to the end of the world (*ad extremum Mundum*). [42:302]

The significance of the break caused by the Flood is further accented by his opposing the first world to the future world (42:280). In emphasizing the Flood as the major crisis in history, Luther appears to be in contact with an ancient exegetical tradition which goes back to Origen, Philo, and ultimately to Jewish speculation on the figure of Noah. According to this tradition the seven prediluvian generations corresponded to a primitive period of happiness. Living in the eighth generation, Noah represented a new beginning after the cosmic week. Coming at the end of the old humanity and the beginning of a new one, he was a type for Christ just as the ark was a type for baptism.[12] Luther does not accept all aspects of this elaborate typology. To him Noah represents more a sign of the end than a figure of Christ and a new beginning. On the other hand, by claiming the appearance of a new humanity and a new Church

12. J. Daniélou, "Déluge, baptême, jugement," *Dieu vivant, 8* (1947), 97–112.

after the Flood, he indicates an awareness of this exegetical tradition and involves his thought in a typological scheme of periodization.

With this exception Luther conforms to the conventional scheme of periodization. In the *Lectures on Genesis* he refers to the first five chapters down to the Flood as being the first book and the story of the Flood to Abraham as constituting a second book (42:264). He considers as a single period of two thousand years the patriarchal governorship of the first world and first Church (42:428). When he turns to the appearance of Abraham in his exegesis of Genesis, he adds:

> You have now the history of the first world shown faithfully by Moses, so that one may be certain as regards the perpetual propagation of the promise concerning Christ. If, therefore, you call this the history of the first Church, you have not erred. [42:427]

A study of the first age's character indicates the comprehensiveness of the Church and of Church history. The most significant feature of the first millennium is that the age reveals itself as Church history, while world history remains still implicit and derivative. If world history constitutes that which God accomplishes in the worldly Regiment, no formal and explicit manifestation of this Regiment exists until the Tower of Babel. If world history involves that which stands in opposition to the Word and alienated from God, it manifests itself in the actions of the Cainite church and within the context of the twofold Church. In his *Lectures on Genesis,* Luther states that the Church is instituted prior to the economic and the worldly Regimente. God constituted the economic with Eve, and the worldly Regiment or *politia* followed as a result of the Fall (42:79–82). Adam labored in the economic and political orders as well as in the ecclesiastical and was father, king, and priest all in one (42:159). The actual constitution of the worldly Regiment, however, remained long delayed. In founding the first city out of a desire to dominate and to persecute the true Church, Cain acted within his own church, which was not the worldly Regiment but a perverted form of the spiritual Regiment (42:232). Undeniably the worldly Regiment exists implicitly within the Church of the first millennium, for immediately prior to the Flood, Luther mentions that all three orders have become corrupted because the Church had been dissipated by idolatries and impious cults (42:284). Not until after the Flood, when God bestows upon men the power of life and death among men, does the civil law appear. Only then does God institute the magistracy and constitute *politia* (42:360–61).

In the last great work of his life Luther's presentation of this development, and of the peculiar character of the patriarchal authority, remains somewhat confused and uncertain. With his earlier treatment of Genesis in the sermons of 1527 he indicated more clearly the nature of authority in the Church of the first millennium and how the patriarchal authority (*veterliche oeberkeit*) contained and exercised implicitly the power of the worldly Regiment (24:237). Luther begins by conceiving the worldly Regiment not as derived from God's command for man to rule over the animals and fish but as inherent in the fourth commandment. God expressly established with Adam this authority of the elders over children and servants. The paternal authority is greater than that of all kings and emperors and is the nearest to God. In this matter of educating the children in the Word and of caring for the servants, God has made the father bishop and minister of his household, and He has given to the father the office of the worldly sword by which he can sell and even kill his child. Luther is consequently able to explain why God ordained and commanded the worldly sword with Nimrod and subsequent representatives of a distinct worldly Regiment: immediately before the Flood children no longer were obedient to their elders; with the passing of these elders God did not want the world to be disorderly and thus ordained that authority which henceforth became customary in the worldly Regiment (24:223; cf. 16:353–54, 494–95).

Despite the existence of a worldly Regiment in the second half of the first epoch, no such Regiment exists in the society ruled by the patriarchs until the time of Abraham. The unique authority of the patriarchs within the Church arises first from their longevity which allows each to see his children and their children, and secondly from the high esteem in which the household and the marital state are held. The identification of household and Church, which becomes a decisive feature in the time of Abraham, has long been established. All the patriarchs have lived with one another in a single spiritual Regiment (24:237).

In considering these first millennia, Luther envisaged the Church as bearing the world in its embrace regardless of the Church's extent. The few righteous sustain the world, which would perish without the doctrine and the gospel of the Church (43:664–65; 44:346). In his respect for the order given to mankind by the Church and its patriarchal administration, Luther differs noticeably from his contemporaries. Both Carion and Melanchthon accepted the literal reading of Elias' prophecy that the first two millennia were groundless and empty (*inane*). The former attributed such a condition to the absence of a worldly Regiment, while the latter thought that it referred to the existence of areas still uninhabited by human society.[13] For Luther, however, this early period surpasses all others.

With his idea of the golden age, Luther indicated once again the comprehensiveness of redemptive history and his belief that what took place within the Church determined the character of the epoch. In order to appreciate Luther's treatment of an ancient and widely known idea, it is necessary to understand those elements of the idea which he appropriated before considering his own addition to the idea. Furthermore it should be recognized that Luther bestows the term "golden age" quite freely on several periods. Often he applies it to his own age when considering the restored light of the gospel (42:321; *WAB* 7:418); and even more disconcerting is its applica-

13. Carion, *Chronica*, B1ᵛ. *CR* 12:717.

tion to the age of the great Jewish prophets (53:97). Nevertheless, its frequent use does not impoverish the content of the term, for the identification of the golden age with the period of the patriarchs rests solidly upon several common features which are germane to the idea of a golden age.[14]

Although Luther occasionally expands the period of the golden age to include the time of Abraham (43:42), it properly pertains in its full implications to the age before the Flood (42:260). Furthermore, the age of the patriarchs stands nearest to the source and possesses in a fragmentary way some of those transcendent virtues which had been enjoyed in the state of innocence. For despite man's sin and fall, Luther makes it clear that though Paradise was inaccessible after Adam's disobedience, it still remained down to the Flood (42:68, 75). Thus the first millennium has its roots in the period of man's pristine condition, traces of which linger in the golden age.

The first millennium saw practically nine generations of patriarchs live together harmoniously in the promise of Christ (42:251). In presenting reasons for their longevity and in describing the nature of their life, Luther appeals to several characteristics of primitivism. He represents the culture and the economics of the golden age in terms of a hard primitivism and esteems the age for its frugality, simplicity, and moderation. Partly as a means of magnifying the virtue of the patriarchs in this period, partly as a means of attacking the luxury and wantonness of his own age, Luther depicts the patriarchs as shunning any form of flesh, fish, or wine and as being vegetarians who sustained themselves from roots, seeds, and herbs (42:156–57). Simplicity and frugality also marked their dress, for silks, gold, and silver were not known, and such readily available commodities as water, plants, and roots provided abundantly (53:45–46). All things were more vigorous and salubrious in the golden age, which helps to explain the longevity of the patriarchs (42:250).

14. For the classical origins of this idea, see Arthur O. Lovejoy and George Boas, *Primitivism and Related Ideas in Antiquity* (Baltimore, 1935).

Finally there is an indication of a cultural primitivism. Luther attributes to the children of Cain the invention of music and the contriving of other arts; however, he does not attack the corrupting influence of culture. Instead he decries the work of clever men in trying to achieve domination and glory (42:234). Luther directs his hostility against a contrived knowledge rather than knowledge itself. He associates Cain with books and education, and yet Adam, who lived by the Word of God, was more learned than Luther's contemporaries with all their books (14:179–81). In a sermon of 1527 he characterized the time of Noah as having innumerably more learned, clever, pious, and honorable people than his own age, for the world was then still young (27:174).

The congruence of the external features of this golden age with those of classical writers is obvious. Nevertheless, Luther's recognition of this fact and his appropriation of the idea pose a problem. In the first place it has been noted that the editor of his *Lectures on Genesis* may have elaborated the idea of the golden age beyond Luther's original statement in the *Reckoning*. Thus where Luther speaks elsewhere in a rather disparaging way of the classical poets having indulged in dreams about this age (53:46), Veit Dietrich may have changed this expression to read that the poets remembered it from the tradition and even from the conversation of the patriarchs.[15] If the Melanchthonian school had a greater interest in asserting the superior antiquity and priority of the patriarchs, Luther himself certainly did not disagree with the general notion that all culture and religion derive from the Hebrews (cf. 42:4; 1:405). Aware of the golden age's literary expositors, Luther now carried one step further this appropriation of a classical idea into a Christian context. When he describes the golden age in terms of the superior virtue of the patriarchs, which manifests itself by their simplicity, moderation, and vigor, he never fails to preserve the religious nature of these external qualities. Concomitantly, he pursues an argument

15. *WA* 42:263. Cf. Meinhold, *Die Genesisvorlesung*, pp. 318–19.

for the superior faith of the patriarchs during the first age in history. Although he does not effectively relate the golden age, marked by its superior virtue, to the first millennium, marked by its superior faith, he associates the two ideas with the patriarchs in the same period of history. Consequently, the role of faith in the idea of the golden age becomes a problem.

To appreciate the superior faith of the patriarchs demands a brief inquiry into the means of revelation. If a superior degree of faith serves to set this age apart from other ages, it is the difference in God's elaboration of revelation which distinguishes one epoch from another. Luther maintains that two general ways exist by which God communicates with man—commonly through the public ministry of the Word and by special revelations. On account of his controversy with the Enthusiasts, Luther seeks to limit these special internal revelations to the most unique occasions; and in claiming that the Holy Spirit after Christ does not teach beyond the ministry of the Word, he manifests a thorough distrust of all dreams and visions (42:321; 44:246–49). These types of revelation do not co-exist but follow each other in time. Just as the Word, keys, baptism, and Supper present God in a common, intimate, and fully adequate way to all men in the final epoch, God appears in the period of the patriarchs through special and unique revelations, which assume the form of a dream, a vision, or the voice of an angel. It would seem that the directness and immediacy of these special revelations are superior to the common and public manifestation of God in the Word and that the patriarchs possessed an advantage which later men never enjoyed (42:666–67). The contrary, however, is the actual situation, for the patriarchs had to live in the promise of Christ's advent.

Indeed, the patriarchs lived in a period when revelation was relatively dim, but their faith and longing were all the more distinctive. Both Eve and Lamech exemplify this patriarchal longing and hoping for the resurrection of the dead and the liberation from sin.

That horrible ingratitude of our age now becomes apparent because these holiest men whose shoes we are unworthy to clean manifest everywhere so great a longing for the future life. How much does the possession of a thing differ from the desire for the same thing? These patriarchs were the holiest men crowned with the highest gifts like heroes of the whole world. In them we see the greatest longing for the future seed. For them it is of supreme value and thus they thirst, hunger, burn, and long for the Christ to come. We, however, who have Christ present, manifested, given, glorified, sitting on the right hand of God and interceding for us, we contemn and consider Him much more vile than any other creature. . . .

We see therefore what is the difference between these ages (*seculorum differentia*). The first epoch (*Mundus*) is the best and holiest. There exist at this time the noblest jewels of the entire human race. Even after the Flood there are some distinguished and great men among the patriarchs, kings, and prophets, who, although they are not equal to the patriarchs before the Flood, yet in them also shines the distinctive yearning for Christ. . . . Our age (*seculum*) which belongs to the New Testament in which Christ is manifested, is as the shell and dregs of the world; for it holds nothing to be more vile than Christ, as compared with which the earlier epoch and race (*Mundus*) held nothing more precious. [42:260]

We are more richly provided than the patriarchs because we have the revelation itself. But they held in greater value less revelation and were like lovers of what was promised. We are however that fat, thick, distended servant because we abound in the Word and we are buried in our very opulence by it. [42:261]

This trust in God's promise and this passionate longing for the future Christ make the first millennium a golden age in a sense which transcends its purely external features of austerity and simplicity. While the idea's classical elements appear to be ill-digested in Luther's thought, a relation does exist between the distinctive faith of this period and the virtues of the golden age. The virtues which distinguish Luther's conception of the golden age serve to emphasize the heroic nature of the patriarchs. Their superior faith now completes their heroic dimensions. Luther even suggests that their unique vigor derives from their superior righteousness (42:250). Thus, faith enters the complex of Luther's conception of the golden age, and his application of the term to periods of extreme trial becomes more understandable. Perhaps no more dramatic evidence exists in support of this fact than his statement concerning the preservation of the just during the Flood: although the whole human race perished except for eight souls, it was still a golden age (42:264). Ultimately faith alone provides the only criterion for Church history.

The identification of the holiest and golden age with the first millennium accents the idea of a degeneration in history. In establishing the golden age in the most remote past Luther did not claim for it an absolute purity and perfection, because the same period saw the Fall of man, the Flood, and the fate of Sodom. Nevertheless, mankind in that age possessed a faith and a majesty—a virtue in the broadest sense of the term—which, when compared with the abject nature of his own age, made the first period seem golden. The idea of a decline, which results from a belief in both the absolute and the relative virtues of the early millennium, embraces all of history in a universal degeneration. Luther traces this degeneration in every aspect of life down through the age of the patriarchs. With a decline in the nutritive quality of food and water, there has been a decline in the vigor of the body and in longevity (42:250–51). In remarking that the French disease was unknown to Germans when he was a boy but that now children in the cradle contract it, Luther finds positive support for the idea of a decline in man's health (42:154–55). The beauty of womanhood, the strength of the body, the virility of men, the talents and customs of people—all participate in this degeneration (42:479; 43:435, 448; 44:309). Deprivation even enters the moral life. In contrast with Otto of Freising's moral and rational education of mankind preceding the advent of Christ, Luther sees a pattern of increasing punishments with increasing sins.[16] Since the time of Noah and the Flood, which temporarily destroyed the wicked, there exists a progressive moral decline with a corresponding rise in punishments (42:154). In the light of such a total understanding of degeneration, Luther views his own age as the extreme senescence of the world (43:39).

This adoption of a classical idea finds its biblical support in the statue interpreted by Daniel to Nebuchadnezzar (42:161). But Luther extends its application beyond world history to Church history. Because faith and revelation are inversely related, the increasing clarity of revelation down to Christ occurs concomitantly with a diminution in the intensity of faith. Luther recognizes the logical consequences of his assumptions and accepts them. The patriarchs emerge as veritable heroes of faith, for when the divine revelation was still dim, they manifested an intense hope and trust (cf. 42:260–61). While Abraham, Isaac, and Jacob continue this superior faith in the promise, with Ephraim and Manasseh there appears in the later patriarchs a gradual decline (44:688). Writing from the perspective of his own age, yet with reference also to the age of the patriarchs, Luther describes succinctly the ordinary fortune of the Church: the more fully the Word is revealed, the greater is the ingratitude of men (42:515).

The Second Epoch: Abraham and the Law of Moses

In a forceful statement at the outset of his treatment of Abraham, Luther asserts that with this patriarch begins a new epoch and a new promise—a new generation and even a new Church. The promise

16. Otto of Freising, *The Two Cities,* trans. Charles Christopher Mierow (New York, 1928), p. 220.

of the future Christ who will reconcile men with God represents a new light of revelation which will guide the Church down to Christ (42:430). The epoch that begins with Abraham and ends with Pentecost has as its most distinctive feature the clearer revelation in the new promise and in the law of Moses. Consequently, the problem of Church history in this epoch becomes one, first of relating the law of Moses to the promise, and secondly, of distinguishing that law from the gospel of Christ.

Luther saw the cornerstone of Christian belief in the promise given by God to Abraham and its reception in faith. Following Paul, Luther brought to the exegesis of these passages in Genesis the entire armory of his theological and religious outlook. God's promise to Abraham is both temporal and spiritual in its content: temporal because it refers to Abraham's posterity as a great people that will have kingdom, laws, ceremonies, Church, and to whom God will reveal Himself and be worshiped; spiritual because this people will last to the end of the world and enjoy eternal life. To the promise Abraham's faith stands as the necessary complement. This man, who has recently been called from idolatry and who possesses a sterile wife, realizes none of these temporal blessings in his own lifetime; yet, by his faith he sees in the Spirit and rejoices. The importance of the promise can hardly be overestimated for Luther. All the sayings of the prophets concerning Christ and His kingdom, the remission of sins and the gift of the Holy Spirit, the preservation of the Church and the punishment of the unbelievers derive from the promise given to Abraham. The entire life and fortune of the Church to the end of the world become apparent in the example of Abraham. What occurs in the Church occurs by virtue of this promise which begets faith and distinguishes unbelief (42:442–51).

In Abraham's justification by faith emerge the second aspect of the promise in a spiritual and eternal heredity as well as the distinction between the law and the promise. That Abraham should be considered righteous four hundred and thirty years before the law, the works of the law, and even the people of the law serves to confirm Luther's belief: justification comes not from the law, and the sons of the promise are a spiritual rather than a carnal people. No preparation, no faith formed by works, but simply the reputed mercy of God justifies Abraham in the midst of his sins and doubts. God thus willed to give the promise long before the law in order to reveal that righteousness comes from the promise alone and that the father of the Jewish nation was justified before and without the law. The promise is a gift offered by God to us which we apprehend in faith and accept through the divine mercy. Nevertheless the law also exists, for God not only promises, He commands and prescribes. The law pertains to obedience not to righteousness; it requires works not faith. And while the law and works do not justify, the law must still be taught and works must be accomplished so that men may recognize their own misery and all the more eagerly accept grace (40/1:382–83; 42:563–67).

Without denying their relationship, Luther distinguishes the promise from the law in a way which is instructive for understanding his distinction between Old Testament and New Testament. His argument does not rest simply with the priority of the promise; it urges that the promise is the permanent fact of Church history and alone pertains to justification. The evangelical conception of justification to which Luther had fought his way excluded any sense of a change or renewal of man and emphasized the imputation of Christ's righteousness.[17] At the end of his career Luther remarked that before his discovery of justification by faith he made no distinction between law and gospel—Christ did not differ from Moses except in respect to time and perfection. Only afterward did he realize that the law was one thing and the gospel another (*TR* 5518). Christ is therefore always active in history, and man's response to faith remains at all times the same with respect to its content and nature. Abraham's faith differs from ours only in that he believed in the

17. On Luther's evangelical understanding of justification, see Saarnivaara, *Luther Discovers the Gospel,* particularly pp. 14, 41.

Christ to be manifested, whereas we believe in the Christ now manifested (42:567).

To explain why the law was added later, Luther refers to the existence of a special people and the transmission of ceremonies which prefigure the revealed Christ. The law serves to guard and preserve a certain people in the world who have the Word and testimony concerning Christ. This people sighs for liberation through the seed promised to Abraham. Because the ceremonies prescribed in the law foreshadow Christ, the promise has not been abolished by the law or ceremonies but rather has been further confirmed by these signs (40/1:465; 14:601–02). In fact the promise given to Abraham organizes the history of the Church throughout the generation of this patriarch which lasts until Jesus Christ. The covenant between God and Abraham ratifies the promise and is sealed by the sign of circumcision. It promises the corporal blessing of possession of the land of Canaan, and the spiritual blessing of an eternal benediction by which God locates the Church in the family of Abraham and makes him the father of many nations. The sons of Abraham who believe in the promise live in the land of Canaan or Egypt. The generation of Abraham lasts until the Incarnation. As the author of a new generation, Christ does not change the covenant but merely the sign of the covenant (42:627–31). Thus Church history moves on the permanent basis of God's promise and manifests itself in the transmission of signs of the promise and in the preservation of a people that believes in the promise.

Abraham's circumcision marks more than a decisive moment in the transmission of signs; it serves to emphasize the fact that with God's promises as a permanent element in Church history, temporal succession has been limited to the change in the external signs. Circumcision does not justify Abraham because he was already righteous before this act. Rather than being righteousness, circumcision is the sign of righteousness during a certain period in the life of the Church. With every promise God adds a sign or memorial so that the promise may be served all the more faithfully. Thus God accompanied Abel's salvation with a sacrifice and Noah's reassurance with a rainbow. After the sign of circumcision bestowed upon Abraham, He gave the fleece to Gideon and the child Immanuel to Ahaz. All these different signs proclaim the promise of God. Circumcision represents the distinctive sign of righteousness in a particular period to be supplanted by baptism and the Lord's Supper in the period after Pentecost (6:518, 532; 42:620).

> For the signet of circumcision is given to him so that through the righteousness of faith which is in Abraham, all might be saved and the Church might be transferred from the sacrifices of the earlier fathers into that one circumcised Church. [42:628]

Within the Jewish people that will possess the land of Canaan exists the Church of the later patriarchs. In the lives of these great athletes of faith Luther discovers truths that demonstrate and confirm his own understanding of the Christian life and doctrine. To him, Abraham appears as the greatest of the patriarchs not simply because he illustrates most clearly the evangelical doctrine of justification but because of the frightful *tentationes* that he suffers (43:201). Abraham excels all St. Anthonies in humility, faith, love, and hope (43:130). His obedience and abnegation are superior to those of all prophets, apostles, and patriarchs (43:209). Yet, while holier than all the saints in the New Testament, Abraham does not disdain such lay work as planting trees. In contrast with the present Anabaptists, Abraham does not deny the obedience and responsibility owed to the civil authority; he shows by his action that the Church confirms and supports the other two Regimente (43:198–99). And if in Abraham's exile of Ishmael and Hagar the idea of the hidden, persecuted Church appears momentarily to have foundered, Luther hastens to add tears to the event, upbraids Moses for his laconic treatment of the matter, and uses the occasion to praise the unfaltering obedience of a distressed Abraham to a divine command (43: 161–65).

The location of the Church in the household of Abraham affords numerous opportunities to represent domestic trials and responsibilities as an integral part of the Christian life and to appreciate Isaac and Jacob in their human as well as in their heroic dimensions. Luther finds the blessings of marital life taught neither in canon nor in civil law but in Scripture (43:299). On the other hand he is not blind to the suffering and tribulation of wedlock. When he represents the trials of the patriarchs in their wandering exile, he shows the superior religious nature of the household life to that of monks untroubled and untested in their fixed, ample abodes (43:433, 493). Present trials (*tentationes*) are so much lighter than those of the patriarchs who have borne and suffered more than the martyrs (43:469; 44:51). In describing these heroes, Luther wishes to show them not as blocks of rectitude but as real beings with weaknesses and sins (44:111). Their lapses serve to demonstrate human infirmity and divine forgiveness (43:357). By their lives they illustrate the fusion of the most menial economic and political tasks with their spiritual exercises (44:261). In their faith and temptations, their obedience and suffering, they present the paradigm of the common Christian life.

The institution of the law of Moses marks a turning point in the period of the second epoch: the Church of the patriarchs becomes the national Church of the Jewish people. The constitutive elements of hiddenness, so salient in the age of the patriarchs, are now displaced, though not removed, by the legal ordering of the religious community. While Luther recognizes the magnitude of this event, he indicates no concern for the way in which the institution of this law fits into the greater scheme of the periodization of Church history. The age of the patriarchs cuts across the first and second epochs and ends with the law of Moses. Here one encounters the danger of requiring from Luther a precision and concern for periodization, which he quite obviously lacked. It may be suggested, however, that the national Church had long existed—first in Abraham's faith in the promise and secondly in the fact that the Church of the later patriarchs constituted the Jewish people. The patriarchs had the Decalogue, and the bestowal of the ceremonial law together with the entry of this people into the land of Canaan reveal the fulfillment of the temporal blessings given to Abraham in the promise. Finally, both the generation of Abraham and the ministry of Moses terminate with the fulfillment of the spiritual blessing in Christ.

Luther's religious understanding of the law vitally affected his outlook upon Church history and his view of this second epoch. The complexity and greatness of his mature attitude to the law of Moses can only be appreciated in the light of the fundamental issues involved. He sought to maintain the unity of Scripture together with the dialectic between law and gospel; yet, at the same time, he had to distinguish the temporal and historical from the permanent elements in this law. It is significant that he arrived at his mature understanding of the law of Moses in his controversy with the Enthusiasts. In exposing here the temporal, local, and historical nature of the ceremonial and judicial elements of the law, he envisaged the work of Moses as the Jewish popular law and recognized the law's double use. Pressing inward to the source and core of the law, Luther discovered the entire law of Moses contained in the Decalogue, which he identified with the natural law. Finally the Decalogue itself was only an elaboration of the first commandment, which expressed most profoundly the spiritual nature of the law and which reflected the unity of Scripture itself. Just as Scripture embraced but two things—promises and threats, benefits and punishments (43:36)—so in this original commandment threats which work wrath were to be found with the promises. This threefold consideration of the Mosaic law as simultaneously being a spiritual law and a popular law and containing the natural law became of essential importance both for the relation of the Old Testament to the New Testament and for his total understanding of Church history.

The connection between the natural law and the Decalogue demonstrates first that the God of the Jewish people is also the God of all peoples and secondly that He effects a special purpose in the Jewish people during the generation of Abraham. God has given to all people the knowledge that He has created and does preserve everything. These truths are impressed upon each person's conscience with the purpose that he should honor God and show concern for his neighbor. Yet in addition to this natural law written in each person's heart God has given to the Jewish people a written law, the Decalogue, which represents the clearest single expression of the natural law (16:431–33). Natural law does not come from Moses but only finds its best expositor in him, and any contemporary application of the Decalogue depends upon its conformity with the natural law.

As the very substance and distillation of the Mosaic law the Decalogue, however, is not limited to the natural law. Spiritual and eternal as well as local and historical elements are included in it. Given to a particular people in time, it teaches how to live well both spiritually and corporally and institutes an internal realm of conscience, a civil polity, and an external mode of ceremonies (14:545). Through the very local and temporal features of this law God works a spiritual purpose. While little or nothing of these external laws exists now, in their time God sought to bury His people in them so that by being pressed with such a multitude of external laws, they would be reduced to self-knowledge and thirst for grace. At the same time, God wished to provide this people with a civil administration that they might be further brought to obedience (14:601–02). Concerning the worldly Regiment of the Jewish people, its direct subjection to the divine will, expressed in the Mosaic law down to the finest detail, eliminates any individual responsibility or free use of reason in this Regiment and removes the distinction between the two Regimente. As in the case of the patriarchs, this subjection avoids being a purely legal obedience by deriving its authority from the ethical and spiritual basis of the fourth commandment.[18] The controversy with the Enthusiasts now compelled Luther to distinguish the purely local and historical from the universal and permanent elements within the law of Moses.

Luther differentiates the Decalogue as natural law from the ceremonial and judicial law. The law of Moses applies to Luther's contemporaries only to the extent that its demands agree with the natural law written in the conscience of each man. Whatever is not written there belongs to the ceremonies and injunctions necessary to the people of Moses and not binding to present Christians (14:622). The rulings on images and the keeping of the Sabbath demonstrate the derivations of the ceremonial law from the Decalogue. The case of images has a special significance, for it is embedded in the first commandment itself. Luther used it as an illustration of this ceremonial law which is only binding on a particular people at a particular time. The carnal and literal meaning of the first commandment does not apply to Christians living after Christ. To destroy images and to kill offenders were injunctions specifically imposed on the Jewish people alone at this time along with many other laws concerning wives, contracts, and all external ceremonies. Luther attacks those prophets who boast of having destroyed images. If they find nothing of the law's historical and local nature in this first commandment but maintain that all must be done necessarily, they are compelled to kill everyone who has an image. Christ has abrogated this ceremonial and temporal part of the law, and Christians may slay and destroy only with the sword of the spirit (14:619–20).

While divinely bestowed, the law of Moses is historically conditioned. Luther's emphasis upon the temporal and local aspects of parts of the law arose from his religious motivation rather than from a historical appreciation of the law's institution. Yet a shrewd sense of becoming, which has been attributed to him, cannot be

18. Hayo Gerdes, *Luthers Streit mit den Schwärmern um das rechte Verständnis des Gesetzen Mose* (Göttingen, 1955), pp. 58–59.

denied in this instance.[19] He saw the Mosaic law less as a creation of Moses than as old Jewish popular law accumulated in time. Moses had retained the early patriarchs' cult and ceremonies, which could be seen in the case of circumcision. Many laws were assimilated from custom and from the tradition of the patriarchs, and to these Moses as legislator had added others for his own time (43:54; cf. 44:315). Luther attributed the Decalogue to the patriarchs; only the constituting of the Levitical priesthood and the ceremonial law belonged to Moses (43:442). In his treatment of the signs, Luther gave the clearest expression to the relation between the permanent and the transitory—the law as spiritual authority and the law as the product of a people's life.

> Here it is fitting to separate the external works, signs, and times from our works, signs, and times. Nevertheless, through the same faith moves the same God, the same Spirit; the cross is with us as with them. Indeed these externals represent a model (*vice exempli sunt*) so that we may know how to believe properly in our signs as they in theirs. If we wish to appeal to their signs, it is not permitted because it is fitting for us to act according to the command of Scripture which prescribes to us other signs. The use of one sign passes away, the model (*exemplum*) nevertheless remains; circumcision passes away, the model nevertheless remains. Just as they practiced their faith in their own external sign, thus we in our signs practice this faith. In their exodus from Egypt we have one sign which is Jesus Christ who does not descend as then in a cloud and pillar but has spoken in the incarnate Son. This now is our sign to which we fly with equal intensity of faith as once did the Jews. [14:599]

Against the permanent basis of faith and the gospel Luther recog-

19. Cf. Heinrich Bornkamm, *Luther und das Alte Testament* (Tübingen, 1948), p. 107. Hereafter cited as *L.A.T.*

nizes change, although it is not a historical change inherent in the process itself. The change is called into being by God; for with the change of signs according to the command of Scripture, the times change.

As a popular law, the law of Moses has no application to present Christians and its influence upon the religious life represents a veritable poison to the Christian conscience. Yet as a spiritual law, which works God's wrath and prepares the conscience for the acceptance of the gospel, the law of Moses receives from Luther the highest praise and respect. The law is spiritual and no one has better exposed the precepts of its Decalogue than Moses, who shows the force of the law which almost kills man by leading him into the unbearable knowledge of his own sin (14:604). The spiritual use of the law first reveals itself in the Decalogue, which, insofar as it expresses natural law, establishes the universality of God's wrath in our consciences. The right fulfillment of this natural law must wait upon the action of the gospel and the Holy Spirit, and until then the Devil works to darken the law in man. Even beyond the natural law the spiritual nature of this law contains a concealed gospel, which becomes apparent only in Luther's understanding of the first commandment. He develops this commandment as both promise and prohibition; man here experiences God in his unity as command and promise, judgment and salvation. Within the very opposition of law and gospel the unity of Scripture stands forth.[20] As Luther had previously written in his *Treatise on Good Works:* Faith is the true meaning, fullness, and virtue of the first commandment; faith rules and works in all these commandments and actions. Nothing is more fully consoling, nothing is harder and more severe than this voice of the first commandment: I am the Lord thy God (14: 638, 640).

In the strained atmosphere of his polemic against the Enthusiasts, Luther sought to limit and define the work of Moses by understanding it Christocentrically. Moses must be confined to the period

20. Ibid., pp. 111–12, 140, 149–51.

of Abraham and his seed; he is not given to the entire world as teacher but to the Jews as prophet, guide, and marshal. He applies to present Christians only with respect to his prophecies and promises and as an example of faith (16:161–62). Nevertheless, Moses is a Christian and a teacher of Christians (54:85). Although the ministry of the gospel under Christ displaces Moses' ministry, still the latter represents the supreme temporal expression of the law. There was none like Moses, for the Lord spoke to him face to face; subsequent Hebrew leaders stand to him as pupils and inferiors. Only to Christ does Moses yield. In his time, therefore, Moses expounds a law which cannot be improved upon, and when Christ comes, He comes not as a new legislator but as one who fulfills the law (14: 675, 744).

The departure from Egypt and the crossing of the Red Sea present dramatic and decisive evidence of God's redemptive activity in history. With the Israelites out of Egypt and in the desert, God's revelatory activity assumes prominence. God had provided for the worldly Regiment in Genesis 1:28 but there had not yet been any ordering and instituting of both spiritual and worldly Regimente. God now has Moses establish the worldly Regiment and ordain the offices of chiefs and judges. Between this and the spiritual Regiment which Christ rules there appears a third, partly spiritual and partly worldly, that comprises commands and external ceremonies for guiding man's relations to God and other men (16:352–54, 370). In order to confute the use of Moses by papists and radicals, Luther insists upon the historical nature of this threefold Regiment. An external and harsh law has been instituted to discipline and contain an external and crass people. The New Testament dispenses with two aspects of this Regiment—that of the sword is clearly separated and given to the Emperor, the Turks, and the king of France; the external spiritual Regiment marked by ceremonies and prescripts disappears with the advent of the Kingdom of Christ (16:530, 572, 588; cf. 10/3:371).

In significant opposition to previous exegesis, Luther did not consider the Jewish cultic community as the prototype of the Christian priesthood. The Levitical priesthood of the Old Testament does not continue into the present Church. From his early years as a reformer Luther had been quick to reject the claim that the priesthood of Christ has been translated from Moses to Peter (2:19). It is a shameful distortion of Scripture to represent the high priest of the Old Testament as prefiguring the pope (2:211). In fact the priesthood according to the order of Melchizedek has existed from the beginning of the world. At first it had been promised obscurely and then more clearly to Abraham, Moses, and David (43:263). There are thus two true and divinely instituted priesthoods: the Levitical one of Aaron and Moses, which is temporal; and the Christian, which is not visible and external but spiritual, common, and eternal (8:415, 458; 41:175–79). Continuity is not conceived institutionally as existing in the Judaic cultic community but in the community of faith.[21]

For Luther the national Church of the Jewish people attained its most perfect form during the reign of David. In another context Luther had compared the kingdom of Judah-Israel under David to that of Egypt under Joseph. Both rulers had been diligent in promoting the Word through their exercise of spiritual as well as of political authority. If heresy, impiety, and idolatry still remained in the kingdom of each ruler, these kingdoms were holy and pious on account of the Church, which, despite admixture, existed at this time in the Israelite people. With respect to Joseph's work, however, the fact remains that rather than pressing circumcision or any rites and ceremonies upon the Egyptians he contented himself in bringing them to a true knowledge of God (44:674–75). In David's kingdom, on the other hand, the lines of cult and of political authority are identified with this Jewish people that contains the hidden Church.

In its own context Luther represents the reign of David as a marvelous and blessed age for reasons both religious and political.

21. Ibid., pp. 183–84.

While the political factors constitute an integral part of the Church at this time, the specifically religious alone demand consideration. David is praised for his struggle against heretics and his establishment of the true worship of God. Yet what most distinguishes his rule is the composition of the Psalter—an unparalleled accomplishment. Luther maintains that there lived at this time more people trained in Scripture than at any other time and that for the promotion of Christian learning and true doctrine, David's university has never been surpassed (53:82; 51:234). His reign presents one of those rare moments in history when true doctrine, wisdom, and virtue are supported by political power. Luther cannot deny the valid greatness of the Church during this moment of external strength and relative prosperity.

The sufferings of the prophets under Manasseh constitute a golden age (53:97, 99). This abrupt accenting of the crucified and persecuted nature of the true Church produces a shift in perspectives and necessitates an inquiry into the relation of the hidden Church to the national Church of the Jewish people with its amalgam of the threefold Regiment. When Luther declares that exaltation and glorification comprehend all the stories from Abraham to Christ (5:613), he would appear to exclude the hidden Church from the second epoch. Yet the hidden Church can never be absent in the course of God's redemptive purpose, for the abiding presence of the Word will always produce such a Church. Unquestionably the hiddenness of the Church only pertains to the conditions of the New Testament but Luther never forgets the figure of Abel and finds the state of the New Testament present in the Old (5:609). In treating the prophets he is particularly sensitive to the attributes of hiddenness in the true Church (19:134, 374–75, 381).

Whether the prophets define an actual period within the second epoch seems questionable.[22] Such a period would lack that clarity of definition which Augustine gave it.[23] Throughout the Old Testa-

22. But cf. Bornkamm, *L.A.T.*, p. 182.
23. *City of God*, XVII, 1.

ment Luther sees God as evoking one prophet for each time: Moses was alone in the exodus from Egypt; Elijah alone in Ahab's time and Elisha was alone after him; Isaiah in Jerusalem, Hosea in Israel, Jeremiah in Judea, and Ezekiel with the Babylonians—each was alone (7:311). Rather than constituting a distinct period subsequent to the national Church the prophets within this Church preserve its true character and serve as its conscience. Joel, whom Luther places prior to Isaiah, lived at a time when the kingdom of the Jews flourished and there existed peace. But Joel recognized this condition as a plague (13:89). While admonishing the people and directing their prophecies to Christ, the prophets have also the important task of consoling the people and holding them in faith and hope until the future kingdom of Christ appears (19:396). As this time approaches, tension grows and their task becomes more difficult. More than the prophets themselves, the Babylonian Captivity comes nearest to distinguishing a period in the course of the national Church.[24] Never before or afterward were the people so beset and scattered. What happens to the people following the captivity is but a short and painful preparation for Christ's coming (19:351–53; 23:502).

As the advent of Christ approaches, the distinctive features of the national Church indicate senescence (14:744). In interpreting Daniel's seventy weeks Luther perceives the end of the Jewish Church. He recognizes that the period represents four hundred and ninety years but he rejects the Jewish belief that at the end of this period a worldly Messiah would appear and the Jews would do penance, become pious, and serve Him. Christ comes during the seventieth week, dies, and lives again. By destroying the Temple, the Romans conclude the period of the Seventy Weeks. The national Church has ended. David and his children have become the Kingdom and people of Christ. Jews and heathen are now brought together in one uniform people and in a new Jerusalem without any more sacrifices and ceremonies (53:492–500, 548–551).

24. Cf. *City of God,* XVII, 1.

Pentecost marks the beginning of the Church in the third epoch. The pouring out of the Holy Spirit is accompanied by signs and miracles which serve to confirm the Word. If the Spirit is poured out on all and revealed to all, it is not given to all. The entire world sees this manifestation of the Spirit in the preaching of the apostles and by this preaching God demonstrates that there exists no revelation beyond Scripture itself. The divisions and discord introduced into polity, economy, and religion by the building of the Tower of Babel now become healed, and men of all nations are brought together in one body whose head is Christ (42:413). At Pentecost the new Kingdom of Christ is instituted with the priesthood of all believers and the sacraments of baptism and the Eucharist (13:80, 110–11). Such doctrines as the Trinity, familiar to the patriarchs but unknown to others, now become publicly clear at this time of the revealed light of the gospel (44:185–86). What before had been known to a few and had existed under the fear of the law now enjoys the public ministry of the Word (13:113).

In Luther's understanding of Christ's historical appearance the fact of uniqueness, which argues for development and fulfillment in Church history, contends with the fact of Christ's continuing presence in time. If the Incarnation is unique and provides the only focus in Church history, then there exists a development and fulfillment in time. However, if Christ is present at all times, history essentially unfolds on a single plane. The reconciliation of this apparent conflict and an assessment of the Incarnation's real significance require a closer study of the way in which the two testaments are related.

The Incarnation is truly unique. In completing God's revelation of himself and in fulfilling His plan of redemption, it distinguishes a development in history—if not an education of mankind. As the process of divine revelation history moves through three stages like the appearance of the three tabernacles in Hebrews 9: from darkness and silence, through prophecy and public worship, to open and spiritual conversation in the light of day (16:596–99). As the divine plan of redemption, history indicates a development toward the public manifestation of God's saving work. Luther sees the Old Testament as a disciplining of a recalcitrant people and their education from an external holiness and piety to an inner holiness (16:396). The entire Old Testament is nothing other than a preparation and precursor of the New (19:351). Indeed, the movement would seem to describe the increasing universality and clarity of God's revelation and purpose from a household, through a specific people, to mankind.

Luther's appeal to typology emphasizes the uniqueness and centrality of the Incarnation as well as the passage from the shadows of the Old Testament to the fulfillment in the New. By typology is meant here the exegetical practice of relating a thoroughly historical and concrete event in the Old Testament to one in the New Testament through the reference of both to the divine plan or framework within which both events or facts exist. For the fathers and for the entire Middle Ages, typology was more than simply an hermeneutical device; it provided a figural interpretation of events and of the entire course of history which related the Old Testament to the New and which established each event within the divine providence.[25] Working within this heritage, Luther recognizes the Pauline type of Adam and Eve wedded as pointing to its antitype in Christ and His Church (42:174). From Noah's ark the second flight of the dove represents a type for the redemption in the New Testament (42:376). The whole story of the Passover is an obvious type for the later Christ (16:264). In the case of Joseph, his descent into the pit, his sale into bondage, and his eventual forgiving of his brothers make him an elaborate and extended type for the entire Crucifixion and Resurrection of Christ (44:284–303, 466, 618, 681). Similarly, the relation between prophets and evangelists demonstrates the historical position and central significance of the Incarna-

25. Cf. Erich Auerbach, "Figura," *Scenes from the Drama of European Literature*, trans. Ralph Manheim (New York, 1959), pp. 49–60.

tion. All the prophets have but one meaning, one scope; all direct themselves to the future Christ and His kingdom. Prophecies and promises move toward this central event (13:88, 71; 19:351). In contrast with prophecy, the Gospels teach what is present and fulfilled (10/3:65).

On the other hand there stands the mighty fact of Christ's continuing presence in time. When Jacob struggled with the angel, he struggled actually with Jesus Christ, the eternal God and future man (44:107). For the benefit of the Sacramentarians, Luther explains that the manna received by the Hebrews in the desert was the flesh and blood of Christ (16:305). With respect to its defining a dispensation, the Old Testament admittedly precedes the New; but with respect to content, the New Testament has existed from the beginning and long before the Old. The latter derives its name from the fact that it has ceased. In contrast, the New Testament never ages (16:589). This attitude emerges in Luther's use of typology. In the case of Joseph, his sufferings call to mind the Crucifixion and derive meaning from the Crucifixion. Thus Luther manages to subordinate the typological bond between foreshadowing and fulfillment to the existential bond between an actual individual and the gospel story whose fruit extends backward as well as forward in time. Finally, prophets and evangelists have the same faith and differ only in respect to time: the former had faith in the Christ to come; the believers living in the period after Pentecost have faith in the Christ who has manifested himself (44:813).

Rather than opposing each other, the unique and decisive nature of Christ's Incarnation and His continuing presence in time coexist. The activity of Christ in the Old Testament derives its ultimate support from the belief that He will once become man. The Incarnation stands as a truly historical event. Jesus Christ, the God/Man, represents the fulfillment not of a temporal progressive development but of a promise which has borne a community of believers down through time. And while the Incarnation, Crucifixion, and Resurrection express the ultimate revelation of God to man in one moment of time, the Church at all times has lived by the necessity for this redemption in Christ. The redemptive effectiveness of this event has been present, if concealed, since the Creation and cannot be confined by any temporal conception. Luther universalizes the fruit, not the drama, of the redemption.

The final revelation in Jesus Christ constitutes for Church history the central event in the light of which everything before and after must be judged. Moreover it brings about the most significant change in the life of the Church. What previously had been veiled and confined to a single people now becomes public, fully manifest, and common to all. In the Old Testament, works had been required and conditions added so that the promise might be urged through the law; with the New Testament, God's grace gives the promises without conditions and beyond respect for all our works. In a striking passage Luther makes clear the relationship between the two testaments:

> The New Testament is the oldest and has been promised from the beginning of the world even before the world began, as Paul says to Titus, but only fulfilled under Christ. The Old Testament, promised under Moses, has been fulfilled under Joshua. There exists, however, this difference between them: the New Testament is supported by the sole promise of God to the poor in spirit and to the faithful without any human works; the Old Testament, however, is supported by human works. [14:602]

Luther states that with Abraham the third age began and that he was its governor as David was the governor of the fourth millennium. But behind this conformity to the conventional patterns of periodization there towers the vital fact of Christ's abiding presence in time which produces a more significant understanding and ordering of events. Neither in time nor in content does the Old Testament take precedence over the New, for both are in the history of God's people during this epoch and exist beside each other.[26] Both derive from the promise given to Abraham. While the temporal promise is realized in the possession of the land of Canaan and endures to the end of the ministry of Moses, the eternal promise is fulfilled in Christ and continues beyond the generation of Abraham, the ceremonial law of Moses, the Jewish kingdom, and all the temporal and local aspects which clothe the Church at this particular time. The signs change, the promise persists.

The Third Epoch: the Persecutions

Christ has come. The law has been fulfilled. The Kingdom of Christ is established. In contrast to the league and House of David, which had appeared well ordered and serene, now, after Christ, His kingdom, if universal, surpasses all others in being disordered and wasted (54:78). With the fulfillment of the promise in Christ, time is at an end and nothing more remains (16:53). Heretofore the unfolding of the divine revelation had determined the periods of history. Now the revelation of God to His people has attained its ultimate clarity and expression. It would appear therefore that history has in effect been concluded, that the prophecy of Elias is inapplicable and the remaining time meaningless. If there is a period of time after the fulfillment of God's revelation in Christ, that period obviously presents a problem.

With some truth a Roman Catholic can attack Protestant historiography for implying that the Incarnation has arrested the course of history, for the Church does not appear as continuing God's work and the time after Christ brings no increment of real value.[27] In respect to Luther the accusation proves illuminating. Because he is unable to conceive the Church primarily in institutional terms, Luther would never grant to it any growth independent of God's

26. Bornkamm, *L.A.T.*, p. 216.
27. Jean Daniélou, *The Lord of History* (London, 1958), pp. 10–11.

direct action and according to some inherent law of its own. The Church remains pre-eminently the arena of God's continual redemptive action, manifesting in a believing people new decisions and new acts of faith. Thus, if salvation has been revealed and completed in Jesus Christ, God allows the world to survive only in order that His name might be further honored and glorified (12:293). Growth and expansion mark the Kingdom of Christ, for the gospel does not rest but runs its course and expands throughout the entire world until the Last Judgment. Only this kingdom continues to grow and attract (19:164; cf. 10/1/1:601). Admittedly, St. John claims that it is the last hour, but his statement refers not so much to the brevity of time as to the finality of the revelation in Christ (20:668). The Incarnation does not preclude the growth of a Church which is now universal and must go out over the whole earth until God brings the world to an end.[28]

Although Luther does recognize a period after Christ in which the hidden Church expands, it would be equally misleading to stress this aspect in his understanding of the third epoch. The distinctive feature of the last epoch is most emphatically eschatological. The end of the world begins immediately after the resurrection of Christ (47:625–26). The pressing imminence of the world's end pervades the whole period and the remaining time, regardless of its dura-

28. On the grounds that they understood the mission to the Gentiles to have been exhausted at the time of the apostles, the reformers have been accused of neglecting missionary activity. See Oscar Cullmann, *Christ and Time,* trans. Floyd V. Filson (Philadelphia, 1950), pp. 166–67. See also Franklin Hamlin Littell, *The Anabaptist View of the Church* (Boston, 1958), pp. 114–17. This judgment has been seriously contested and qualified. Cf. Walter Holsten, "Reformation und Mission," *ARG, 44* (1953), 1–32. In Luther's case, it certainly does not represent all his views on the subject. By distinguishing between the apostles' authoritative proclamation of the gospel and the hearing or reception of the gospel, Luther explains why Germany was converted eight hundred years after Pentecost and how in his own day the newly discovered Americas have not been aware of this grace. In short, while the apostles proclaimed the definitive and final doctrine to all the world, this proclamation is on the way and has not yet arrived at the less important places (10/1/1:19–23). Luther's later efforts to circumscribe missionary activity resulted from his opposition to the radicals. Nevertheless, his passivity has been exaggerated (cf. 16:472).

tion is narrowly squeezed between the Incarnation and the Last Judgment. The evening of history has arrived and nothing remains but to preach the gospel and look forward to the end (16:222–23). In this last epoch man lives under the growing pressure of a new time already fulfilled but not yet completed. With this mood of expectancy Luther again recaptures an essential element of the New Testament. The imminence of the end of history appears as a necessary consequence of the fulfillment of the promise; after God's revelation of Himself in Jesus Christ nothing more can be expected other than the Last Judgment. Therefore the end and the signs of the end replace revelation in providing order and periods to this epoch pressed between the "already" and the "not yet." Finally the early appearance of the Antichrist accentuates the eschatological nature of the last epoch.

In order to appreciate the problem of Luther's periodization in the time after Christ, it is necessary to consider briefly the medieval use and understanding of giving periods to history. Insofar as one recognized a historical, terrestrial course of the Church, this awareness centered upon the two limits—Christ and the Last Judgment. This recognition could be extended to the beginnings of the Church in the *ecclesia primitiva* of the apostles and to the end of the Church in the time of the Antichrist. Secondly, revelation and particularly prophecy determined reflection upon history. While the book of Daniel provided the pattern for the understanding of world history, the Apocalypse of St. John presented somewhat more uncertain keys to the disclosure of the Church's course in time. By the symbolic application of such a sequence as that of the seven trumpets or the seven seals, a pattern of periods might result. But the tradition of Tychonius and the fathers generally prevented such historical speculation and attempted to preserve the unity of each sequence. Notable exceptions were the identification of the sixth trumpet and seal with the final persecution and Bede's understanding of the second, third, and fourth seals as representing a triple attack upon the Church by the Devil, the heretics, and the hypocrites. Beginning with Richard of St. Victor there appeared a conscious effort to conceive the first four of each sequence as pertaining to four stages in a temporal succession.[29]

This particular development culminated in the thought of Anselm of Havelburg. Anselm posed the significant question—how is mutability possible in the Church of the unchangeable God? In his answer he identified the fundamental movement of the Church with its growth through preaching, and attributed change and differentiation to the attacks of the Devil made possible by the weakness of men. When he came to define the seven stages of the Church's life (*status Ecclesiae*), he went well beyond Richard in giving these divisions historical content. As representative of a developed medieval scheme of periodization they deserve a brief mention: the first state comprised the Church of the apostles; the second, the persecution of the martyrs by unbaptised rulers; the third, the persecution of the heretics; the fourth, the period of the hypocrites and false Christians; with Anselm, as with most exegetes, the fifth remained undefined; the sixth was the frightful persecution by the Antichrist; and the seventh state of the Church was the eternal blessedness.[30] Although Rupert of Deutz elaborated a more complicated scheme, Anselm's work reveals the main features of medieval efforts at periodization. According to this scheme, prophecy rather than historical experience or observation provides the periods of the Church's course in time; consequently, periodization becomes a function of symbolism rather than of events in the past of the Church. These periods serve to typify the Church's life at a given time and do not seek to express a causal development. Furthermore, to the extent that there exists change in the history of the Church, it is comprised under the idea of persecution, which serves to comprehend the events of each period.

In his own attempts to give divisions to the Church's history

29. Wilhelm Kamlah, *Apokalypse und Geschichtstheologie* (Berlin, 1935), pp. 47–51, 62, 116. Hereafter cited as *A.u.G.*

30. Ibid., pp. 63–70.

since the Incarnation, Luther was affected by this outlook and its ideas. Nevertheless, the role of experience and personal judgment came to exercise a greater influence within the old framework. If at first he rejected the Apocalypse of John as containing nothing of Christ, in 1530 Luther found it useful in his struggle against the Papacy. By a novel attempt on his part to elucidate Scripture through history, he compared the future events predicted therein with the difficulties which, according to standard histories, the Church had actually encountered (*WAB* 7:408). While there was nothing final in the results of these speculations, Luther's preface to the book demonstrates the importance of this idea of persecution in ordering the facts of Church history and indicates a definite emphasis in interpretation.

Luther begins by giving experience or history a determinative influence, but he understands the work of the four bad angels doctrinally and symbolically rather than historically: Tatian, Marcion, Origen, and Novatus represent respectively "work-righteousness," enthusiasm, philosophy, and the quest for absolute purity—all of which plague the present clergy. Luther's treatment of Tatian demonstrates the typical and doctrinal nature of his thinking. He explains the priority of Tatian on the ground that the doctrine of work-righteousness must be the first to oppose the gospel and will fittingly remain the last, although it will receive new teachings and other names like Pelagianism. The remaining bad angels he considers to be the three woes through which physical and spiritual persecution merge. Arius, the great heretic, is the first; he persecutes the true Christians both physically and spiritually. Becoming progressively worse, the second woe, Mohammed, follows, and finally there comes the Papacy in which persecution culminates with a shadow church (*WAB* 7:410, 412).

While Luther did not adhere to the periodization adumbrated in this work, his exegesis revealed two significant features. In the first place it indicated an emphasis upon the Church's final persecution and tribulation in the Papacy. This emphasis remained a fundamental feature of his understanding of Church history, and any attempt at periodization must recognize the intensity of Luther's opposition to Rome. Secondly, by the typical and symbolic nature of his judgment upon events, he disclosed his ties with the past.

If the scheme to which Luther most frequently appealed had certain affinities with the exegetical tradition of the Apocalypse, it derived nevertheless from a different source. In the *City of God,* St. Augustine had expressed dissatisfaction with the prevalent notion of ten persecutions, which he considered quite arbitrary and which often omitted important trials in the Church's experience.[31] Living after the Constantinian settlement, Augustine suggested a different scheme in another work. Here the idea of persecution assumed the subtler form of trial or tribulation, and the danger of weariness and contempt for the Word received greater emphasis. Augustine conceived the four periods in terms of a temporal succession and attempted to relate them to the experience of the Church (*MPL* 36:866–70; 37:1421–22). In the twelfth century, St. Bernard adopted this simpler formulation and expressed the idea that the worst trial of all was the last—to have peace from the pagans and heretics with unrest and discord among the Church's ostensible members. Bernard directed the reformative edge of the idea against the avarice and spirit of commercial gain in his day (*MPL* 183:768–70, 958–59).

From his own awareness of peace and complacency as extreme threats to the Church's life, Luther perceived the value of this idea. In his first lectures on the Psalms he adopted this Augustinian-Bernardian scheme and had frequent recourse to it. He understood the effect of the tyrants, the heretics, and now the present wicked ones of Antichrist as both persecution and trial for the Church. His recognition of the value and purgative nature of persecution for the Church tended to make him idealize the period immediately after Christ (3:340, 433). On the other hand, his insistence that the supreme tribulation was to have none gave a reformative significance to the characterization of his own age as being one of peace and

31. *City of God,* XVIII, 52.

security (3:410). Repeatedly, he emphasized this lack of true fervor in the present age and attacked the existing religious conditions by pressing the accusation of peace and security. Prosperity was the Church's greatest adversity and the peace which assailed it bred the sin of torpor (*accidia*) (3:416–17, 424).

There can be no question that for Luther, the young reformer, the Bernardian periodization of Church history proved quite satisfactory. It explained the facts of the Church's past as Luther understood them prior to his break with Rome, and it also possessed a reformative value. Preuss has supplied a massive body of references which demonstrate the reformer's adherence to this idea of three persecutions, and the matter need not be labored further.[32] Unfortunately, however, all the references derive from Luther's writings prior to 1522. The question therefore arises whether this periodization is equally valid for the later period in Luther's life, which saw his open opposition to Rome, his struggle with the Enthusiasts, and the development of his mature theology.

Luther does undoubtedly utilize this scheme of periodization during the latter part of his life: first with respect to the exegesis of Ephesians 6:11 in 1530–31; secondly in a sermon preached at Schmalkald in 1537; and thirdly in a letter written to Wenzeslaus Link ten years later. Yet in each instance he changes either the content or the application of the third persecution and severely tests the elasticity of this entire scheme in trying to adjust it to the facts of his present experience. In the earlier instances he states that the Devil attempts to destroy the Church first through the tyrants, next by entering into Scripture itself and working through the heretics, and finally by establishing a righteousness derived from good works and by attacking the articles of faith (34/2:381–84). Here Luther expands the content of the third persecution to include the fact of the Church's subversion by the Papacy. Nevertheless, at the same time, Luther extends the application of the third per-

32. Hans Preuss, *Die Vorstellungen von Antichrist im späteren Mittelalter, bei Luther und in der konfessionellen Polemik* (Leipzig, 1906), p. 87. Hereafter cited as *Antichrist.*

secution to the Enthusiasts; the latter assume an equal place with the Papacy as persecutors of the Church and tend to dominate his consideration of Ephesians 6:11 (32:156–57).

The sermon delivered at Schmalkald provides the most decisive evidence that the idea of three persecutions persists in Luther's understanding of Church history. To appreciate its meaning for his periodization of the last epoch, one needs to recognize the fact that Luther explicitly attempts to apply the three temptations endured by Christ in the wilderness to what each Christian must suffer as well as to the sufferings of the Church (45:27). Although he preached on the text of Matthew 4:1–11 on twelve separate occasions during his life, only in one other instance did he formally and consistently apply these temptations to the history of the Church as well as to the life of the individual Christian (cf. 52:171–77). After describing the first two temptations which clearly define the periods of the martyrs and the heretics, Luther comes to the final and most terrible persecution of the Antichrist itself. While the element of peace and security is not completely absent, Luther elaborates this eschatological abomination largely in terms of a self-devised Regiment and of an idolatrous human tradition (*traditio humana*) (45:37–41; cf. 37:306; 52:175).

Finally, in his letter of 1541 to Link on the occasion of Nuremberg's apparent defection, he restored both the content and the application of the third persecution to their proper and original use: he directed the idea against his own kind. In this last clear expression of the whole scheme, he outlines the three trials as being against the Father, the Son, and the Holy Ghost: the tyrants are followed by the graver trial of the heretics and are succeeded in turn by the most deadly trial of all—that which comes with peace (*tentatio in pace*). He describes this condition in its original sense of living in security and of holding the Word in aversion; he even uses the term *fastidium* which Augustine had employed in expressing this third persecution. Luther continues to assert that the real danger does not lie with the pope nor with the tyrants nor even with

Carlstadt, Müntzer, and the Anabaptists but with those who claim to belong to the Church and yet mock and contemn the Word (*WBr* 9:510–11).

What conclusions can be drawn from Luther's continued use and further elaboration of the Bernardian-Augustinian scheme? Undeniably, the scheme retained its vigor in Luther's thought, but whether he intended it to represent an ultimate and definitive statement of the last epoch's periodization remains questionable. In the first place the contemporary publication of patristic and conciliar sources and the Renaissance's effort to discover the primitive Church had the effect of obliterating the lines distinguishing the period of the martyrs and that of the heretics; the two periods defined by Scriptural exegesis tended to merge in the period of the early Church. Here the conflict is between a periodization based upon a symbolic use of Scripture and one arising from the increasing historical knowledge of the early Church.

A second type of difficulty appears when Luther attempts to bring his own experience and his understanding of the Church's past within the category of the final persecution. If he intended this scheme to represent a valid periodization for the Church, then too much had occurred in the history of the Church since the time of the heretics to be included within this single last tribulation. Luther indicates this apparent dilemma by changing the content of the third persecution or trial each time it must encounter a new, major phenomenon in his understanding of the Church's life. The accusation of spiritual laxity, which was originally embodied in the idea of the third trial, satisfactorily expressed the condition of the unreformed Church in 1514 and the disappointing faith of the evangelical party in 1541. But it did not satisfactorily express the magnitude of the Antichrist which had wasted and corrupted the Church, nor did it express the eschatological intensity of judgment and grace manifested in the contemporary restoration of the gospel. In the Schmalkald sermon of 1537, Luther was able to include these vital factors by shifting the content of the third persecution and applying it with advantage to the appearance of the Antichrist. At least in respect to the last persecution experience and Scriptural exegesis now moved together. Thus these two types of difficulty make necessary a discriminate understanding of this scheme of periodization.

The interpreter of Luther is confronted with an obvious dilemma: either he must accept the reformer's view of the Church after Christ in terms of the idea of three persecutions, which conforms only partially and imperfectly to the events of Church history as Luther knew them; or on the basis of these facts he may suggest a pattern implicit in the writings of Luther. It would be misleading to represent Luther as one who feels his own experience and understanding of the past constricted by an inherited scheme of periodization, although the possibility cannot be excluded. Our problem must not be made Luther's, for it arises from the difference between the basic presuppositions behind a modern and a medieval conception of periodization. In the former case, the period is understood in the perspective of a crucial event which relates itself causally to subsequent events; periodization becomes a function of empirical evidence as perceived by the historian. In the latter case, periodization is freed from the historical evidence and operates as a function of symbolism in prophecy or revelation; at most the period represents the type of trial suffered by the Church during a particular span of time. If the present problem is to be understood, the difference between the thinking behind each view needs to be noted.

Insofar as Luther concerned himself at all with providing divisions to the course of the Church, he stood well within the latter type of thinking and never explicitly rejected a scheme which conformed quite imperfectly to his own knowledge of the Church's past. Both the conventional attitude to periodization and Luther's own application of the Augustinian-Bernardian scheme help to explain this incongruity. In the former case, the periods of persecution, which at the time of Tychonius and Augustine may have conformed in a fair degree to the experience of the persecuted Church, tended to become stylized through many centuries of the privileged Church;

later exegetes considered these satanic persecutions as attacks of the Devil upon the individual rather than as historical persecutions.[33] In a similar way Luther argues that Jerome and most of his contemporaries could not understand Paul because they were not exposed to the necessary tribulations; if one is to arrive at the true sense of Scripture, he must be exercised externally by tyrants and heretics and internally by the terrible weapons of Satan (40/1:634). Thus Luther had recourse to the Augustinian-Bernardian scheme when it suited his purpose. And even within the medieval understanding of periodization Luther's use indicated that he considered these persecutions less as periods in Church history and more as necessary constituents of the Church's life and the Christian experience.

In attempting to understand the periodization of this last epoch, one can reject the use of this conventional scheme only with a full recognition of its importance. It cannot be simply suppressed. For Luther the scheme continued to possess a reformative and polemical value. It illustrated the belief that the Church undergoes essentially the same experience in different ages because of the permanent nature of the Word. Nevertheless, a rigid application of the idea of persecution and its triadic periodization obfuscates more than it clarifies his view of the last epoch. While Luther could agree with the common notion that the persons change but the issues remain the same,[34] he was supremely sensitive to the increased intensity and magnitude of these same issues in his own day. Along with the recognition of the permanent features of the Church's life went an awareness of the unique, for his were the last times. Furthermore, the eschatological magnitude of the Antichrist's appearance, in which he understood his entire opposition to Rome, stood in an entirely different dimension from the persecutions of the tyrants and heretics, about which he had comparatively nothing to say.

33. Kamlah, *A.u.G.*, p. 62.

34. Hans Volz, *Die Lutherpredigten des Johannes Mathesius* (Leipzig, 1930), p. 90.

Within the conventional scheme of the three persecutions he was not able to express adequately these distinctive features of his view. His exegesis of Matthew 4:1–11 in 1537 stands as a possible exception. By this formal and extensive application of the third temptation to the Antichrist, he captured part of the paramount importance which the period of the papal abomination occupied in his total thought: as an eschatological reality, the Antichrist extended throughout the entire epoch; as the dominant ecclesiastical authority, the final abomination of the Papacy crowded the other periods of the Church into the corners of this epoch. The light of the gospel which preceded and would terminate this major period defined relatively brief, if vitally significant, periods.

Without claiming for Luther an implicit scheme of periodization, one can discover a certain pattern by observing the continual return of his attention to crucial moments in the Church's past. The rise of the Papacy and the eschatological significance of his own time distinguish three periods: the early Church, Antichrist, and the last times. While these divisions may appear to be the result of a presumptuous application of modern historical presuppositions to the facts as Luther knew them, such a periodization does not lack a basis in Scripture. For the 1530 edition of the New Testament, Luther wrote a new preface to the Second Epistle of Peter in which he stated that the first chapter endeavors to show how the Christian people stands at the time of the pure gospel, the second chapter shows how it is to appear at the time of the pope and of human traditions, and the last chapter shows how people will despise both the gospel and all doctrine and will believe nothing in the final period before Christ's return (*WAB* 7:315).

During his life as a reformer, two central experiences served to shape Luther's understanding of this final epoch in Church history. The first was his opposition to Rome, which crystallized in his recognition of the Papacy as the Antichrist; the second was the restored light of the gospel, which he interpreted in the context of current eschatology. Concerning the first event, the reader of Luther's works is confronted with a bewildering mass of conflicting dates which refer to such matters as the corruption of the episcopate, the introduction of the Mass as a sacrifice, and the extinction of pure theology. But the establishment of papal primacy and the revelation of the Antichrist embraced all these corruptions and remained the subject of more than passing observations. He dated the origin of the Antichrist with the investiture of Boniface III as pope in 606 (sic); but the further elaboration of the Antichrist in the development of scholastic theology and canon law awaited the beginning of the sixth millennium. In one of his more apocalyptic works he suggests that Satan was heretofore bound but now is free and rules this final millennium (53:152–53). Despite the undeniable growth in the activity of Satan from Gregory VII to the Council of Constance, the Papacy as the Antichrist assumes eschatological proportions as a historical entity that has arisen since the death of the last bishop of Rome, Gregory I.

The reappearance of the Word in its full vigor and the consequent ingratitude of the world come almost as a coda to the long suppression of the Church by the Antichrist. Eschatologically, these final events belong to the period of the Antichrist as its consummation. Yet the complexity and the intensification of the issues create a period of separate consideration, for the restored gospel now intensifies the struggle between the realm of Christ and the realm of Satan. Grace and judgment become most apparent, and Luther can refer to this period both as a golden time distinguished by a pure theology and as an age characterized by the most extreme incredulity and licentiousness. The menace of the Turk, the agitation of the Enthusiasts and the miraculous signs in the sky attest to the imminence of the end.

The mass of evidence that indicates Luther's concern with the fact of the Antichrist and the event of the restored gospel establishes these two events, which in themselves distinguish three periods: that of the Church's degeneration from the time of the apostles to the establishment of the primacy of the Papacy, the disclosure of the Antichrist, and the period of the gospel's restoration together with the signs of the end.

The Fall of the Church

The idea of the fall in Luther requires independent consideration, for if it continues to occupy an unqualified place in the understanding of Luther's view of Church history, the main features of the present study can be discounted.

While any effort to establish clearly Luther's position concerning the fall must rely heavily upon an analysis of the terms used, the problem of the fall of the Church is not a mere quibble over words. The idea of the fall has a distinct meaning associated with particular religious groups. It belongs to the world of medieval sectarianism; formally introduced into Church history by humanists, the idea found ready acceptance among the Anabaptists and the radical reformers in Luther's day. The idea essentially claimed that at some time in the history of the Church the pattern had been lost. For the Anabaptists, who placed the fall at the time of Constantine, the idea involved the glorification of the first three centuries after Christ, an awareness of the Church's decline in association with the empire, and an impelling sense of restitution.[35]

Erich Seeberg represents probably the greatest exponent of the idea's presence in Luther's thought. In his monumental study of Gottfried Arnold, Seeberg attempted to understand Church history according to two opposing principles—the idea of tradition and the idea of fall, or more precisely decline (*Verfallsidee*). The former principle maintains that the Church possesses a pure, uncontaminated, divine substance, which it bears in its succession down through time. The second principle conceives Church history as a progressive decline of the Church through a deprivation of revelation beginning in a fall, defection, or apostasy (*Abfall*).[36] Seeberg discovers both

35. On the idea of the fall, see Littell, pp. 46–78. Erich Seeberg, *Gottfried Arnold: Die Wissenschaft und die Mystik seiner Zeit* (Meerane i. Sa., 1923), passim. Hereafter cited as *Arnold*.

36. Seeberg, *Arnold*, p. 259. I would like to acknowledge the receipt of a letter from Professor Heinrich Bornkamm, who kindly warned me at the beginning of my research not to adopt Seeberg's categories.

the catholic conservative strand of tradition and the radical, spiritualist strand of decline operative in Luther's view of Church history. In applying the latter principle to Luther, however, Seeberg's interpretation becomes ambiguous. There is no question about the location of the fall at the time of the agreement between Phokas and Boniface III. Yet in referring to this moment as the antichristic decline, Seeberg understands it first as the actual caesura in Church history; then immediately afterward he claims that for Luther there exists no radical break with history but only its ecclesiastical rejection.[37] In a later work he clarified his own understanding of the idea in Luther's thought by interpreting it as the loss of a previously pure pattern in the history of the Church. Seeberg has Luther confront the chaos of the decline and assert that what was before him has fallen, been disfigured, destroyed, depraved. The great Church has fallen from its own nature.[38]

The present task is not to impugn the obvious merits of Seeberg's work, a great achievement of German scholarship. The task is first to adduce those texts in Luther where the reformer employs the term and to assess its meaning according to the particular context and to the underlying principles of Church history for Luther. Secondly, it is to determine whether Luther's use of the term in his understanding of Church history conforms to the existing idea of the fall with all its implications.

The early works of Luther and especially the first lectures on the Psalms provide the principal support for the presence of the idea. At this time when his ecclesiology still remained undefined and his self-awareness as a reformer was to be redefined, there was abundant material for the construction of such a theory. The Church has been cast down from its first glory (3:216), and the early period of the martyrs appears as the springtime of the Church (3:25). Yet in his most extensive treatment of fall (*cadere*) in Psalm 91, Luther

37. Ibid., pp. 435–36.

38. Seeberg, *L.T.G.*, p. 166. See also Erich Seeberg, *Luthers Theologie* (Stuttgart, 1937), *2*, 439; but cf. also p. 397.

has the meaning refer to a fall into sin and secondly to a falling away of Jews and heretics from the true Church (4:67, 72–73, 77).

Subsequently, he gives the notion of fall either the sense of erring or of apostasy. By emphasizing the fall (*casus*) of Aaron in his exegesis of Exodus, Luther seeks to show that even the elect can err and none except Christ may presume to be above error (16:614–17). When he turns to the institution of the private Mass, he asserts that the Church fell into error and needed to be purged (39/1:165). In a late treatise, *Against Hans Worst,* where one would most expect to encounter the idea of a lost pattern, Luther claims that the papists accuse the evangelical groups of having fallen from the old Church and of making a new church. In reply Luther refers to the papist church not in terms of the fall but as being apostate (*abtruennig*) (51:478–79, 485). Significantly, the German word *Abfall* also contains the sense of apostasy among its meanings, and Luther himself in one instance defines each term by the other, although he makes it clear that any sense of fall refers to a fall from the commandment of God, not from any institution or community (24:221:26). In this late treatise Luther claims to be in line with the old Church and that the papists have absconded. The imagery of apostasy is not that of the loss of some original pattern but rather that of a group departing from God's commandment and setting up a false community in opposition to the Church (cf. 51:497:17, 501:28). Except that this present apostasy concerns the appearance of the Antichrist, it is the old case of the *duplex ecclesia.*

Another passage, which appears in the late *Lectures on Genesis,* reveals the inner complications of any theory of a fall and provides a tentative answer to the problem:

> Indeed, the Flood did not come because the Cainite generation might have been corrupted but because the generation of the just, who had believed in God, had been obedient to the Word, and had practiced the true worship, fell away (*prolapsi sunt*) into idolatry, disobedience to the parents, sensual pleasures,

> tyranny. Even so, it is not the impiety of the Gentiles, Jews, and Turks that hastens the last day but rather that the Church itself has been filled with errors by the pope and the fanatic spirits and that those who have first place in the Church exercise sensual pleasures, violent desires, tyranny.
>
> This serves, however, to inspire terror in all of us because even those who were born from the best patriarchs began to grow insolent and to depart (*discedere*) from the Word. They gloried in their own wisdom and righteousness—just as the Jews do with circumcision and with their father, Abraham. Likewise also the pontiffs glory in the title of the Church, for having abandoned the knowledge of God, the Word, and worship, they began to transfer its own spiritual glory into carnal luxury. The Roman church was truly holy and ornamented by the most distinguished martyrs. But today we see from what it has fallen (*delapsa sit*). [42:270]

The first fact that may be noted is that in two instances "fall" is used in the sense of a separation from the commandment of God; at the same time, however, Luther can employ the term to denote a decline from a previously established reputation. Secondly, the passage reveals that one cannot speak of a single fall or apostasy in Church history for there have been several which can be said to constitute the very core of the Church's struggle in time. Finally, Luther allows for a fall of a church but it is a particular, territorial church—the Roman church—which at one time had demonstrated by its martyrs such great vitality but has now declined from its earlier existence.

Further evidence confirms the view that the problem concerns the biblical idea of repeated apostasies rather than the humanistic or sectarian notion of a single loss of a pristine pattern. Luther can apply the concept of apostasy to either aspect of the *duplex Ecclesia*. Usually the false church is the apostate and the Antichrist represents the greatest apostasy (cf. 47:575). In respect to the Old Testament prophets, however, he can refer to their apostasy in leading the people away from the priests of God in order to preserve the Church in its obedience to God (53:235–36; cf. 7:411). Luther never denies the fact of apostasy in Church history. Indeed he recognizes continual apostasy as integral to its nature. Nevertheless, the true, hidden Church always remains:

> For the Church is ruled by the Spirit of God; the saints are led by the Spirit of God. And Christ remains with His Church up to the consummation of the world. And the Church of God is the pillar and buttress of truth. This, I say, we have known. For thus the creed of all of us asserts—I believe the holy catholic Church. [18:649–50]

Thus a case can be made for an idea of a fall peculiar to Luther; however, such an idea would have little to do with the humanist or sectarian idea of the fall in Church history. There have been repeated apostasies from the true Church, and, as will become evident later, there has been a decline in the institutional Church. But there is no fall as a sudden break in Church history. Since the term does not clarify anything and leads rather to an obfuscation of all the issues, it may be urged that the idea of the fall be omitted from further consideration of Luther. To impose the idea upon his view of Church history is to introduce him into a world alien to his thinking—a world of sectarianism and spiritualist ideas in which all the wrong syllables of thought are accented. One cannot treat Luther's understanding of Church history from the foreshortened perspective of the Incarnation, because it begins with the Creation and reveals not one fall as a break in the life of the Church but a series of apostasies that express the nature of Church history. Furthermore, the fall involves the idea of legitimacy in the past. But for Luther no period, not even the age of the patriarchs, is normative; legitimacy does not exist in a community's congruence with a past period of the Church but in its obedience to the ever-present and active Word of God. Lastly, the idea emphasizes discipleship rather than faith as the true mark of the Church. But Luther, despite all his eloquence concerning the period of martyrs, is too conscious of the doctrinal foundations of the Church's life to be misled by its outer appearance. Faith, not blood, constitutes the Church.

It has been necessary to indicate the internal distinctions in Luther's use of the term and to consider the logical implications of the current ideas of the fall in order to free his view of Church history from a misleading conception. There exist not two strands operative in his view of Church history—a radical revolutionary one and a conservative, traditional, or Catholic one—but rather the single bond between the Church and the Word. For the Word not only preserves and bears the Church down through time, it also creates division, discord, and the opposition evident in the fact of the *duplex Ecclesia*. The pattern of Church history itself is one of apostasy, struggle, and degeneration made supportable by the faith and the reality that Christ is present to the end of the world.

Thus if there was any radical or revolutionary strand in Luther's view of Church history, it existed not in accepting a spiritualist motif but in his placing the entire temporal course of the Church squarely under the conserving, bearing power of the Word. The view was at once most radical, most catholic.

4. THE EARLY CHURCH

In the period which Luther identified with the early Church, the modern historian may move with greater assurance. The institutional aspects of the Church now become more evident. Furthermore, Luther himself demonstrated here a fair degree of historical criticism. The relevant historical material includes the actions of apostles and fathers, martyrs and heretics; the institutions of episcopacy, councils, and monasticism; and the use and development of ceremonies and sacraments. The present task, however, is not to adduce all of Luther's factual knowledge of this period; nor is it to organize this material in a coherent development meaningful to the modern historian. The present problem consists in the discovery and elucidation of Luther's relation to this period—its institutions, events, and dominant figures.

Luther's approach to the material of history, and to the period of the early Church specifically, began with his quest for the origin of papal primacy. Previously, during the controversy over indulgences, he had appealed to the penitential practices of the early Church (1:551, 661). But only when confronted with the problem of the Papacy's origin did he undertake a formal investigation of the sources. Behind his accumulation of historical material, motivating and shaping it, stood the conviction, derived from Scripture, that the Papacy was of human origin. At Leipzig he linked histories with rational demonstrations and advanced an argument from history along with his more fundamental argument from Scripture. This agreement between the evidence of history and Scripture lay well within his theology, and for polemical and utilitarian purposes he could exploit it. Almost twenty years after the great debate, Luther reiterated this essential agreement and claimed the value of history in supplying proofs through specific cases (50:5).

Historical evidence provided examples that represented God's grace or God's wrath and revealed man's faith or unbelief. Since the meaning of God's Word remained clear, there could only be agreement or disagreement. Luther used the historical evidence of agreement to support his own doctrine and conception of the Church and to refute others; he used the historical evidence of disagreement to explain the workings of an alien force within the Church. History possessed a demonstrative power which was not independent of the authority of Scripture. In his approach to the history of the early Church he discovered evidence for agreement with Christian doctrine and also evidence of innovations, degeneration, and the intrusion of human traditions. In either case he found in the history of this period ammunition for his polemic against Rome.

The Early Church as a Tentative Norm

One of the most significant features that distinguishes Luther's understanding of history from humanistic reflections upon the past is his rejection of any historical period, person, or event as normative.[1] His successful avoidance of the lure provided by historical norms arose from his belief in the authority of Scripture and the

1. On humanism as providing past norms for present instruction and conduct, see Paul Joachimsen, "Der Humanismus und die Entwicklung des deutschen Geist," *Deutsche Vierteljahrschrift für Literaturwissenschaft und Geistesgeschichte, 8* (1930), 419–80, especially pp. 419–30.

activity of the Word in history. Yet in his use of the material concerning the early Church after Christ, he often found historical facts which were in such profound agreement with the nature of the true Church that he tended to make them tentative norms. If it is justifiable to isolate as one of two strands in Luther's attitude to the period this exploitation of history in terms of its implicit or explicit agreement with the Word of God, then Luther's success in keeping these norms merely tentative constitutes the thematic focus in the examination of this first strand.

Luther's discovery and appropriation of the history of the Council of Nicaea presents the most significant single example of the exploitation of the historical argument and its effective use as a tentative norm. From his early appeal to the canons and history of this council and throughout his struggle with Rome, Nicaea held a pivotal position in his view of this period; it provided specific definition to the claim that there had been a time when the Roman church had not been above all the others. During the controversy over indulgences in 1518, he suggested that until the time of Gregory I the Roman church had not been superior to all the rest and that at least it had not been able to enforce its penitential canons on the Greeks (1:571). In the famous thirteenth thesis for the Leipzig debate Luther used the canons of Nicaea as a vital part of his argument. In general he claimed the entire history of the Church up to the formal appearance of canon law for proof against papal primacy by divine law. During the debate, however, he indicated that papal primacy might have to be placed much earlier, for the struggle over this question was not four hundred but rather twelve or even fourteen hundred years old (2:287). He continued to have recourse to Nicaea during the debate and asserted that at least down to this council the Greeks could not be considered schismatic; they were true members of the Church and not subject to the Roman pontiff (2:285). He came away from Leipzig speaking of Nicaea as the holiest of all councils (*WBr* 1:473). Nicaea came to represent the keystone in his historical argument (*WBr* 1:518).

The Council of Nicaea offers an entry into Luther's interpretation of this period as well as into his use of history. In order to appreciate what he intended by his extremely favorable judgment of this council, one must examine his own reasonings on this historical fact before proceeding to his interpretation of the specific canons of Nicaea and the circumstances surrounding this council. In a protracted correspondence with the Leipzig professor, Jerome Dungersheim, Luther revealed his method and intentions with respect to the use of Nicaea. His opponent had advanced an argument through papal decretals and the standard histories, and he had claimed additional canons for the council. In reply Luther maintained that he possessed the Greek text and limited the number of canons to twenty. He then proceeded to distinguish his argumentation from that of his opponents. While Eck argued only from the universal, he, Luther, argued from the particular. Consequently, if he was able to discover one particular example against the primacy of the Papacy by divine law, the entire universal collapsed, for divine law ought to be observed uniformly. Because he denied the possibility of logical contraries, either the Papacy was not of divine origin or the fathers of the council were heretics. In concluding, Luther guarded himself against making Nicaea an absolute norm: he would not weigh all men according to the Nicene Council, but with it he would dissolve contradictions (*WBr* 1:567). While Dungersheim and Luther may have entertained different conceptions of tradition, the significance of denying a divine origin to the Papacy could be lost on no one.

Nicaea provided Luther with the clearest proof that there had been a period in the history of the Church when the primacy of Rome had not existed. Luther was quick to note that at the council itself the bishop of Antioch and not that of Rome had assumed first place. Furthermore he sought unsuccessfully to maintain that the council had attributed the primacy of honor to Jerusalem, not to Rome (2:238, 285). At the time of the Leipzig debate Luther used an examination of the sixth canon to reduce even further the claim of a

Roman primacy to what involved a limited episcopal authority. It was from custom and not from divine law that Nicaea had recognized the authority of Rome among the churches of Italy and in the surrounding area, just as Alexandria and the other great sees had administered their respective realms of authority (2:238). Thus Nicaea, and more specifically its sixth canon, presented Luther with a picture of equality rather than of hierarchy and subordination in this period of the Church. Yet this picture never assumed the force of an absolute norm—three years later Luther could discover in the same canon the origin of the papal tyranny of legislation (10/2:218; cf. 50:537–38).

By his interpretation of the fourth canon of Nicaea, Luther confirmed his view of the equality among the great sees in this early period. The original canon read that the bishop was to be elected by all the provincial bishops or at least three of them and to be confirmed by the metropolitan. To meet the needs of his own argument in opposing the view that the Roman bishop had controlled all episcopal ordinations from the beginning, Luther gave the metropolitan a merely cooperative and consultative position among the bishops.[2] In his *Address to the German Nobility*, written in the following year, Luther pursued this idea further and urged that this canon should be reinstated in order to meet the contemporary situation in Germany and the need of the Bohemians for an archbishop of Prague. Here Luther presented the canon as providing that confirmation of a bishop could be accomplished by the two nearest bishops or by the metropolitan (6:429, 455). Luther's interpretation of the Nicene ruling on episcopal consecration seems to have been shaped by his knowledge of Rufinus' version of the council's canons together with the letters of Cyprian. Although Nicaea said nothing about a popular election of bishops, Luther appropriated this idea from Cyprian and claimed that Ambrose, Augustine, and Cyprian

2. *WA* 2:238. Cf. C. J. Hefele, *Histoire des conciles*, trans. H. Leclercq (Paris, 1907), 1/1, 539–40.

himself had been elected in this way and confirmed by other bishops.[3]

At Leipzig, Eck had brought Luther to realize the differences among councils (2:399, 404). Twenty years later in his tract *On Councils and Churches,* Luther turned this knowledge to good advantage. Here the question was not one of establishing the human origin of papal primacy; rather, it concerned the type of reform to be sought. While the historical argument retained its same relation to Scripture as it had held in the earlier period, Luther reinterpreted Nicaea in a new light in order to meet the contemporary needs. Instead of suggesting the normative qualities of certain canons of the council, he now emphasized the impossibility of using Nicaea as a norm for the present reformation. The recognition of the divergencies between council's canons on the one hand, and ecclesiastical practice and Church doctrine on the other hand, proved Luther's argument that Scripture alone could be normative. Though the immediate problem was different, Luther's attitude to Nicaea did not substantially change; it revealed a greater concern for this council in respect to its total purpose, rather than in respect to particular canons.

Although Luther may have earlier overemphasized the unanimity expressed in this council against the Arians, he never considered it as pure or as providing a program for present reform (31/1:208–09; 28:52). In the tract of 1539 Luther devoted an extensive study to the Council of Nicaea together with the three subsequent universal councils in order to reveal the nature and purpose of councils. He gave particular attention to Nicaea as the first and greatest of the four universal councils which he accepted. If he could show its canons to be the product of a particular period and inapplicable to the present situation, then the other councils would appear even more irrelevant. Consequently he emphasized the inapplicable nature of its rulings on penance, purgatory, warfare, monasticism,

3. *WA* 6:408. Walther E. Koehler, *Die Quellen zu Luthers Schrift "An den christlichen Adel deutscher Nation"* (Halle, a. S., 1895), pp. 70–72. Hereafter cited as *Quellen.*

and rebaptism (50:532–38). All these canons represented solutions to external and accidental matters which were pertinent and useful at the time, but which had become irrelevant and were not to be taken as permanent laws or articles of faith. Luther urged his readers to understand the immediate causes which forced these councils to assemble, but he denied that they were convoked in order to rule on these external matters. The latter did not require the presence of the Holy Spirit but could be solved by reason on the local level of the diocese (50:559–60, 553). Luther submitted the work and effects of these great councils to a rigorous criticism in order to indicate the four councils' true authority and purpose which remained in accord with the Word of God.

Having destroyed the possibility of applying the particular ordinances of councils as models for present action, Luther ascribed to these great councils a normative value congruent with Scripture by considering their fundamental purpose and the place occupied by the emperor in them. The purpose of a council and the reason for its convocation were not to establish anything new in respect to belief but to strengthen against innovation the old articles of faith given by the Holy Spirit at Pentecost. In accordance with his knowledge of these first four universal councils and the council of the apostles at Jerusalem, Luther maintained that a council had no power to create new articles of faith but had the power and responsibility to condemn articles which were not in harmony with Scripture and the ancient faith. For this purpose Nicaea was called to condemn the Arian heresy, Constantinople the Macedonian heresy, Ephesus the Nestorian, and Chalcedon the Eutychian (50: 551, 607; cf. 39/1:187–89).

As councils, these four possessed a normative quality beyond the fact that they had worked to preserve the true faith in the early Church. Their convocation and control provided a model for considerable reflection. Luther could think of Nicaea together with the three subsequent councils as being relatively normative because they had been convoked by the emperors. He represented the threat posed at this time by the increasing activity and authority of the bishop of Rome who built up the hierarchy and subordinated other bishops. If it had not been for the power of the emperors in assembling these four universal councils, they would have been called and held at Rome (50:523). Previously, when he was preparing for the Leipzig debate, Luther began to clarify the distinguished place of the emperor in the early Church. Following I Peter 2:13, Luther asserted that the emperor was pre-eminent in sacred as well as in temporal matters by divine law; both laity and clergy were subject to his secular authority and what liberties he had granted to the latter were revocable (2:220). Furthermore, the first Christian emperor appeared to Luther as a model by his decisive intervention in the controversy between Arius and Athanasius (31/1:209). In his admiration for the imperial cooperation with the Church at this time, Luther presented an idealized portrait of Constantine, who dominated the council of Nicaea (50:548–50). In explaining his later defection to the Arian party, Luther claimed that the emperor had remained a good Nicaean and had never intended to undo the work of the council; rather, he had been misled by the deceptive language of Arius' argument (50:572–74). In this way Luther retained the link between the authoritative nature of the first four councils and their imperial convocation.

Luther's emphasis upon the imperial responsibility in respect to councils had a definite bearing upon the contemporary situation in 1539. In his later thinking it held a somewhat more permanent place. A year before his death he reiterated the normative nature of the four universal councils with respect to their imperial control and referred to their convokers as the four greatest Christian emperors (54:221). The imperial authority, whether in the early Church or in the sixteenth century, represented the only bulwark against the almost inevitable control of a council by the pope. Thus if Luther doubted the possibility, he could not suppress the hope that there might be a council after the manner of the four great councils, and of Nicaea and Constantinople in particular, where the secular authority would convoke the bishops and where a Constantine would dump the obsolete and irrelevant on the fire (50:622–23).

With respect to the problem of potential norms in Luther's knowledge of the early Church, Nicaea and the three subsequent councils have occupied considerable attention because they illustrate Luther's use of history, the relationship between the picture of the past and the needs of the present, and, furthermore, his success in controlling a historical example and in refusing to make it absolute. Luther's two main pronouncements on councils, given in 1519 and 1539, are different although not conflicting and represent not so much a development as the reacting of his historical judgment to the needs of two different situations in his own time. In the earlier statement he urged the normative nature of particular canons as a means of criticizing the papal primacy. In the later statement he revealed the irrelevancies and contradictions amidst the greatest councils. Yet in his desire to indicate the nature of a council and the danger of its control by the pope, he discovered a limited norm in their preservation of the old articles of faith and in their imperial control. In both instances Luther deepened his view of the early Church and subordinated to the authority of Scripture the tentative norms supplied by history.

The significance of the fathers as a potential norm represented even less of a threat than did the early councils. If Luther's use of patristic authorities appeared haphazard or opportunistic, it only served to underline the scriptural principle as a critical and authoritative norm. Fully aware of the continuing difficulty to reconcile the fathers, he praised the work of Peter Lombard and naturally preferred his achievement to that of Gratian (50:543). Because he could find no consistency among the fathers, there existed no norm and thus no danger of any competition with Scripture. Frequently Luther seemed to delight in noting the lack of agreement and the conflicting opinions between individual fathers. But even if he could find only patchwork here and no consistent norm in doctrine or ecclesiastical practice, this belief neither prevented his appropriating patristic statements of doctrine which agreed with his own, nor did it neglect the religious significance of their lives. In this respect Luther's attitude to Augustine provides an example of his complex attitude to the fathers. It is well known that St. Augustine served as Luther's outstanding patristic authority. Nevertheless, Luther's appeal to him was occasional, qualified, and normally to the anti-Pelagian writings of the father. The Augustine of the *Confessions,* on the other hand, always held the respect and affection of Luther, for here the German reformer came in contact with the personal faith and the religious content in the life of the great Christian thinker.[4] In short, Luther turned to the fathers not for doctrinal definitions but for polemical support and most particularly for the religious import of their lives and works. In what they had written and done he would glean the evangelical fragments (54:115).

Impressed by the differences among them and guided by his axiom that nothing in them should be embraced which did not conform with Scripture, Luther used the fathers when it suited his purpose. In *Councils and Churches* he had to oppose the patristic irenicists as much as the conciliarists. He emphasized the difficulty of reconciling the fathers and used Augustine to support his contention that the Church was not to be brought back to their doctrine (50:539–41, 525). At times he could be quite generous in his appreciation of them and at other times rather condescending, as on several occasions when he noted the faultiness of their exegesis because of the decline in languages (15:39–41). The controlled respect with which he regarded Augustine contrasted markedly with his continual condemnation of Origen and Jerome as the allegorizers of Scripture. He appealed to the fathers when they promoted or agreed with the gospel. In 1529 he approved Lazarus Spengler's effort to turn canon law against its creators; by a reading of selected passages, one could perceive how different the papists were from the old patristic doctrine and life as well as from their own law

4. P. Courcelle, "Luther interprète des Confessions de Saint Augustin," *RHPR,* *39* (1959), 235–50.

(30/2:219). Again when confronted with Oecolampadius and the Sacramentarians in 1527, Luther was willing to speak their language; without needing the argument himself, he nevertheless claimed the support of Augustine, Tertullian, Irenaeus, Hilary, and Cyprian for his doctrine of the Eucharist (23:209–41). On the other hand, regarding his doctrine of justification, he averred that it was not to be found in Gregory, Augustine, or Jerome but in Scripture alone (32:244–45).

When Luther formally repudiated the doctrine of purgatory in 1530, he happened to make some significant pronouncements concerning the authority of the fathers and their interpretation within the Church. He argues that in their numerous writings the dear fathers have made a number of ill-advised but well-meaning utterances which were never intended to be taken as absolutely authoritative. The Papacy has willfully twisted some of these to its own ends. The fathers would have been the first to resist this distortion of their statements into articles of faith (30/2:380–83). Here Luther does not assail so much the ecclesiastical practice of receiving texts as he does the way in which the received and approved work is applied. For example the pious St. Gregory in his *Dialogues* never intended that his unfounded notion of purgatory should become an article of faith, but the knavish sophists have imposed it on Christendom. Not everything in a received text is right, and nothing should be added to what already exists therein (30/2:385; cf. *MPL* 77:396–97). To reassert the norm of Scripture, Luther quotes one of his favorite passages from St. Augustine: in writing to St. Jerome, the great Church father explains that they themselves and all other works must be judged according to their agreement with the books of Scripture and to the canonical authors alone can be given an unqualified adherence and respect (30/2:384; cf. *MPL* 33:277).

In one respect, however, Luther had frequent recourse to the fathers for his view of the early Church. At the time of the Leipzig debate he adduced Jerome as his authority for the equality of all bishops by divine law and as his historical proof that in the early

Church no bishop had been preferred to another. Likewise presbyters and bishops had been the same by divine law; their equality had been a historical reality which only custom had altered. At Alexandria for a while the presbyters selected the bishop from among themselves and appointed the deacons (2:227–30, 423, 434; *WBr* 1:392). In the last years of his life Luther re-emphasized this view and went so far as to publish the central text, Jerome's letter to Evagrius. Jerome's commentaries revealed presbyter and bishop to be one reality, differing only in designation. All bishops were alike in being joint heirs of the apostles regardless of a city's size. Preachers and chaplains had administered the church at Alexandria and only to guard against sects had they elected a bishop (50:84; 54:229). Luther revealed this historical situation to the German public not because the authority of Jerome was so great but to demonstrate the human origin of the Papacy and its wide divergence from the condition of the old or primitive Church. Luther's constant intention was a frontal assault on the Roman hierarchy. He claimed that at the time of Jerome, Ambrose, and Augustine, there had been no archbishops, patriarchs, metropolitans, or popes—all were equally bishops (50:341).

In conjunction with the historical witness of Jerome, Luther appealed to the authority of Cyprian to demonstrate the equality and integrity of the episcopal office in the early Church and its subsequent decline and destitution. For Luther, Cyprian possessed considerable significance beyond the fact that he had claimed the equality of bishops by divine law; the African father had also asserted that each bishop exists not by the authority of another bishop but by that of his people who may elect or reject him. From the book of Acts, Cyprian showed how the ordination took place in the presence of the people and of the other bishops. The contemporary absence of this former cooperation between people and neighboring bishops caused Luther to ask why this oldest and most sacred rite by divine law has been supplanted by a more recent rite.[5]

5. *WA* 2:230–32. Cf. *Cypriani Opera Omnia,* ed. W. Hartel, *Corpus Scriptorum Ecclesiasticorum Latinorum,* 3/2:737–39 (Vienna, 1871). Hereafter cited as *C.S.E.L.*

To emphasize the integrity of each bishop's authority, Luther used at the Leipzig debate the example of Cyprian on the matter of episcopal equality in the early Church. Luther maintained that any priest possesses the power to absolve a penitent person from punishment and guilt. In protesting against the contemporary appealing of cases and the general confusion of jurisdictions, he adduced Cyprian for the episcopal order which had existed in the early Church and which had been confirmed by Nicaea. Dioceses were not confounded and each bishop had served in his own diocese. In writing as an equal to the Roman pontiff Cornelius, Cyprian had objected to the fact that those who sinned in Africa should run to Rome; better than all this running about was the holding of the process in one's own diocese where the accusers and witnesses of the crime were present.[6]

Luther undoubtedly discovered in the previous practice of binding and loosing sinners a powerful accusation against the existing system and a potential remedy for it. In this instance his use of the early Church as a norm repays closer consideration.

> The Church would not be ruined if the same ordinary bishop were archbishop and pope, and all cohering harmoniously, they might be yoked together, as Cyprian says and as was the practice of the earlier Church. Accordingly, what the condemned article in the Council of Constance reports as regards the reserving of these cases, I do not really care. This I know: the practice was approved and this reserving of cases condemned in the primitive Church and in the institution of the apostles. Now also as the most lamentable experience of the Church teaches, it would prove most useful and beneficial for the punishment of sins and the removal of the detestable confusion among dioceses which we see today. By what cause, however, it may have been changed in its time I pass over.

6. *WA* 2:378–79, 264. Cf. *C.S.E.L.* 3/2:683–84.

> Here I discover the mutable. I leave this to the decision of the judges. The hour has passed. [2:379]

Except for a very brief interchange with Eck, these were Luther's last words at Leipzig and must have left the assembled audience much to ponder.

The precise nature of the alteration which Luther announced in this passage may be temporarily deferred. In passing, one may note the practical nature of his suggestion and the admission of his concern for the mutable. The immediate problem is to determine the extent to which the historical example of the early Church's episcopacy or ministry presented an absolute norm.

In the first place, it should be recalled that Luther does not depend upon the authority of Cyprian and Jerome for his view of the early Church's ministry. These two fathers are merely useful historical witnesses for the presence of this ministry in the early Church. Luther discovers its fundamental authority in the apostolic provision, divine decree, and rite of the Holy Scripture (8:429). Yet in appealing to the actual practices of the apostles relating to the ministry, he uses a norm derived from the *historia sacra* of Scripture. This fact becomes more evident in his *Preface to the Instruction* of 1528. Here in attempting to prove the visitorial nature of the original episcopal office, he appealed to the ministries of Samuel, Elijah, and Elisha as well as those of Peter and Paul: whether pastor or archbishop, the ministerial task of visiting and supervising remained the same before a worldly splendor entered to create false distinctions and tyrannous dignities (26:195–96). Although Luther did not claim to find in Scripture a complete church order that could be applied to the present, he did maintain the divine institution of the equality of ministers. But the ultimate basis for this equality and all practices relating to it did not lie in the historical witness of the early Church nor in the *historia sacra* of Scripture. It existed in his doctrine of the priesthood of all believers and the congregation's calling of members to ministerial office.

The right of a Christian congregation to call and depose its own ministers affords another opportunity to examine Luther's appeal to, and possible dependence upon, practices belonging to the early Church. In 1523 he was asked to present scriptural support for the preaching office. Luther readily adduced the examples of Paul, Titus, and Timothy to demonstrate that a bishop may confirm a minister but only the congregation can choose and call him. Yet even these examples Luther will renounce because the extreme distress of the present makes it impossible to meet these conditions. With the corruptions of bishops and the consequent destruction of souls, the Christian congregation cannot wait for a minister to be confirmed but must assume this responsibility and install one (11: 413–15). Thus the necessity of proclaiming the Word transcends the authority of examples offered by *historia sacra*.

As one moves back toward the age of the apostles in an examination of tentative historical norms, their absolute nature and influence as models appear to become more pronounced. Martyrdom represents such a permanent feature of the Christian condition for Luther that his treatment of it as a period in the history of the Church must be isolated from his consideration of it as a spiritual condition. Luther quotes Tertullian's statement that the Church is nourished by and thrives upon the blood of the martyrs, and he claims martyrdom and tribulation to be the true form of the Church (16:17; 5:308–09). This suffering and persecution constitute a good sign. Christians represent Christ's garment, and when Christ wishes to clean and purify this garment, He has the members of the Church suffer. Thus Luther can say that at the time of the martyrs following the apostles, Christ assumed a new garment (10/1/1:478). In his early lectures on Psalms, Luther's admiration for the period of the martyrs as the spring of the Church has already been observed. In 1520 when he contrasted a righteousness based on good works and its effects with justification by faith and its effects, Luther asserted that the theology of the cross made martyrs, and for this reason the Church flourished most fully during the time of the martyrs (7:148).

Yet in order to assess the full weight of the period of the martyrs as a possible norm, it may be noted that three years later Luther wrote to a community in the Netherlands comforting and congratulating its members on having been the first to suffer. He proceeded then to describe the return of the gospel's light and time with the same imagery that he had used a decade earlier to describe this early period of the martyrs (12:77–78; cf. 3:25). The vitality of the gospel as evinced in the martyrs, and not the garment of martyrdom itself, commended this period to Luther's admiration.

In history nothing stands nearer to Christ the source than the apostles and their age. The influence of this period as a historical norm can only be determined by observing the distinction between the apostles as members of the early Church and the apostles in their relation to the Word of God. The present problem concerns the apostles of the book of Acts, not those of the epistles. Luther reacted in different ways to the various features that he discovered in this period. From an early moment in his career he saw in the age of the apostles a time when the Church had been properly subject to secular authorities in matters pertaining to the worldly Regiment (56:477); and more than once later in his life he maintained that his own respect for the secular arm merely duplicated an attitude which had once been a fact at the time of the apostles but had since disappeared (19:625; 30/2:109–10). On the matter of apostolic communism, however, he recognized the possible subversion of the domestic and the worldly Regiment in the efforts of the Anabaptists to transform a local and historical measure into a norm. Luther emphasized that the pooling of property by the apostles had been limited to the church at Jerusalem at one moment in time and had not been observed by the other churches. It had worked because all had believed and there had been few children (52:588–90). Nevertheless, Luther's respect for and attachment to the period of the apostles was far from tenuous. The apostles themselves had associated with Christ and had received special revelations (42:323). The fact which distinguished them in the eyes of Luther from their predecessors, the prophets, and from succeeding bishops was their unanimity in preaching one faith; to this agreement in the gospel he attributed their accomplishments and their conversion of the world (8:13–14). No more favorable judgment could Luther pass upon his own time than to claim that not since the age of the apostles had the light of the gospel shone so brightly (11:208; 17/1: 389).

The significance of these potential norms in Luther's view of the early Church can now be determined. The structure of Luther's historical investigation is that of adducing examples from the past as rational demonstrations for delimiting periods in the Church's history which were free from later corruption introduced by the Papacy. A twofold reason exists for preserving the original form of Luther's historical knowledge of the early Church. In the first place it cannot be overlooked that his representation of the early Church assumes the nature of a number of auxiliary arguments to the central argument from Scripture. In his view of Church history the theological argument claims precedence over the strictly historical argument. When the original form is dropped and the context of polemic and practical reform forgotten, the period of the apostles, of the martyrs, or that up to Nicaea stands forth isolated as a potential norm for the total life of the Church; it no longer remains as supporting evidence for the validity of a particular doctrine, practice, or institution. Although Luther may appear inconsistent on the less important issues, one only magnifies unnaturally this impression by transforming these rational demonstrations from history into absolute historical norms and then attempting to locate a fall of the Church amidst them. From this very danger arises the second reason for presenting Luther's historical view within its original form: the existence of these arguments as tentative historical norms provides an effective instrument for studying the transformation which the Church suffered and also for investigating further the idea of the fall—the validity of which depends upon the existence of a normative period in the past.

By theological definition, the community of believers, the hidden

Church, does not fall; there are apostasies from it. Once this basic principle of Church history has been grasped, Luther will allow ample room for the degeneration or decline of the institutional or territorial Church as a community that includes both the wheat and the tares—in fact, degeneration constitutes another principle of Church history. There have been times when the lines of the true Church have more nearly approached those of the institutional Church, as with the age of the patriarchs and the apostles. But the area in which the Word is preached can never coincide with the area in which it is both preached and believed. Although Luther was a man of the Word, this truth should not be allowed to disguise the fact that he was thoroughly concerned with the external life and organization of the Church. And if he could not discover in Scripture a definite form for the ordering of the territorial Church, he recognized that some external conditions were more favorable than others for the preaching and believing of the Word. By a brief consideration of the relationship between the external ordering of the Church or face of the Church (*facies ecclesiae*) and its actual life, an assessment can be made of Luther's understanding of the early Church, his relation to it and the change that the Church suffered.

In his preparation for the Leipzig debate Luther had deplored the proliferation of laws, exemptions, privileges, and regulations that had distorted the face of the Church during the previous four hundred years. Human traditions had come to suppress the public gospel. Luther referred to this general corruption as the ruined state of the Church (*ecclesiae occasum*). The term which he employs can mean both condition, state, and setting, or destruction, decline, and even fall. If Luther used it in the sense of fall, it would still apply not to a break or departure in the past but to the total state of degradation in which the present Church (*hodierna ecclesia*) existed (2:226). Here the external corruptions intruded far into the actual life of the Church, which is the proclamation of the gospel; indeed, they threatened to choke this life entirely.

Luther fully recognized the fact that the Church as spiritual

Regiment had suffered a terrible disfigurement and decline in the past one thousand years. He even went so far as to identify his own party with this degraded Church (*untergengliche Kirche*). The pope and his followers had renounced their responsibility, absconded from this Church and left those remaining in the Church to provide for it (50:514). While always asserting the continuity of the hidden Church maintained by God, Luther could measure this decline in terms of the difference between the temporal appearance of the present Church and that of the early Church. In considering the period of the martyrs, he could observe how far the contemporary Church had receded from the face (*facie*) or external condition of the early Church (5:308). Or simply through an examination of the *Decretum* he could be struck by how greatly the condition of the former Church differed from that of the subsequent Church (50: 341). Much as Luther admired the ministry of the early Church, it was not to this fact nor to any specific practice that he sought to restore the contemporary Church. What he discovered in the primitive Church for the most part, and what he sought to restore, was not its entire outward appearance but its relative freedom from human traditions in order that the gospel could effectively operate. Yet this same condition of freedom depended upon the proclamation of the gospel itself. With such a view in mind he wrote Spalatin from the Wartburg, urging him to have Melanchthon preach to the people at midday. Luther envisaged the consequence to be the introduction of liberty and the restitution of the face and customs of the ancient Church, by which he meant the public recognition of the priesthood of all believers and lay preaching. The rest of the letter indicated that he valued these conditions, which had once been evident in the Church, because they advanced the free proclamation of the Word (*WBr* 2:388–89; cf. 12:35–37).

The face of the Church was important, but it was the face of the gospel within the Church that Luther sought to restore. In attacking the commentaries and traditions which had come to obscure Scripture, he asked:

> When we believe the holy, catholic Church to have the same spirit of faith which it received once at its origin, why is it not permitted today to study sacred letters alone or primarily as it was allowed to the primitive Church? [7:97]

Thus he admired the entire period of the early Church because it represented a condition of relative freedom for the promulgation of the gospel. And just as the historical argument remains subordinate to the theological argument in his thinking, likewise in his view of Church history, the practical conditions of ecclesiastical life remain subordinate to the condition of the gospel. Writing from the Wartburg in the first flush of reform, he reminded his followers in Wittenberg of their responsibility in being made the first to see the pure and primitive face of the gospel (*primitivam Evangelii faciem*) (8:476).

The Early Church and the Antichrist

The accepted understanding of Luther's attitude toward the early Church is that he considered it relatively pure. This assessment of the reformer's view of the period rests upon a definite type of evidence which, in associating arguments from history with arguments from Scripture, presents a basic agreement between the Word of God and the work of God. Luther does not consciously elaborate the institutions of the early Church under the concept of God's grace in the same sense that he elaborates the advent of the Antichrist under the concept of God's wrath. But he does feel free to embrace at will various elements discoverable in the early Church in order to promote the authority of Scripture. When he accuses the papists of having condemned the entire first Christendom as well as Christ, it would appear that the early Church represents a relatively pure period (38:225, 269–70). Yet such an assessment rests upon evidence that derives from a context of polemic and the need for practical reform. The consequent judgments on Luther's part represent the product of a dialogue between the contemporary Church of his day and the Church at a former period. In this evidence the institutional aspects of the early Church constitute a major concern. Because this assessment of Luther's attitude neglects another aspect of the problem and another type of evidence, it does not comprise his total attitude to this critical period.

When in his preparation for the Leipzig debate Luther claimed the support of eleven hundred years of Church history, he did not fail to admit that well within this period the popes had promulgated their decrees and the struggle over the primacy had raged (2:225, 227). If the bulk of Luther's formal historical investigations sought the elucidation of earlier periods when the Church had been free from papal primacy and papal corruptions, he could still recognize in the same material evidence for the origin of corruptions established later. In his tract *On Councils and Churches* he pressed more vigorously a counterargument. But this other aspect of his attitude to the early Church finds its main source of evidence in scattered statements and references to the introduction of new corruptions after Christ. Although this material is hardly less polemical than the first type and might even be considered mere *obiter dicta,* it constitutes in many respects a more important source for establishing his view of the early Church. For it is more closely associated with prophecies in Scripture and relates directly to the working out of God's wrath in the revelation of the Antichrist. Here once again the accent falls with greater emphasis upon the hidden Church in its suffering and destitution.

It would be difficult, if not misleading, to draw together the numerous statements pertaining to this decline of the Church and attempt to present a coherent picture. Fortunately, however, Luther himself supplies a brief but extremely significant statement concerning the corruption that befell the Church after the apostles. In explaining the grotesque cults and monstrous ceremonies which grew up among the Egyptians after Joseph's ministry, Luther claims that the Egyptians abandoned the Word and retained only the shell of ceremonies received from Joseph; consequently, they aped the appearance of the saints rather than imitating their faith. This abandonment of faith and the promise for an increased emphasis upon externalities and ceremonies sheds some light on the fate of the Church after Christ.

> Thus in the Church of the New Testament the heretics immediately followed the apostles. Then came the bishops who did not know the Lord, after them the monks, and finally the whole Papacy and the universal abomination standing in the holy place. And all these have clamored: We serve God far more ardently and with greater piety. For the apostles have neglected much that must be added to the Church; the fathers have had a paucity of vows and ceremonies; we[7] accumulate more rites and forms of worship. In this way ceremonies have been multiplied in the Church, the Devil mixing the true with the false and subsequent generations steadily hastening for the worse. [44:676]

The statement is important for it not only presents the succession of calamities which beset the Church but also emphasizes the factor fundamental to this decline—namely an alien conception of tradition.

Notwithstanding Luther's respect for the age of the apostles, he recognized that the community of believers had maintained an extremely tenuous existence and the spirit of the Antichrist had won an early start. At the time of the council of the apostles when the Church was still young, vigorous, and filled with many believers, God allowed all to err except three or four (12:417). Sects soon arose to pervert the work of Paul, and the rapidity with which heresies followed the time of the apostles caused Luther to estimate that hardly fifty undisturbed years had elapsed since Pentecost

7. The sense of this passage makes the *nos* of the Erlangen edition preferable to the *non* appearing in the Weimar edition. Cf. *EOL* 11:74.

(40/1:610–11; *TR* 4123). Although the early bishops had at first repelled the heretics and had been strong in doctrine and sanctity of life, they had not proved as unanimous in their faith as the apostles. Where this unanimity was lacking, human doctrines and works had replaced faith and the gospel (42:137; 8:13–14). With works and ceremonies the realm of the Antichrist began to advance immediately after the time of the apostles (7:747). These two dangers—the proliferation of heresies and the multiplications of human traditions—are related for Luther, and as historical movements they appear to attack the primitive Church simultaneously. But each of the two evils requires separate consideration. The heretics may here claim precedence, for the fathers managed to suppress them; the traditions of men, on the other hand, came to suppress the Church.

As might be expected, Luther's understanding and his treatment of the early heretics are doctrinal rather than historical; they conform to his general conception of heresy itself. In its desire to excite and attract, in its craving for novelty and absolute purity, and in its contempt of the common revelations provided by the Word, heresy appears as a revolt against God and His entire *potestas ordinata* (42:666; 43:495–96; 32:519). In noting how a bad generation always seems to follow a good one, Luther asserts that wherever the gospel arises, factions and sects must follow to spoil it; wherever God builds a church, the Devil builds his chapel next to it (32:474). Luther observes that immediately after Christ there appeared ungrateful people, who despised the light afforded by the present Lord and sought to be like the patriarchs in having immediate revelations (43:225). With the perversion of the schools and the advance of sects, Scripture itself became a book for heretics who proceeded to chop it up to conform with their own notions (23:65). Amidst the welter of heresies Luther perceives their common source and common goal. For all error arises from a neglect or misconception of the main article of the Christian faith which claims that Christ is the God/Man who died for us (50:267–68). John wrote against the followers of Cerinthus and against the spirit of the Antichrist which early began to deny that Christ had come in the flesh (*WAB* 7:326). Likewise the Manichaeans were in part the Antichrist by denying Christ's humanity, as were also the Arians in denying His divinity. But heresy in respect to the person of Christ is not so great as that in respect to the merit or fruit of Christ, and only with the invasion of the head of the gospel's doctrine did the full and true Antichrist emerge (20:669). Luther could therefore recognize the future Papacy as the culmination and distillation of all these early heresies (*WAB* 4:710).

Arianism is the most outstanding of the first heresies, and Arius appears as the great heretic, who, in uniting spiritual with physical persecution of the Church, led to Mohammad and ultimately to the Papacy (*WAB* 7:412). Luther can equally understand these heretics in the light of his own experience with the radicals, for Arius like the Anabaptists promoted an acquired wisdom (42:120–21). This poison, which lasted three hundred years among Christians, was accepted because it offered something new (50:574; 43:90). At its height Arianism produced one of the darkest periods in Church history, yet it demonstrated the hiddenness of the Church's continuity in history. This crisis supplied historical proof for the fact that the greater part of the institutional Church could err (2:347). The heresy overran all mankind, launched the most severe persecution, and even deceived the Emperor Constantine; scarcely three bishops in all of Christendom preached correctly (20:566–67; 50:569–73). Athanasius and Hilary were among the few who resisted, and their care for their flock and for the ministry of the Word while in exile remains exemplary (49:582; 5:230). Elaborating upon a commonly held opinion, Luther declares that shortly after the suppression of Arianism by the fathers, Mohammed came from this heresy.[8]

Far more dangerous for the Church than the acclaimed heretics

8. *WA* 50:575. On the medieval basis for this idea, see Rudolf Pfister, "Reformation, Türken und Islam," *Zwingliana, 10* (1956), 356.

is the growth of human traditions (7:724). While both produce a fragmentation of the common Christian life by an excessive piety and by special distinctions, the introduction of human traditions proves more dangerous, because it enters the abode of the holy and clothes itself with the trappings of the Church. The growth of traditions arises from an improper division of the Word, causing threats and promises to become confused; at the same time, human traditions involve the presence of ceremonies and the ecclesiastical power to legislate. In warning against ceremonies shortly before his death, Luther stated that ceremonies grow into laws, which in turn become traps for consciences and the suppression of pure doctrine follows. For this reason he found an excessive effort at legislating and harmonizing ceremonies to be unwise (*WBr* 11: 132–33). While Luther here contrasts the example of the early Church with the experience of the papal Church, elsewhere he recognized in the later stages of the early Church a growth of ceremonies, laws, and human traditions.

The first great problem for the early Church was whether the law of Moses should be observed (42:608). In an effort to preserve the freedom of conscience and the supremacy of faith, Paul had made the keeping of the law optional. Guided by this solution, the Church had permitted Judaic ceremonies down to the fourth century, when Jerome sought to compel the abolition of the law with an ordinance. In opposition to this effort, Augustine maintained the Pauline view during his lifetime, but with his death Jerome's attitude prevailed. Luther conceived this controversy as a significant step toward the subsequent legislation of the popes. From the elimination of one law had grown a thousand laws (56:495; 10/3:18–19). With the conclusion of the great persecutions wrought by the tyrants and heretics, the bishops who were contemporaneous with Jerome began to feel secure, failed in the gospel, and introduced their own traditions (40/1:634).

Luther does not limit this growth of ceremonies and traditions during the fourth century to the less responsible bishops but extends the accusation to the fathers. In criticizing their consecration and ordination of ministers, Luther maintained that they had ornamented that calling with excessive splendor. Thereupon a distinction had been made between the called and the common members of the priesthood and a new type of priesthood had been produced. By their multiplying of ceremonies with consecration and by similar elaborations the fathers had meant well, but the religious zeal and good intentions of one time became vexation, error, and idolatry later (38:228). Furthermore, because the fathers had endeavored to eliminate the dissension and godly quarrel which Scripture and the freely preached gospel engender, they had contributed substantially in the shift from Scripture to purely human things. Through their collaboration, deliberate or inadvertent, the Church sought its security no longer in faith but behind human walls. The result was the unanimity and obedience in the glosses of the fathers and the see of Rome (23:67, 69; cf. 7:633, 636).

In connection with the fathers' responsibility for the accumulation of ceremonies, Luther accomplished in one instance a significant work of historical criticism; he attacked Pseudo-Dionysius as a proper authority for the existence of six of the seven sacraments in the early Church. Luther rejected the apparent antiquity of Dionysius on the ground that there existed nothing in the other fathers which could justify the presence of extra sacraments. He deduced therefore that Dionysius must have lived after the fathers and that his writings had promoted new inventions. Luther went on to discover in his mystical theology little of Christ and much of Plato. While he admitted his inability to identify the man, Luther inferred that Dionysius must have been subsequent to the great Latin doctors (6:561–62).

It would be futile to attempt to construct from Luther's statements a temporal succession of progressive decline. Nevertheless, his frequent references to the period contemporaneous with Jerome would suggest that from this time until the establishment of the Papacy the growth of traditions and special works accelerated.

Important corruptions had appeared before Jerome's time. Luther correctly judged ecclesiastical celibacy to have originated about the time of Cyprian through the institutional Church's establishment of a previously voluntary practice.[9] Far more significant for the future papal tyranny was Rome's claim after Nicaea to the right of establishing laws as well as that of simply judging (10/2:218). But Jerome witnessed the growth of monasticism and the first signs of a distinct spiritual estate.

Luther was not concerned with monasticism as an economic and cultural reality except insofar as he considered its foundations originally to have been Christian schools and only later to have become eternal prisons (6:439; cf. 50:211–12). He was primarily concerned with it as representing an enduring perversion in the religious life of man. Incited by the Devil, man sought what was different, special, and better than what God commanded (32:301). At the same time Luther could recognize the distinctive characteristics of the monks in this particular period. Originally the religion of monkery, as he called it, had possessed no orders; each monk had been a hermit and had lived truly alone (50:535). For Luther there existed a relationship between Stoicism and this early form of monkery. The monks had simulated the Stoics, and their apathy had deceived many people into emulating them (44:553–54, 556, 563). According to Jerome, Evagrius had composed a book on apathy or imperturbability for monks. This work in Rufinus' translation had been spread widely throughout the West and had proved a portent of subsequent excesses in monasticism and the entire religious life. Jerome condemned only certain aspects of these superior Stoics, whom no true Stoic would ever have been able to recognize. Jerome's own admiration for the great hermits of the period indicated that monasticism, at least in its less exaggerated form, was still the custom of the age (54:110–11). The four great councils did nothing to restrain this new holiness, and the suckers began to obscure the true, old tree (50:609).

9. *TR* 4688. Cf. Koehler, *Quellen,* p. 81.

In his tract *On the Abolition of the Private Mass,* Luther set forth the calamity that had befallen the Church. Here he sought to describe in its full dimensions the fact of the papal abomination, and he was not concerned in establishing the temporal sequence of corruptions with the growth of the Papacy. Nevertheless, both from internal evidence supplied by the document and from the external evidence of other statements, it can be said that Luther related the origins of these corruptions to a time contemporaneous with Gregory the Great. In the tract he directed his attention to an idea that occupied a crucial place in his entire polemic against Rome. This idea was the destruction of the Church as a community and the fragmentation of the common Christian life.

Luther understood the injuries suffered by the Church at the hands of the papists as a threefold attack. The first violence had aimed to destroy the priesthood which had been made common to all Christians. In its place emerged another priesthood specially shaved, garbed, and consecrated. Because its ordination lay beyond the Word of God, it derived not from the Church but from the synagogue of Satan under the name of the Church (8:417, 419–20). Luther discovered that the fathers had called the priestly estate a priesthood. Thus custom had already entered and separated the laity from the clergy, and the fathers together with human doctrines had confirmed this innovation (7:633, 636). In attacking this contrived distinction between laity and clergy, Luther claimed that the new priesthood conflicted with the only two divinely ordained priesthoods. Founded on the traditions of men, this new priesthood of Bethel opposed both the law of God and the Levitical priesthood as well as faith and the Christian priesthood (8:471).

The second violence wrought by the papists was the transformation of the Mass into a sacrifice. Formerly, the sacrifice had applied to all Christians in common as a sacrifice of their lives and persons and the sacrifice of praise to God (8:420–21). Instead of accepting Christ's promise for the remission of sins, the papists had denied this gratuitous gift and had labored with His sacrifice to accomplish their own new remission (8:445). Luther objected that Scripture never used the term, and a year earlier he had explained this confusion of the idea of a sacrifice with the testament and promise of the Lord's Supper. The word had come into the Mass at the time of the apostles; it had originated from a practice, current during the Old Testament, that Christians should bring together food, money, and necessities and distribute them before the apostles to those who needed them. Both the terms "sacrifice" and "collect" derived from this practice, which had not been confused with the Mass itself (6:365–66). Through the priestly control and understanding of the Mass, the ministry of the Word which had been committed to all Christians in common now became the property of an estate. This transference of the teaching office to these priestly intermediaries constituted the third and final violence (8:422–25).

In Luther's treatment of Gregory the Great, one discovers the crucial figure for the final corruptions that led to the establishment of the Papacy. Luther attributed to Gregory the innovation of the private Mass, which was the greatest abomination in the Church instituted by Christ (40/2:106; cf. 39/1:141, 165–66). What had been intended for the living now came to be misapplied to the dead. Luther considered Gregory to have been deceived by the soul of his monastic steward when the great bishop wrote that some dead have appeared and have asked for help and that a response should be made. The Church father was extremely superstitious; assisted by the Devil, he had seized this particular occasion for terrifying consciences and stabilizing the traditions of men (8:452–53; cf. *MPL* 77:420–21). Besides the institution of the private Mass and the fables concerning purgatory, Luther considered Gregory's influential statements on penance to have proved equally detrimental to the Church and to the Christian life. His excessive scrupulosity and his cultivation of doubt and fear both contributed to the establishment of excommunication and of the Papacy itself (40/2:140). Luther granted that only in time had Gregory's injudicious actions and views hardened into abominations, and in the same way he went on to discover that Gregory had inadvertently been the cause of other corruptions. The Roman bishop's correct assertion that the sacraments could be given just as effectively by impious as by holy priests had been misconstrued and distorted (6:525). And concerning the title of *Servus servorum Dei,* Gregory understood it as belonging to each Christian in that he must wash his brothers' feet and practice humility. But the popes had retained the title for themselves (50:87).

Yet Luther spared Gregory in the end; like Jerome and Bernard, Gregory was saved by a final recognition of his dependence upon God's promise (40/1:687). Luther's generous attitude toward the Roman bishop cannot be explained on properly religious grounds. Although at Leipzig he argued that Gregory had been the last pastor in the Roman church (2:197), Luther entertained a mean opinion of him as a teacher. In attempting to show that since St. Peter there had been no occupant of the see of Rome who had preached the gospel, Luther maintained that Gregory's sermons were little better than trash. He considered him to have been certainly holy and pious in his life, but his teaching accomplished no good results and his knowledge of Christ and the Word, if it had existed at all, appeared extremely tenuous (12:388–89; 32:347; 44:759). Luther's ultimately favorable judgment of Gregory resulted from his view of the role that Gregory had played in Rome's claim to episcopal supremacy.

In a sense Luther's knowledge of the early Church began with his use of the pontificate of Gregory to delimit a period and to establish a fact in Church history. It was during the controversy over indulgences when he first observed that up to the time of Gregory the Roman church had not been superior to other churches. While preparing for the Leipzig debate, Luther discovered in Gregory's correspondence ample evidence that he had protested against the title of *universalis episcopus* as much for himself as for the patriarch John of Constantinople (2:201, 232). Luther seemed to value this evidence so highly that at the debate itself he sought to explain away the facts that Sixtus III and Victor I had employed the title and that the Council of Chalcedon had accorded it to Leo the Great; humility and restraint rather than any claim of Roman primacy by divine right had informed those pontiffs' understanding of this title (2:309). At the end of his life Luther elaborated his portrait of Gregory without changing any of the essential features. The pious bishop had refused the title on the grounds that none of his predecessors had possessed it. While he admitted that the Roman bishop was greater than others, he had rejected the controversial title that had ostensibly been offered by the Council of Chalcedon.[10] Following Platina, Luther emphasized the piety and humility of Gregory by repeating the story that Gregory had vainly begged the Emperor Maurice not to confirm his election. Such was the last bishop of Rome (54:229–30).

To Luther, the murder of Maurice by Phokas and the granting of the disputed title to Boniface III constituted a turning point in Church history. His selection of this event to mark the establishment of the Papacy warrants careful consideration. This date was crucial for Luther's view of this last epoch; furthermore, the event later assumed great importance in Protestant historiography and served as a vital weapon in the armory of Protestant polemic.[11]

Though Luther remained quite consistent in his assertion of Gregory as the last acceptable figure of the early Church, he showed some hesitation in determining the event which had established the Papacy and had secured the growing corruptions. At Leipzig he suggested a time in the latter part of the seventh century; although the bishops of Greece had not recognized the act, Constantine IV had legally granted to Rome the primacy of honor (2:236, 280). For nearly two decades during that period of his career when he was not specifically concerned with the past of the Church, Luther made no apparent effort to redefine this judgment. He did indicate

10. See Hefele-Leclercq, 2/2, 834–35, on the question of this title at Chalcedon.

11. Cf. Preuss, *Antichrist*, pp. 234–36. Polman, *L'Élément historique*, pp. 164–66, 497.

his awareness of the fact that the appointment of a patriarch for Constantinople had initiated a protracted struggle between the two sees for the primacy; and in one instance he insinuated that Rome had not emerged victorious until the time of Charlemagne (*EA* 60: 200; cf. *WA* 50:577). Apparently, not until 1538[12] did he locate the establishment of the Papacy in 606 with Phokas' granting to Boniface III the primacy of honor. Significantly, he associated this event with the appearance of the Turk and with the prophecies concerning the realm of the Antichrist (*TR* 3104b). By the frequent reassertion of this date during the remaining years of his life, Luther indicated his definite acceptance of the event as the crisis for the early Church (cf. 39/2:74; 50:578; 53:142, 170; 54:218 ff.). In his last tract against the Papacy written a year before he died, Luther described in more than usual detail the circumstances surrounding Boniface's acquisition of the long-sought supremacy from a man who had murdered the entire imperial family (54:229–30).

There can be no question that Luther committed himself to the rapprochement of Boniface III and the Emperor Phokas as the event which had established the Papacy. Yet it appears somewhat peculiar that he should have articulated the idea so late in his life. On the other hand, his apparent silence concerning this act does not prove that he was unacquainted with the idea and did not accept it prior to 1538. Moreover, the importance of the event did not originate with him. Among some of the Hussites the work of Phokas had rivaled that of Constantine for marking a terminal date in the corruption of the Church. The idea entered popular literature very early in the Reformation and seemed to enjoy some currency.[13] Therefore, the more relevant problem is that of determining the reason for Luther's shift from the later date of Constantine IV to the earlier one of Phokas.

At Leipzig, one year before he publicly came to identify the Anti-

12. A passage in the *Table Talk* of 1533 cites this date, but this passage appears to be a later insertion on the part of Aurifaber. Cf. *TR* 507.

13. Preuss, *Antichrist*, pp. 53, 194–95.

christ with the Roman Papacy, Luther had expressly adduced the fact relating to Constantine IV's decree in order to emphasize the superiority of the imperial authority and to prove the imperial establishment of the Papacy (2:280). Once Luther had recognized the Papacy as the Antichrist, its imperial origin did not suffice; the satanic and eschatological elements had to be included. Therefore, it is hardly surprising that when Luther returned to the problem several years later, he should have selected the date for the lurid events surrounding Phokas, by which he could more easily relate the Papacy with the origin of the Turk and the prophecies concerning the Antichrist. In his initial observations he established these points and compared the fratricide that began the Roman Empire with the fratricide which brought the imperial Papacy into being (cf. 50:578). Finally, in his last tract against Rome, which asserted in its title the devilish foundation of the Papacy, he described the concrete introduction of the satanic element into the Roman church at this time. Once having obtained the necessary recognition from the Emperor, the popes had immediately begun to publish decrees which claimed the Papacy to have been founded neither by emperors nor by councils but by Christ himself (54:230, 236). And concomitant with this first appearance of the Antichrist, the eschatological nature of the entire epoch became more prominent.

Both Luther's knowledge and his understanding of the early Church terminate with Gregory the Great; the growth of the satanic and eschatological elements belongs to another period. Luther's complex attitude toward Gregory reflects essentially his relation to and view of the early Church. As in human life itself, nothing escapes corruption, and no period in Church history is pure. The work of heretics, the elaboration of ceremonies, the growth of human traditions all seek to destroy the proclamation of the gospel. Ultimately, however, Luther could accept this period of the Church, as he could accept Gregory, for in each he discovered historical witnesses opposing the abomination of the Antichrist which now sat in the very temple of God.

5. THE APPEARANCE OF THE ANTICHRIST

If a critical attitude distinguished Luther's relation to the period of the early Church, scriptural prophecy determined his view and understanding of the subsequent centuries. With the earlier period he had benefited trom the more abundant and accessible source material, and his knowledge and use of these documents had tended to obscure, if not to eliminate, the distinction between the period of the tyrants and that of the heretics. But with the later period, which was long to remain comparatively uncharted by historical investigation, no such threat presented itself to the application of scriptural prophecies to the past of the Church; and Luther's own experience served to confirm these prophecies. To understand the calamity that had befallen the Christian faith and which confronted it in his own day, Luther turned to Daniel, Paul, and John. He discovered there his answer in terms of the abomination of the Antichrist which marked the last time of the Church, and consequently of the world.

Luther's identification of the Papacy with the Antichrist naturally afforded great polemical opportunities. Yet it would be a gross misjudgment to limit this identification to the level of expediency and religious controversy. Such an interpretation disregards the general outlook of the sixteenth century and the Christian understanding of history. Man had long lived in the shadow of the Antichrist and in the expectation of the end. There had previously been numerous identifications of existing or expected ills with this dreaded figure that marked the last time.[1] Based upon his own experience and the prophecies in Scripture, Luther's recognition of the Papacy as the Antichrist had a determinative influence on his entire view of Church history and provided the groundwork for his understanding of the last time. The concrete reality of this Antichrist together with all its implications appeared unquestionable, and what for Luther was a conviction became later a matter of official doctrine in the book of Concord.[2]

To account for this subversion of the Church during such a number of centuries, Luther gave an answer that conformed to the prophetic basis of this abomination and the eschatological dimensions of its historical reality: the papal abomination had neither come from God nor in His name, but through God's wrath it had been founded by the Devil for the punishment of sins. God's wrath allowed the Devil to effect this abomination within the Church for such a length of time (54:232, 235; cf. 40/1:245). Luther could see the entire period since Gregory the Great as belonging to the Antichrist; for nine hundred years the abomination had worked to remove the Christian people almost entirely (45:37). On the other hand, he claimed from his earliest years that the worst perversions had originated only three hundred years previously (1:677). At the end of his life he identified the advent of the abomination with the pontificate of Gregory VII and made Antichrist the governor of the sixth millennium (53:152, 154).

Beyond these simple references to the origin and revelation of the Antichrist, Luther felt little responsibility for the temporal definition of this period of nine hundred years. Instead his efforts con-

1. See Preuss, *Antichrist*, pp. 10–83.

2. Ibid., p. 231.

centrated upon the depiction of the nature of the Antichrist whose countenance he recognized in the contemporary Papacy and whose features he read back into the vague past. Thus the main attempt in the present study is not to discover a sequence of events for this period but to elucidate the fundamental ideas which express the nature of the Antichrist and which explain its relation to the true Church. While not neglecting the prophetic, satanic, and eschatological aspects of the Antichrist, the investigation seeks to examine the relationship between the Church and the Papacy in terms of the two basic ideas of tyranny and apostasy. Tyranny, as it appears in both the worldly and the spiritual Regiment, claims prior consideration, for it best describes the monstrous proportions of the abomination which has now manifested itself in Church history. Inextricably bound up with the notion of tyranny is an idea of apostasy that adheres to the prophecies of Scripture. In the idea of apostasy the continuity of the hidden Church again assumes a central significance. The historical reality of the Antichrist astride the entire life of the Church presents the final and most terrible apostasy in Church history.

Tyranny

In the year 1521 the Antichrist sat for its first formal portrait at the hands of Martin Luther. With his *Reply to Ambrosius Catharinus,* Luther went beyond a mere rebuttal to this Italian apologist for the traditional faith; here he gave full expression to his recently attained conviction that the Papacy was the Antichrist. The significance and vigor of the tract derive from its author's skillful use of scriptural prophecies. The profusion of scriptural citations is not accidental, because Luther asserts in the work itself that, except for Christ, the New Testament bears witness to nothing so much as to the Papacy, and the Old Testament also provides testimony as to this reality (7:722). Indeed the tract assumes the form of a commentary upon the latter part of the eighth chapter of Daniel with appropriate elucidation from the ninth chapter of Revelation and the crucial text in the Second Epistle to the Thessalonians. These passages establish the tone and setting for understanding Luther's view of the Antichrist. They refer to the last flickering gasp of temporal government and to the unnatural abomination which comes to dominate the Church in the closing days of the divine wrath. Upon the solid structure of scriptural prophecy Luther now raises his accusation against the tyrannical nature of this satanic and eschatological reality.

In his conception of the Antichrist, Luther parted company with all the popular notions and with earlier attempts to locate it in some aspect of a corrupt Roman Church. Rather than associating it with any person or pope he squarely identifies it with the entire institution of men and succession of those ruling the Papacy. Luther's explanation of the Antichrist's nature hinges largely upon his exegesis of Daniel 8:23, where he gives separate treatment to the two ideas of being replete with external forms (*potens faciebus*) and of understanding the darkness of human laws (*intelligens propositionum*) (7:728–40, 740–48). The two major aspects of this tyranny emerge —the anomalous character of this new power and the extradoctrinal quality of its traditions. Concerning the former, he understands the papal tyranny to have risen up and grown out of the Roman Empire, thus succeeding the fourth and last monarchy. While the title of empire has fallen to the German people, the substance of empire now rears itself as a new sort of tyranny over both bishops and kingdoms which the Papacy fashions according to that absurdity, the Donation of Constantine. The second aspect pertains more to the inner nature of the Antichrist. Luther accuses this tyranny of inventing new glosses and statutes that lead away from the royal road of faith into the fragmentation of the religious life through works (7:722–26). Each aspect needs to be considered more closely.

In respect to the numerous outward forms of this tyranny, Luther does not limit his understanding to the externalization of the religious life in pomp, ceremonies, superstitions, rites, and many other appearances. By frequent returns to the thought that this realm is neither a spiritual nor a worldly authority, he seems to be concerned with an idea greater than mere externalization (7:729). Inward and outward, bound and free have reversed their proper places. The introduction of laws and prescriptions where they were never intended to exist promotes a realm of external forms which possesses in its darker aspect a confusion and subversion of all the divinely ordained orders. Behind the accusation of externalization looms the more terrible fact of a complete anomaly that confuses and overthrows the existing orders. Following the crucial Pauline text, 2 Thessalonians 2:4, Luther refers to the pope as a quasi-god and laments the infamous mixing of Christ and His vicar. The Church of Satan becomes the Church of God and differs from all other realms in that it grows with words and not with arms. It teaches neither mundanely nor spiritually but simulates the latter and achieves the former. While it derives from the Roman Empire, the papal imperium belongs to neither Regiment but confuses them both under its own novel tyranny (7:741–44). By a power not its own and by the oppressive force of its external appearances, it establishes the most terrible tyranny over both the spiritual and the worldly orders. Such an abomination can only pertain to the end of the world (7:750–52).

Luther's understanding of the Papacy's external forms implicitly expressed his notion of the Antichrist's anomalous nature. It was anomalous because it conformed to none of the divinely ordained estates but confused them into a new, contrived order. Indeed the very perversion of vocations and obliteration of the distinction between the Regimente expressed the substance and chief support of its tyranny. This aspect of the Antichrist, which was adumbrated in the tract against Catharinus, became more explicit and pronounced in other works written later in Luther's life. With the Antichrist, the satanic element had entered into the vocations to pervert them; bishops were no longer masks (*larvae*) of God but had become *larvae* of bishops (8:429; 38:229). Worse still was the confusion of the two Regimente which the Devil had successfully welded together (51:239; 7:173). In emphasizing the confusion and destruction of the divinely appointed orders by this quasi-spiritual power, Luther includes the third Regiment, for even marriage has been defiled.[3] Luther's original designation—*Endechristliche Regiment*—best expresses the eschatological and satanic magnitude of this novel, contrived order (cf. 15:43; 26:507). Thus he recognizes no magistracy in the Papacy, because it has ordination neither from God, from natural law, nor from men. The Emperor Phokas did not give the pope authority but merely the honor, which has been scandalously abused to form a tyranny. The Papacy has thus instituted itself with the help of the Devil (39/2:74). In his last polemic against Rome, Luther reiterated the view that the Papacy's assumption of both spiritual and worldly authority, yet its inability to discover its origin in either of the only two divinely ordained Regimente, proved that the papal estate was a human fabrication of devilish origin (54:237–39).

With his consideration of the Antichrist's external aspects, Luther sought to represent the cancerous growth that had risen above and obliterated the lines of vocation and divinely ordained authority. In his treatment of the second major aspect of this tyranny, the abundance of laws, he attacked the substantial and dynamic power of this new authority. For Luther's concern with the injured conscience referred to the usurpation and perversion of the teaching office which had transformed the religious life into a jungle of prescriptions (7:745–46). Here Luther pursues an exegesis of the ninth chapter of Revelation to express the unique nature of this calamity. What follows from the fifth angel's sounding of the horn can only be applied to the Roman bishop and his forming of decrees. No other bishop has ever arrogated to himself this power; with these pontiffs

3. *ARG, 23,* 24–25. The Weimar edition does not include Luther's fragmentary exegesis of Daniel. The definitive edition is that of O. Albrecht, "Luthers Arbeiten an der Uebersetzung und Auslegung des Propheten Daniel in der Jahren 1530 und 1541," *ARG, 23* (1926), 1–50.

alone there has always existed this terrible tyranny in making laws and subjecting others to them (7:737). Following the Pauline text that the Antichrist will sit in the temple of God, Luther presses on to the core of this tyranny and arrives at the heart of his argument:

> But what does it mean to sit other than to rule, to teach, and to judge? For who has ever dared from the beginning of the Church to call himself a teacher of the entire Church except the pope? None of the saints, none of the heretics ever voiced such a frightful expression of pride. . . . For what does it mean to be the Vicar of God but to sit in the place of God? What does it mean to sit in the place of God but to show himself as if he were God? [7:741]

To the Antichrist alone belongs this supreme presumption.

The Papacy's perversion of the magisterial responsibility and the consequent traditions of men have already received considerable attention in this study and require no further demonstration in Luther's other writings. Nevertheless, the relationship of the Antichrist to this appropriation of the divine authority and the deplorable effect of human traditions need to be emphasized. In his reply to Emser written in the same year as that to Catharinus, Luther returned to the Pauline text which refers to the Antichrist of the last time (*Endchrist*) as the man of sin and son of perdition. Through his own law and doctrine this figure of the last time turns all the world away from God and prevents God and mankind from coming together. Idolatry is nothing other than subservience to such human doctrines and all prophets have struggled to maintain God's word in the people against these human doctrines. The distinctive feature of the Antichrist and the magnitude of his tyranny consist in his being present in the Church itself under the guise of Christ, and in his persecuting of all who do not obey his prescriptions (7:664). Theologically, this assumption of a magisterial power within the Church means that Christ is made simply a judge and thus crucified again (40/1:325); religiously, this imposition of new burdens makes the popes butchers of men's consciences (40/2:140). In directing his polemic against the human traditions as the core of this tyranny, Luther indicated that his controversy with Rome was doctrinal rather than moral. It was directed against an institution instead of against particular individuals.

This tyranny rears itself above all the divinely appointed orders and over the two Regimente. As the last persecution and the last apostasy in Church history the Antichrist, according to its nature, engulfs the worldly as well as the spiritual Regiment. The fate of the worldly Regiment together with that of the German people now becomes an integral part of Church history in the broader perspective of the last time. Necessarily dim is Luther's knowledge of the events subsequent to Boniface III which culminate in the tyranny of the Antichrist. The prophecies of Scripture and the idea of the *translatio imperii* provide the basis for his understanding of the papal encroachment upon secular authority. The contemporary criticism of the Donation of Constantine and his own knowledge of canon law serve to shape this understanding.

Luther inherited the idea of the *translatio imperii* from medieval historiography, but in his first treatment of the problem involving the fourth monarchy he made a significant distinction. Against the Roman claim that the pope had taken the Holy Roman Empire from the Greek emperor and had bestowed it upon the Germans, Luther objected that the true Roman Empire, which appears in Numbers 24 and Daniel, had long been at an end. Because the eschatological figure of the Antichrist had already appeared, Luther felt no obligation to maintain the fiction of the Roman Empire's persistence. The Goths had overrun this empire and the rise of the Turkish Empire had completed its destruction; Africa and Asia had been lost, and Venice had arisen to consume what had once belonged to Rome. Luther claims that the pope merely robbed the Greek emperor of the name and title and gave these to the Germans with the intention of building another Roman Empire subject to himself. Only through a gift of God did the Germans transform this title into a second Roman Empire of which the pope in 1520 still held the treasure and the authority, the law and the freedom.[4]

A decade later, Luther pursued further this idea of the imperial Papacy's bestowal of a shadow empire. He attributes to the pope the resurrection of the fallen Roman Empire transferred from the Greeks to the Germans, and he recognizes the two beasts of the Apocalypse in this revival of the last monarchy by an imperial Papacy. He grants that it is more the shadow than the substance of the old empire. Yet in this image he discovers spirit and life, for it possesses estates, laws, members, offices, and it operates to some extent. While the Roman Empire has long since vanished, there still exist some of its lands and the city of Rome (*WAB* 7:414, 416; cf. *EA* 41:239). Aided by the publication of Valla's *Donation of Constantine* and arguing from the evidence supplied by current histories, Luther began to sharpen the basic themes of this interpretation.

Luther's understanding of the developing relationship between Papacy and empire attained stability during the last decade of his life in a view which embraced more of the historical evidence. On the one hand, it gave greater prominence to the role of Charlemagne and the substantial nature of a German Empire; on the other hand, it exploited the myth of the imperial title to indicate the aggressive, tyrannous designs of the Papacy. Luther criticizes the idea of a donation on the ground that the historical evidence disproved the existence of a papal domination of Italy, France, and Germany during the past twelve hundred years (50:75). Secondly, he rejects the whole idea of a papal *translatio imperii* and asserts a theory of division which had earlier been made by John of Paris.[5] The pope did not take the Roman Empire from the Greeks and give it to the Germans because the Lombards ruled in Italy for two

4. *WA* 6:462–64. Cf. 5:649; 7:723, 744, 748. For an earlier example of the limiting of *translatio* to the name or title, see Werner Goez, *Translatio Imperii* (Tübingen, 1958), pp. 176–77.

5. Goez, p. 286; cf. p. 222.

hundred years, and it was not the pope's to take or to give. In the subsequent invasions of Italy, Charlemagne helped the pope. The Christmas Day ceremony merely meant that Charlemagne was Roman emperor in the West, while the Greek emperor continued in the East. The split was not unusual and had occurred several times previously (54:295–97). Actually Charlemagne accepted nothing from the pope; in fact he gave much. The Roman bishop owed the salvation of his see to Charlemagne, who restored the defenses against the Lombard king. Prior to the coronation, Charlemagne held Germany, Gaul, and Lombardy. Indeed he wanted to accept the imperial title from the Greek emperor rather than from the pope. Yet Luther recognizes how vain the weight of historical evidence is, for the papists persist in claiming themselves to be the givers of empire. They seek to revive the old Roman Empire, and having given the title, they hope by an alien labor to acquire the thing itself (50:105; cf. 54:282).

In attempting to relate the origin of the papal tyranny with the number 666 of Revelation, Luther once suggested that the Papacy's lordship over kings had followed immediately after Charlemagne (*EA* 60:200; cf. *WA* 45:41–42). Nevertheless his other statements, drawn from his writings as well as from the *Table Talk,* supported the general view presented in his treatment of the translation of the empire: the German Empire had prospered for several centuries before the Papacy, under Gregory VII, transgressed its proper relationship to the secular authority and moved toward that mixed tyranny which became a fact with Boniface VIII. Down to the eighth generation, Charlemagne and his successors ruled the empire without the pope's having any authority in respect to the imperial election; and down to the fourth generation, no pope was elected without the emperor's knowledge and permission. Luther suggests that at this time the pope ruled Italy as a convenience to the emperor. This satisfactory arrangement collapsed when Gregory VII objected to the imperial control of episcopal elections (*TR* 3620; *EA* 60:208). Driven by ambition and avarice, the popes beginning with Gregory

VII now strove to obtain temporal authority by force of the sword and by the thunder of the ban (*TR* 6457; 53:152, 154). In the subsequent struggle between empire and Papacy, Luther emphasizes the appalling nature of the new realm of Satan by capitalizing upon a single event during the reign of Frederick Barbarossa. Luther depicts the triumphant pope, Alexander III, placing his foot upon the neck of that pious emperor and quoting the appropriate verse from the Psalms.[6] If the pope can perpetrate this most unchristian act upon a person in such a high, divinely ordained office, Luther questions what safety there can be for the ordinary Christian (54: 308–09; 47:581; cf. 22:27–28).

The emperors lacked fortune in their struggle, and the popes banned and condemned them. By the control of investiture and the imposition of oaths, the Antichrist succeeded in assimilating much of the secular authority (54:298; 47:580–81). By abandoning their posts, magistrates allowed the papal bishops to move into the temporal authority (43:189). The papal aggrandizement culminated with Boniface VIII and his extensive use of indulgences (cf. *TR* 3104b). Luther claims that the German emperors still exercised a real authority until the pontificates of Boniface VIII, John XXII, and Benedict XII. Here Luther exaggerates the importance of the Donation and intimates that its impossible claims were seriously pressed at this time. He describes Boniface's jubilee where the pope appeared on separate occasions, first dressed in papal splendor and later in imperial regalia, and demonstrated his assumption of the two swords of authority. Not content with having robbed the emperor of his right of investiture and kings of their feudal rights,

6. Psalm 91:13, "Thou shalt tread upon the lion and the adder: the young lion and the dragon shalt thou trample underfeet." Luther seems to be unaware of the theme's Augustinian elaboration. Cf. Ernst H. Kantorowicz, *The King's Two Bodies* (Princeton, 1957), pp. 70–73. For a general description of Luther's sources and use of the theme, see Hartmann Grisar and Franz Heege, *Luthers Kampfbilder, 3* (Freiburg im Breisgau, 1923), pp. 64–72. For the contemporary application of the theme to Luther himself, see Maurice Gravier, *Luther et l'opinion publique* (Paris, 1942), p. 296.

the Papacy in Boniface VIII raised its throne over God's Word, worldly authority, body, soul, and all the goods of men. With Boniface it became an article of faith that a pope cannot err. It was indeed a time of divine wrath (50:75–77).

Luther names the Antichrist the governor of the sixth age, for even more clearly than the assimilation of temporal authority does the subversion of the spiritual Regiment date from the period subsequent to Gregory VII. The reformer recognized very early in his career that the full effects of this tyranny upon the religious life had appeared only in the past three or four hundred years. With respect to human traditions and the assumed right of legislation, he located the stabilization of this tyranny in the collection of decretals by Gregory IX, Boniface VIII, and Clement V (*WBr* 1:352). With respect to the systematic burial of the gospel he maintained that the Church had believed correctly for twelve hundred years, and only in the past three hundred had Aristotelianism introduced transubstantiation and its false philosophy (6:509). In fact, prior to his late identification of the first pope with Boniface III, Luther admitted the social vigor and ostensible rectitude in the self-devised sanctity and austerity of the early Papacy (32:347; 40/1:685–86). He stared at the gulf that separated these early Roman pontiffs from their legislating successors (6:571). While the forces that worked to obscure the gospel and to establish human traditions had existed in the earlier period, only in the sixth millennium did they attain their full expression and bear their bitter fruit.

The nature of the Antichrist's tyranny in the spiritual Regiment is twofold: the burial of the gospel and the establishment of human doctrines and practices. In his tract *On the Keys,* Luther illustrated this fact when he considered the first abuse in penitential practice. The pope's excessive use of the binding key produces a multiplication of laws and opposes Christian freedom (30/2:473). Luther refers to the second papal abuse as the erring key by which the effectiveness of forgiveness represented by the loosing key is made questionable and comes to depend upon the piety of the seeker

(30/2:483–84). The two aspects are inseparable; once the gospel has been neglected or denied, the way remains clear for the strivings of human merit and the tyranny of human prescriptions (cf. 42:185). For this reason Luther could consider Pelagius the ground and cornerstone of the papists, because he implicitly ignored Christ by believing that sin could be destroyed through one's own power (20:670).

The universities shared almost an equal place with the papal authority in this twofold subversion of the religious life. Luther warns against those who chop up Scripture into as many meanings as syllables, and in the universities he locates the fountain of this study and of so many questions, reasons, and opinions (5:281). This systematic corruption of Scripture has lasted three hundred years (1:677). With the rise of the new, scholastic theology there followed the disappearance of the theology of the Cross and the transformation of the Church into the widow of Christ (1:613, 620). Because it obscured and neglected the Word, scholastic theology degenerated into a philosophy and revealed its more positive aspect in its own doctrines and laws (42:349). Luther identifies the schools with Moloch and claims their governor to be Abaddon, the spirit of the abyss (8:473; 7:739). Aristotle became greater than Christ in these engines of the Devil. Elevated by the authority and work of Thomas Aquinas, Aristotle ruled, reviving free will, teaching moral virtues, and promoting natural philosophy (7:739). Beyond this recrudescence of philosophy and human reason, the study of law led to the neglect of the gospel and the multiplication of laws and practices apparent in the papal decretals (2:226). But the theological faculties represented the gravest danger. They were the fonts of error which produced the new doctrines that devoured the religious life (8:460, 474). From the universities the Roman tyranny acquired the four new sacraments, and by the prestige of these schools they were maintained (6:571). Here Luther discovers the false teachers and wolves of whom Scripture warns. For, rightly understood, Peter meant that there will come universities, doctors, priests, and monks who will introduce orders and ruinous sects and will seduce mankind with false doctrines (14:33–34, 36).

By the burial of the gospel and by the promotion of their own works, the universities have the same effect upon the life of the Church as the papal magisterium with its traditions. The fragmentation and destruction of the common Christian life constitutes the effect of this tyranny, and to understand it one needs to consider the profound significance behind Luther's accusation that the pope is the heresiarch *par excellence:*

> Heresies have always existed in the Church, as has been previously noted. The pope, however, is the universal heresiarch and head of all heretics for he filled the world, as if by a flood, with an infinite number of sects. No monk agrees with another for they measure sanctity by the severity of the orders. Here a Carthusian wants to be esteemed holier than a Franciscan etc. Indeed in the papist Church there is no unity of Spirit, no concord of minds but the greatest discord. There is not one and the same doctrine, faith, religion, worship, and mind but the greatest diversity. On the other hand all Christians are common and the same in the Word, faith, worship . . .
>
> [40/2:114]

Luther was not alone in carrying the charge of heresy and sectarianism into the Roman camp; contemporary cartoons and the outstanding historian of the age pursued similar arguments.[7] For the reformer, however, this confusion of sects had arisen from the subversion of the common order and unity in the Word and the sacraments. Luther could recognize in the Papacy a certain unity embracing this diversity and confusion. Yet it was a contrived unity and did not rest on a common baptism, sacrament, and preaching. Before the Leipzig debate he suggested that the primacy of the Papacy had been stabilized in order to resist schismatics and

7. Sebastian Franck, *Chronica, Zeÿtbuch und Geschÿchtbibel* (Strassburg, 1531), CCCCLXII ff.

heretics (2:186, 229). In this purpose it had not only failed but had in effect produced more factions and sects (50:216). Twenty years after the debate he compared the Papacy to the Pantheon where the Romans had sought to bring all the idols of their gods within one city that they might live happily together and in concord. Similarly, under the Papacy the world is as full of factions and sects as it had previously been under the pagans. To preserve such a unity and peace the pope merely confirms the orders, foundations, churches, pilgrimages, and brotherhoods which seek to be designated as holy. In this particular instance Luther emphasizes the peace and unity which exist within this empire of diverse factions and orders because he wishes to reassert the familiar theme that Christ's presence and the true Church mean division, struggle, and even heresy. Yet the common Christian order, if it brings heresies and sects (*Rotten*), includes no factions (*on secten*) (50:271–73).

Thus the papal unity appears as a merely mundane unity that bears no resemblance to that more profound unity and community in Christ, which withstands the onslaught of heresies and sects. The image of the Roman Pantheon occurs more than once and serves to represent that papal unity which enfolds a luxuriance of heresies (cf. 7:677). Luther can observe that the pope has fastened an abominable disunity on the Church with his sects. One goes into a monastery, another into the desert and each follows his own sense together with what the pope has taught. Baptism and the Lord's Supper no longer suffice (47:586; cf. 10/2:219–20).

This tyranny of sects, which destroys the community of the Church in Christ, requires an examination of what sectarianism or heresy signified for Luther. From his earliest lectures he presented the main characteristics of heresy which he retained throughout his thought. Heretics seek their own wisdom and absolute purity in special works and in an excessive piety beyond the common society of the Church (3:292, 445; 4:77, 93; cf. 32:519; 43:495–96). Only in respect to tradition did his understanding of heresy in these early lectures differ from that in his later thought; once having arrived at his principle of scriptural authority, Luther no longer accused heretics of insisting upon the old and of refusing to move forward but claimed rather that they introduced new doctrines and works (4:345, 366; cf. 50:558). These features, however, are merely attributes of heresy and do not reveal its essential root and nature. Ultimately, the basis of heresy derives from one's partial or false relationship to Scripture or to Christ the Word, which alone creates the priesthood of all believers and the community of the Church.

Luther defines heresy as an obdurate errantry in respect to Scripture. For this reason he discovers that the papists shrink from calling the evangelicals heretics but refer to them as schismatics, disturbers, the new thing, or the protesting estates (54:288). This opposition is an opposition to the Word of Christ which the Spirit communicates through Scripture. Luther observes that the Devil has entered into Scripture; he has transformed it into a book from which all heresies derive (23:65). In the same way he maintains that all heresies are Christological in nature, because each appropriates but a fraction of the main article of faith. This failure of heretics to take the outer Word in the whole of Scripture or to accept the inner Word in the fullness of Christ appears in Luther's earliest writings and persists in his mature thought (3:174; 4:66; 56:251). All heresies arise from neglecting the simplicity of the words of Scripture and from affecting tropes and their consequences (18:701). In characterizing sectarianism, Luther finds that the sectarian does not wish to hear the preached Word but claims to cogitate it in his own heart (37:136).

The basis for Luther's judgment upon the pope as the heresiarch and its meaning for the corporate life of the Church now become apparent. The pope claims to bear all laws within his breast and to possess the Holy Spirit[8] (50:245; 7:427). But still worse is his partial

8. On the actual meaning of this assertion in canon law, see F. Gillmann, "Romanus Pontifex iura omnia in scrinio pectoris sui censetur habere," *Archiv für Katholisches Kirchenrecht, 92* (1912), 3–17.

appropriation of the inner Word. For the distinctive feature of this heresy and of the Antichrist is its propensity to attack the merit instead of the person of Christ. The Antichrist alone invades the main principle of the gospel's doctrine and makes the overcoming of sin a matter of one's own works and merit. Because Christ has died only for original sin, each person must rely upon his own powers after baptism. Thus the ground appears for works, masses, and special orders in the scramble of isolated individuals for salvation (20:669–70, 672; 50:268). In the light of this general conception of heresy and sectarianism, Luther's statements in his tract against Catharinus assume greater significance. The false teachers and their traditions, which produce these sects, create a dissension and fragmentation of the religious life. Rather than denying Christ openly, they deny Him in respect to the doctrine of justification and lead people away from the gospel and the royal road of faith into the divisions caused by the purchase of salvation. Here the neglect of the gospel and the establishment of human traditions cooperate in creating a fatal confidence in the efficacy of good works. This egocentric trust necessarily produces a sectarianism which consumes the common Christian order and marks the last time of the Church (7:724–28).

The growth of a superior piety, the distinction between an elite of holiness and the ordinary Christian, and the proliferation of mendicant and monastic orders reveal the bitter fruit of this righteousness based on human merits. Luther berates St. Thomas for subscribing to the doctrine which the universities have promulgated that monks and priests are in a better estate than the common Christian (12:353). The time of the Emperors Henry IV and Henry V marked the great increase in the number of monks, who in their new holiness of outward works constituted another race of Pharisees (50:610; 32:359–60). While he recognizes the personal gifts of the great saints during these centuries, Luther laments the fact that the imitation of their virtues has created new orders (42:453–54). He objects particularly to the new law of Franciscan poverty and condemns the orders of Francis and Dominic for obscuring the benefits of Christ and burying the gospel (42:495–96; 40/2:180). For St. Bernard, Luther always manifested a definite preference as the most sincere and pious of all the monks. Although he could admire the religious genius of Bernard apparent in his mystical writings, he rejects the bad example set by this most perfect of monks. Imitation of Bernard promoted that life which is opposed both to nature and to the Church.[9] Together with such saints as Francis, Dominic, and Bonaventure, Bernard follows Gregory the Great in being saved not by his monastic piety of external works but by finally breaking through into the Christian common life of faith in Christ (7:774; 8:451–52). And in his apotheosis of Savonarola, Luther discovers in the Dominican friar one who walked by his meditation on the gospel rather than by the statutes, cowl, masses, and works of his order; he lived not by the order of preachers but by the common order of Christians (12:248).

With this conception of vocation and the common life of the Christian, Luther attacked the entire order of special works, special revelations, and a special class of religious virtuosi. Appropriating the language of traditional theology, he imparts a new meaning to the concepts of the contemplative and the active life. He defines the contemplative or speculative life as the apprehension of Christ in faith, and from this justifying faith, man goes out into the active life of charitable works toward his neighbor (40/1:447). While man's contemplation resides in the promise, his action remains in the Decalogue which defines the works of his vocation (44:194–95). Luther deplores the monk's pre-empting of the contemplative life and the whole division and specialization of functions among classes. He objects to the customary exegesis of the passage in Genesis which concerns the eyes of Rachel and Leah: the beautiful eyes of Rachel supposedly accommodate her to the contemplative life, while Leah with ignoble eyes has the political and economic activities heaped

9. *TR* 4472. Cf. Koehler, *L. und K.*, pp. 320–33.

upon her. The contemplative life cannot be limited to the sterile visions of the monk in his cell. But both contemplative and active lives are exercised together, for the political and economic responsibilities pertain to all men who live in faith (43:667–68).

Luther consciously opposes his understanding of the common life of the Christian in his calling to the elaborate system of special orders and functions which has emerged under the Antichrist.

> [As regards] the papist abomination which has been introduced into the Church in the past centuries, the papists provide themselves profusely with tonsures and cowls and refer to all other orders as secular and unprofitable. We are the spiritual ones, they said, we pray for others; you citizens, peasants, princes, nobles, and all secular persons are not able to serve God. Therefore give your gold, silver, coffers, towns, and authority and we will pray for you night and day, while you plow the field, rule the family, subjects etc. . . . How horribly demented and foolish the entire world would have become through the papists, canonists, and sophists who have enclosed the invoking and worship of God within monasteries, as if God is not able to be worshiped and invoked in the common life. . . . Since the wife, the citizen, the prince, the noble is a creature of God and each of us is established in a certain office, therefore people who administer these in their respective positions may consider themselves pleasing to God provided that they abstain from sins. [44:260–61]

Luther's elaborate portrayal of the papal tyranny as the Antichrist derived largely from an intensive use of Scripture to support his criticism of the contemporary Papacy. Yet he did not limit himself to these sources and eagerly appropriated other material that confirmed the basic features of a tyranny which opposed the Word with its own laws and engulfed both Regimente. Luther's exposition of a reported vision, which a Swiss hermit of the fifteenth century had beheld, provides a good example of his adroit application of contemporary material to a basic theme. The substance of the hermit's vision was a frightful head of a man bearing a triple crown and having a beard parted in three places. Six swords radiated from this face; the two swords from his nostrils and the one from his forehead pointed outward. Three swords pointed inward toward the eyes and mouth respectively (26:132).

Luther had known previously about this vision, but in 1528 he applied its meaning to the Papacy as the Antichrist (26:130). The horrible face represents a bloody Regiment which rules over both body and soul. The first sword, which comes from the forehead, signifies human doctrine and human wisdom that destroy the Word. The sword from the right nostril represents canon law by which the Papacy rules in spiritual matters, and the sword from the left nostril represents its own worldly Regiment which dominates temporal affairs. Concerning the three swords which point inward on this terrible face, the one directed against the mouth is the Word of God, and the swords directed against the eyes signify the same Word in its respective opposition to the Papacy's encroachments upon both Regimente. The threefold beard represents those relying upon their own good works—monks, priests, and nuns; the learned—jurists, theologians, and teachers; and the powerful—kings, princes, and lords. The sword with its point at the hilt signifies that the Papacy supports itself on corrupted and misunderstood texts of Scripture (26:135–36). Luther continued to depict the Papacy as the Antichrist, but the main features of this portrait had been disclosed by the time of this little tract's appearance.

Luther's attack upon the Roman Papacy signified even more than a reformulation of the Christian tradition. It implied the rejection, if not the dissolution, of that superb universal order which had evolved in Latin Christendom from the time of Nicholas I to Innocent IV. The polemic against the Papacy, which Luther had initiated in his early *Lectures on Romans,* he had sustained with growing vehemence until his death. In its political and social implications his polemic directed itself against the idea and fact of hierarchy which had commingled the spiritual and the secular orders. In striving to distinguish these two authorities once more, Luther appealed to Paul and suggested an affinity with Augustine (30/2: 110). In fact medieval Christendom had obscured the independence of the secular authority held by Augustine and had developed the Augustinian elements which promoted the hierarchy. Without explicitly appealing to St. Augustine, Luther presented in his criticism of the papal hierarchy a certain parallel to his great predecessor. At the depth of his torrential abuse against the Papacy moved a most important aim: to reassert the mutuality of the two authorities and to subject the secular authority once more to eschatology rather than to ecclesiastical hierarchy.[10]

How had it been possible for this unique tyranny to confuse all orders and authorities and to break up the community of Christ with its burdensome traditions and special distinctions? According to Luther a single explanation and cause existed. He attributed the terrible deprivation and perversion of the Church to the wrath of God. This wrath had given the papists over into a reprobate sense for so many centuries (40/1:245). He distinguished between two counsels within the divine Providence. Not by a gracious but by a wrathful counsel of God has the pope risen above all bishops and as a plague on the world oppressed all mankind (6:321). Even the very failure of histories to account for this abomination he ascribed to the wrathful counsel of God (50:4). The Papacy belongs to the divine operation in time, but it represents a work of God's wrath, not of His grace (26:168).

10. For the medieval replacement of eschatology with hierarchy, see Walther von Loewenich, "Das Neue in Luthers Gedanken über den Staat," *Von Augustin zu Luther* (Witten, 1959), pp. 210–24. See also Ernst Kinder, "Gottesreich und Weltreich bei Augustin und Luther," *Gedenkschrift für Werner Elert* (Berlin, 1955), pp. 24–42, for an excellent comparison of the two thinkers on the problem in its larger context. H. -X. Arquillière, *L'Augustinisme politique* (Paris, 1934), especially pp. 67–72, traces the medieval departures from the political thought of St. Augustine.

Apostasy

In 1533 appeared the tract on *The Private Mass and Priestly Consecration.* The work represented Luther's chief polemical writing against Rome during the middle period of his mature thought. According to its author, the tract intended to attack private consecration and the private Mass and to present a distinction between the Church and the Papacy (38:255). Its significance for determining the relationship between the hidden Church and the Antichrist is apparent. In this tract the problem of ordination claimed particular attention, for Luther's conception of being called provided the ground upon which two priesthoods confronted each other, two Churches clashed. By presenting the issues of the sacraments' validity and the Church's continuity during a millennium of apostasy, the tract brought into focus the main themes of Church history.

In a preliminary sketch to his work, Luther outlined the peculiar situation and dilemma of the Church during this period. The presence of the Antichrist in the midst of the Church itself creates the problem. Luther asks how the throne of God can continue to retain its identity if the Devil sits upon it. Appealing to the indispensable Pauline text, 2 Thessalonians 2:4, he depicts that situation of the Church in which it appears simultaneously opposed to and yet dominated by the Papacy (38:188). Later he describes the Antichrist as standing in the holy place, corrupting the Word of God; and while the Church exists under the abomination, it is so closely mingled with the Papacy that only the Holy Spirit can distinguish the temple of God from the abomination which has assumed its name (38:219, 222). This peculiar relationship between the Church and the Papacy provides the context for Luther's conception of the validity and continuity of the ministry and the sacraments during this last time of the Antichrist. Furthermore, it leads to an understanding of the apostasy.

Luther's argument endeavors to reveal the insufficiency and invalidity of priestly consecration under the Papacy and to root ordination and the calling in the Christian community. While the Church must continue on earth, the fact remains that under the Papacy neither pastors nor preachers but only private priests were consecrated. The latter were certainly consecrated and anointed, but they were not called or ordained and brought to office. Their special consecration is distinct from the ordination and calling to the common Christian office of preaching and the ministry. Although the papists claim to have called no unconsecrated persons to the ministry, their consecration does not ordain a pastor or Christian calling within the community of Christians but only a private priest (38:220–21). Consecration itself had once constituted simply a calling to office. In time, however, the original institution of Christ had been perverted. A private consecration replaced the consecration to ministerial office; private priests for private masses followed, and a definite distinction arose between the true Christians and the priests of the Devil (38:228–29). Luther presents the picture of the entire hierarchy of these private priests from the lowest to the pope himself. This imposing structure calls itself the holy Christian Church, but actually it is the abomination in the abode of the Holy. It constitutes a people that lives for itself—a private rather than a public ministry which performs no service either in preaching or praying, baptising or ordaining, but only consecrates its own private priests (38:223, 229, 234).

Throughout this terrible trial the preservation of the Church rests as always with God. He maintains the sacraments under this abomination, and even if their use is against the Church, God has instituted them, and it is to Him, not to the administer or to the recipient, that they belong. Thus, despite its perversion, the calling remains legitimate (38:188). While the tract describes how the private consecration has corrupted all the sacraments and the entire ministerial calling, the deprivation suffered by baptism assumes a central significance for Luther's argument. Baptism provides the basis for the ministerial calling. The private consecration directly jeopardizes the meaning of baptism because it claims to accomplish something far higher and greater than baptism by making the consecrated priest superior to the common baptised Christian (38:227). With his consecration the bishop attempts to create *larven* priests, but according to the priesthood of Melchizedek one is born and called priest and has inherited his priesthood through birth from his mother and father. This last fact together with baptism makes one a true priest among the Christian people (38:229).

Once having reasserted the integrity and full significance of a common priesthood based upon baptism, Luther proceeds to locate the valid ministry amidst the abomination. For in baptism one is born a priest but not a preacher, minister, or teacher. To those offices one must be chosen or called (38:230). The ministry, its calling, and the proper consecration to the preaching office have suffered along with the sacraments from the private consecration. Nevertheless, against the abomination Christ has maintained by His power the office and the calling to the preaching office in His Church. Ministers and the preaching office have at all times been outside and over the special consecration; they have been bestowed by princes, lords, cities, even by bishops, abbots, and other estates, and through this investiture have remained the calling and the correct consecration to the ministry. Baptism and God's Word provide the basis for ministers and preachers. Through their election by the community, they are ordained and confirmed (38:236). In the Papacy, Christ has preserved His ministerial office under the abomination, and this ministry has pursued its proper office of changing or making nothing but simply giving or extending the gospel commanded by Christ (38:243, 239).

To explain the difficult question concerning the existence of the true Church during the period of the Antichrist, Luther reasserted many of his basic doctrines. The Church endures through the Word of God and Christ's institution of the sacraments. The central sacrament of baptism and the community's calling of persons to the ministerial office give a concrete reality to the common, public nature of the Church. Furthermore, this tyrannous and proximate relationship of the Papacy with the Church distinguishes the period of the Antichrist.

An examination of Luther's later statements confirms this view of the Church's relation to the Antichrist and its preservation during that trial. If his position appears somewhat more conservative and the Papacy seems to participate more fully in the sacraments and signs of the Church, the basic conception agrees with the statement of 1533. In *Against Hans Worst,* where he seeks to ground his evangelicals in the reality of the old Church, Luther's argument assumes an apologetic character and is therefore more restrained in its purpose. Significantly, he claims that baptism constitutes the first and pre-eminent sacrament and that both evangelicals and Catholics derive from the same baptism (51:479). He admits that both Churches stem from the old Church and have the same baptism, sacrament, keys, and text of the gospel. But while the evangelicals have held to the old nature of the Church and have received everything from the churches under the papists and not from the papists, the latter have not remained in the Church but have absconded to the Devil. Both parties are truly baptised, but the papists who live beyond the age of seven or eight renounce their blessedness and participate in the whoredom. With baptism and the Word, the true, old Church remains even under the Papacy (51:501–02, 506).

Likewise in his statements from the *Lectures on Genesis,* Luther sought to establish the validity of the contemporary ministry. At the same time, however, his conclusions suggested answers to the period in question. Luther cannot deny that through the ministry of the papists and their baptism the evangelicals have come into the fellowship of the true Church. Yet here his admission is not as great as would first appear, for he reminds us that the sacraments belong to God and an impious administer does not impair their validity. The papist ministry is valid only to the extent that it retains the substance in baptising, giving communion, and absolving (43:158). He grants that the papists belong to the Church because they have baptism, absolution, the Bible, and because many pious people exist among them. Since Christ and Belial cannot stand together, however, he claims that insofar as the papists have the pure Word and baptism, they belong with the evangelicals to the true Church; insofar as they retain human traditions along with the baptism and the Bible, they remain members of the papist Church (43:597–98). To the accusation that he and his followers have departed from the old Church, Luther answers that the statement would be true if they had departed from the Word. But since he and his followers have returned to the Word and are not apostates of the Word, they retain through it all the essentials of the true Church (42:334–35).

The Church, which has become the holy abode of the abomination, persists during this last time through God's power and wonderful action. Luther becomes quite specific in stating those elements which have served to maintain the Church: first, baptism; secondly, the text of the gospel in the vernacular; thirdly, the forgiveness of sins and absolution both in penance and in the fourth element, the sacrament of the altar which has been offered to the Christian at least during Easter and in one form; fifthly, the calling or ordaining to the ministerial and preaching office, and the general care of souls by which many persons have been recalled to Christ on their death beds; and finally, prayer, which here includes the Psalter, the Lord's Prayer, faith, the Ten Commandments together with many good songs and hymns both in Latin and in German. Through these elements have Christ and the Holy Spirit operated to preserve the Church (38:221).

Admittedly, the faithful have been few and the sacraments so obscured by traditions that the elect have come to participate in this corruption. Luther returns repeatedly to the image of Lot before Sodom and Elijah with the seven thousand; they express God's extrication of a small number from the great mass that rushes toward destruction (38:206, 221). Luther claims that there were some who benefited from the text of the gospel and used baptism correctly, while others like Bernard, Bonaventure, and many lay individuals wanted to believe in Christ when they were in the extremity of death (39/2:167–68). On other occasions Luther could discover the seven thousand in the Eastern Church which had never known the perversion of the private Mass (5:563; 39/1:140, 166).

In his fragmentary exegesis of Daniel, Luther defines a tripartite people that the Antichrist did not manage to seduce. First are the Edomites, the red colored ones or martyrs, who have permitted themselves by the pope, bishops, doctors and particularly by those blood hounds, the preaching orders, to be strangled, drowned, and burned throughout all the world up to the present. The second group is the Moabites or confessional ones of whom Bernard provides the model. Although they have not been public preachers, in dying they have left themselves to Christ and not to a private Mass. The first of the children of Ammon constitute the third group. As Ammon and Moab were brothers, Luther tends to relate these to the confessional group. He understands them to be those recently born into the people of God through baptism. Not having had a chance to consider the papal abomination, they neither strengthen nor weaken it as do the Edomites and Moabites. Such are the three orders of the saints—*Martyres, Confessores, Virgines* (*ARG* 23:36–37). And even within the Roman Church itself Luther postulates the existence of some Lots and their daughters who recognized the abominable nature of the Papacy (54:233).

For the sectarian groups of the Reformation, the Church existed among the heretics throughout the post-Constantinian period. For Luther the Church continued as it always had in the main stream of the divine operation, maintained and preserved through the Word and through the sacraments instituted by Christ. Partly because he saw the past of the Church in the light of his struggle with Rome, partly because of the essential vigor in the biblical outlook upon history, the period of the Roman abomination placed no strain at all upon Luther's understanding of Church history. The Church must always exist under, amidst, and even in the possession of its adversaries (39/2:183). In his conception of this last and greatest apostasy he explained the intimate involvement of, and yet distinct separation between, the hidden Church and the possessory Papacy:

> For we claim the Papacy not to be the holy Church nor any part of it, and we are unable to cooperate with it. Rather it is the horrid abomination and the Antichrist of the end, the enemy and adversary which devastates the Church, God's Word, and order, and sets itself over and against them like a god over all gods as Daniel and St. Paul have prophesied. And while we or the holy Church are not able physically to separate or detach ourselves from the abomination, Papacy, or final Antichrist until the Day of Judgment—for as Christ teaches the abomination should and must stand not outside but in the place of the Holy, and the Antichrist must sit not outside but in the Temple of God, and the Papacy must not be outside but in the Church—so we must continue to recognize ourselves spiritually and with a right understanding separating ourselves from him, guarding and preserving ourselves from his devastation. Thereby we remain pure in the right faith of Christ, resisting and defending ourselves against his excrements and vermin. [38:251]

In order to comprehend the nature of this apostasy in Church history, the eschatological and prophetic elements must be recalled and the historical reality of the Antichrist must be reaffirmed. If the previous passage suggests that the period of the Antichrist continues to the end, that idea is precisely what Luther intends. Not only does this terrible reality control the life of the Church until the Lord's coming, but its presence was discernible even while the apostles lived. Therefore, the events of the Church since Christ's Resurrection occur in an eschatological twilight provided by the presence of the Antichrist. With the massive support of prophecies drawn from Scripture, Luther's thought moves relentlessly toward its conclusion in defining the nature of the Papacy's apostasy:

> Pestilence, hunger, and sword signify that the pulpit and the Regiment of the Church are supposed to be entirely against the Church. Such an event St. Paul calls an *abfhal* just as the monks name those who have betaken themselves out of the cloister—their absconding monks. In German we call it the denier of Christ when in the Christian people such an *apostasia* or *abfhal* should occur that the absconding Christians are supposed to rule the Regiment and the true Christians are supposed to be deprived of it. [47:575]

Luther took seriously the prophecies concerning the revelation of the Antichrist in the last time. Guided by the Pauline prefixes, he understood the relationship between the Church and the Papacy both as an apostasy and as a tyranny. The Church appeared simultaneously opposed by and subjected to the Papacy. More precisely, Luther revealed the Papacy as the Antichrist ruling over the institutional Church and standing against the hidden Church.

6. THE ANTICHRIST AND THE LAST TIMES

LUTHER ADHERED to the common belief that the last period of Church history belonged to the Antichrist. According to him this period had already begun with the agreement between Phokas and Boniface III and would end with the return of Christ. Living at the end of this major period, however, Luther experienced a movement which distinctly opposed the long rule of the Antichrist and in all its aspects revealed the imminence of the end. What is generally known as the Reformation, and what Luther knows as a restoration of the evangelical light, belongs properly to the period of the Antichrist. But the intensification of the issues, the pressure of events, and the increasing complexity of the eschatological scene serve to distinguish the last times from the rest of the period which saw the advent of the Antichrist. Into these last times the Antichrist continues as the outstanding eschatological phenomenon, and in the form of the Papacy it still occupies the central position in Luther's consideration. Concomitantly, the restored light of the gospel involves a number of other issues which occur immediately before the imminent return of Christ. The appearance of the Turk, the growth of sects, and the new forms of unbelief move together with the Antichrist in the last times as signs of the impending Parousia.

The Restoration of the Gospel

After his forced encounter at Leipzig with the work of John Hus, Luther entertained a growing admiration for the Czech reformer. Besides acclaiming him as an outstanding martyr, Luther associated him with the restored light of the gospel. Although Gerson preceded Hus in the return to the reading of Scripture, the latter had given his life for the evangelical light (*TR* 5711). To Luther he appeared as a single man resisting council and world at a time when the Church seemed to be absolutely extinct. With his martyrdom, Luther maintained that the light of the gospel had begun to shine far more clearly in pious minds (44:774, 744). While he recognized the moral nature of Hus' attack upon the Papacy, Luther considered him to be his true evangelical predecessor and read into Hus' life and writings much of his own experience and thought.

In his fragmentary exegesis of Daniel, Luther identifies Hus with that blow which would lead to the final destruction of the Antichrist. The opposition of Lewis the Bavarian and Ockham to the Papacy, the Babylonian Captivity, and the Great Schism leading up to the Council of Constance—all served as the prelude to the blow which Christ spoke through Hus. Like Luther's own protest one hundred years later, Hus' action took place in the context of a sale of indulgences for the church of St. Peter at Rome; and his rejection of Clement VI's bull, which claimed the pope's immediate control of heaven and hell, continues the parallel. Hus made the stake inevitable by his advocacy of two ideas: that the pope, unless a pious man, was not a member of the holy Church; and that the pope was head of the Church by human, rather than by divine, law. While Luther sees these acts as a blow against the Papacy and as portending his own work, he recognizes that the Papacy managed during this period to retain its position, burning Hussites, setting Germans against Bohemians, and even increasing its simoniacal practices and abuses (*ARG* 23:32–34).

Luther's estimation of Hus reflects upon the historical judgment of the German reformer. Luther had first been attracted to Hus by the latter's observation that the papal primacy derived from Caesar (2:159, 279–80). At Leipzig he had concurred with several articles of Hus condemned by the Council of Constance. The most important were those concerning the nature of the Church. In Hus' reassertion of the Augustinian distinction between the organized Church and the holy Church as the number of the elect, Luther believed to discover his own conception of the Church.[1] After reading Hus' book *De ecclesia,* he accepted him fully into the common fold of Paul and Augustine, claimed all his articles condemned at Constance to be evangelical and Christian, and considered him a beginner in the great task of disclosing the light of truth (7:135–36; *WBr* 2:42). A year later at Worms, in restating this new position, Luther gave a more definite reason for considering these articles most evangelical and Christian: they pertained to that all important article—"I believe in the holy catholic Church" (7:612). Moved by a desire to use the support of the Czech reformer, Luther willingly confused an ecclesiology based upon election with one based upon faith.

Luther was aware of differences between himself and Hus. The latter did not go as far as Luther; he could accept the pope as head of the Church and honor him as long as his person was pious. But here the distinction was between the organized Church and the holy Church of the elect (47:585; 50:34). In appropriating Hus' ecclesiology, Luther repeatedly associated the condemned articles respecting the Church with the third article of the Apostles' Creed (*WBr* 2:324). Looking back at the Leipzig debates, he understood himself as having defended Hus' article that the universal Church was the assembly of the elect (5:451). Furthermore, in his public opposition to Rome and his concern for Scripture, Hus appeared to Luther as the first sign of the restored light of the gospel which culminated in his own time. Luther saw a congruence and link between the work of the Bohemian martyr and his own endeavors.

1. *WA* 2:287. Cf. Koehler, *L. und K.,* pp. 198–234.

He repeated the prophecy which Hus had made in prison when he punned that a goose would burn, but in a hundred years a swan would sing and people would listen (30/3:387). Constance marked the beginning rather than the end of a movement, for Hus now spoke through many others besides Luther himself (50:39).

Luther's recovery and apotheosis of Hus necessarily involved the censure of that council which had condemned him and his beliefs (cf. 7:612). Following Leipzig, Luther weakly attempted to uphold a concord between Constance and earlier great councils, but realizing the need to choose between them, he renounced his acceptance of the former. He supported this decision on the ground that the Council of Basle had itself reversed the ruling at Constance concerning a council's being superior to a pope (2:399–400). Thus the problem of Constance which had been raised at the Leipzig debate undermined the authority of conciliar decisions and produced a growing skepticism in Luther's thought as to the efficacy of councils. Within a short time, Constance became for Luther the most impious of all councils and the classic example of how a general and ostensibly legitimate council could err (6:561). The condemnation of those articles relating to the Church and the murder of Hus and Jerome made this council the junto of Satan (5:451–52).

With the increasing tension over the convening of a new council, Luther's attitude toward Constance became somewhat more complex. In 1533 he urged the rejection of the Nuncio Rangoni's proposals for a council on the ground that it would be run not according to God's Word but according to the pattern established at Constance and subsequently at Basle, Pisa, and the Lateran. Later in his remarks he singled out Constance as representative of this dangerous pattern, for it produced an unprecedented spilling of blood between Germans and Bohemians and the martyrdom of many thousand Christians (*WBr* 6:484, 486). Influenced by his rapproachement with the Bohemians and impelled by the approaching council at Mantua in 1537, Luther reiterated the theme of the needless bloodshed between the two nationalities and warned of the example of Constance. He now described the council's supreme care to have been the elimination of the schisms; it had entrusted to monks and sophists the cause of religion and matters of faith. Thus restored by this council from schism, the Papacy raged more fiercely and filled the world with its lies regarding indulgences and vendible masses, its worship of saints and its religion of works (50:23–24, 123–24). But Luther did not forget the fact that Constance had subjected the pope to a council and had deposed three popes (*TR* 5711). In his criticism of the Council of Mantua's postponement, Luther believed to descry the influence of the distant council of Constance which persisted in all minds. In this respect Constance made the popes fear any proposal for a council (50:92; 54:208–09). Despite these compensating features Constance remained in Luther's mind the council of Satan (53:167). Viewed in the light of the Papacy's deliberate policy of procrastination in the convening of a council, Constance contributed to his increasing distrust of and skepticism concerning the worth of a council (54: 220; 42:276).

In Daniel and in the Second Epistle of Peter, Luther discovered scriptural support for the event of the contemporary reformation; in the charged atmosphere of the last time, the major part of mankind would fall into error and concomitantly the gospel would expand its influence among people (14:66). Yet there exist instances in his thought where the contemporary movement appears as an unexpected coda to the last time of the Antichrist. The period of thirty-nine years during which the Papacy was divided prior to Constance signified that the end was at hand (cf. *ARG* 23:33). In considering those persons distinguished by sanctity and erudition who preceded and confirmed his doctrine, Luther remarks that none then knew that it would be later pleasing to God to add beside this sign of the end, the Word of the preached gospel. For Luther this apparently unexpected re-emergence of the gospel prior to the end could only be understood on the ground that God does not relinquish His Church but continues to send it Elijahs (26:123).

To Luther, reformation meant a reformation of doctrine from which all other improvements might follow. In his first statement respecting the nature of this reformation he recognized that its time and execution lay with God. Nevertheless, while he doubted the possibility, he could urge the necessity for a general and legitimate council to meet the more obvious abuses (1:627, 584). Shortly afterward he reiterated the hope that a council might restore communion to the laity in both kinds (6:498, 507). But by the time he came to publish his first commentary on Galatians in early 1519 Rome had become the pronounced enemy and the main obstacle to the reformation which he desired. Seizing upon a distinction made at the recent Diet of Augsburg, Luther expressed his love for the Roman Church while denouncing the Roman Curia (2:448–49). He now believed that it was impossible to elucidate Scripture and thereby reform other churches unless the Roman Curia and the entire hierarchy were reformed from top to bottom (2:609). After having written *To the Christian Nobility,* he claimed that at the time of its composition he had wanted to remain with the Papacy and, in adhering to it, reform it (7:645). To Alveld in the same year he set forth the conditions for this reformation within the established order of the Church: the refusal to accept from men new articles of faith, and his own right to judge all the actions and decrees of the pope according to Scripture (6:322).

By the end of the same year the tension between the two views of authority—the two conceptions of tradition—had become unbearable; Luther would have the papists restore the freedom of the Church and reject all its own laws and traditions (6:537). Shortly afterward against Emser, Luther expressed the nature and intention of this reformation:

> Thus have I advised and still advise that one does not propose a reformation, as Emser prates, which would improve human doctrines and canon law, for it is impossible, but that one should even burn up, junk, annihilate, and overturn them, or

> at least as much as one is able, and against them drive the double office of the letter and the spirit which may not be exercised if human doctrines remain as obstructions. [7:658]

So great was the prevalence of traditions and the tyranny of human customs that his expectations often appeared modest. In writing from the Wartburg to his followers in Wittenberg and with specific reference to the unreformed Castle Church, Luther recognized the limited effects of such a reformation. A general renewal was impossible. But it could be hoped that those working with right faith might sin less (8:474–75).

Such an understanding of the nature and intention of reformation persisted in Luther's thought. At the height of his career he explained what distinguished the present reformation from that of Wyclif, Hus, and others: previous reformers had attacked the morality of the papists; only he, Luther, had the vocation of assailing the doctrine. And while the evangelicals were probably no improvement upon the papists when judged according to their lives, the clarifying of the Word would lead to an improvement of morality (*TR* 624).

With its emphasis upon the purification of doctrine, he did not exclude the practical measures from his conception of reformation but comprehended them in so far as they promoted or derived from the exercise of the gospel. In 1534 he claimed that the gospel had cleared away much of the rubbish which impeded the Christian life but that the two pillars of the papist Church, the Mass and celibacy, now needed to be attacked (38:270–71). Writing to Prince George of Anhalt about the reformation rather than the elimination of episcopacy, he urged those practices that would allow the pure doctrine of the gospel to reign (*WBr* 8:432). In his tract *On Councils and Churches* he illustrated how Scripture alone could provide the authoritative basis for reforming the churches and for eliminating abuses. Shortly afterward he denied the need of a council for reform; a council's purpose was to investigate the churches and bring evangelical doctrine to light (51:529). At the end of his life Luther could see that the order of reformation had been reversed. Instead of beginning with an overhauling of doctrine and then proceeding to the purging of existing corruptions, the majority remained in the worship of a multitude of unknown gods and did not get beyond a concern for externals and vestments. Only the teaching of pure doctrine could bring about a real reformation (44:169–71).

Luther's understanding of himself and his own agency in respect to this reformation was quite consistent with his theology. He saw himself opposing papal indulgences one hundred and two years after Hus' death and almost a thousand years after Phokas had confirmed the Papacy (53:170). He could date the movement from his controversy with Tetzel and trace its development (51:538–42). He could even assert that through himself the whole business had started (*WBr* 2:460–61). But he never claimed the reformation as his own work and instead emphasized how he had been drawn unconsciously and helplessly into the matter (*ARG* 23:40). In describing his relationship to the agency of the Word, he understood himself as being seized (*rapi*) and acted upon rather than acting.[2] At the end of his life he described this action of God upon man as that divine strength which perfects our infirmity. Never does man do something better or holier than when he seems to be impotent and unable to do anything; nor does he perform anything more wisely than when he appears to himself most foolish. For in the things of God it is much safer for man to be seized than to act (*WBr* 9:610). With his conception of *rapi* he raised the human *cooperatio* to the level of religious intensity.

Luther saw himself as standing to the Word of God alone and never in any special agency or calling. At most he claimed to be an evangelist but preferred to emphasize his position as a doctor of theology.[3] The office of a called preacher and doctor in Holy

2. *WBr* 2:39, 149. Cf. Hans Preuss, *Martin Luther: Der Prophet* (Gütersloh, 1933), p. 111. Hereafter cited as *Prophet*.

3. Hans Frhr. von Campenhausen, "Reformatorisches Selbstbewusstsein und reformatorisches Geschichtsbewusstsein bei Luther 1517–1522," *ARG*, *37* (1940), 140. Cf. *WA* 30/3:386.

Scripture demanded from him the response which he gave it (31/1:212). He lacked the immediate self-awareness of the prophet and always wished to have his person disappear behind his work.[4] It is therefore misleading to consider Luther's awareness of himself under the concept of a prophet.[5] He may have made some predictions but they did not relate to any understanding of himself as a seer. Yet if he eschewed the crystal ball, he unconsciously assumed the leather mantle on several occasions (10/1/1:473, 497, 688). The Reformation was not to advance very far before Germany would hear his jeremiads.[6]

The cry of the Word which arose from the pope's own Regiment and which claimed one of the most vehemently antichristic papists, Martin Luther, leading him on from an attack upon the misuse of indulgences, to an assault upon indulgences themselves, and finally upon the entire Papacy—this resurgence of the gospel now located itself in little Wittenberg (*ARG* 23:40). In marveling that God should have raised up His Word in such a remote, insignificant corner of the earth, Luther refers to the popular legends of his native Thuringia which drew upon the medieval Sibylline Oracles concerning the Emperor of the Last Days.[7] He identifies Frederick the Wise with that Emperor Frederick who was to recover the sepulcher of the Lord. The sepulcher itself is nothing less than holy Scripture in which the truth of Christ has been buried by the papists and guarded with lies. While Luther ultimately relates God's election of Wittenberg to His previous election of Judea, he does not reject his own entertaining of this popular legend. Like Erasmus in his *Praise of Folly* he admits that he plays, but plays

4. Karl Holl, "Luthers Urteile über sich selbst," *Ges. Auf., 1*, 382, 397.

5. Cf. Preuss, *Prophet*, passim.

6. Cf. Gunnar Hillerdal, "Prophetische Züge in Luthers Geschichtsdeutung," *Studia Theologia, 7* (1953), 105–24.

7. On the medieval background to apocalyptical thought among the masses, see Norman Cohn, *The Pursuit of the Millennium* (London, 1957), especially pp. 110, 122, 142–48.

prudently.[8] Luther was neither the first nor the last to identify Frederick the Wise with the eschatological Emperor and to recognize in contemporary events the convulsion of the last time.[9]

The consequent struggle and dissension over the gospel Luther understood in the context of the two Churches which God bears down through history—the Church of possession and the Church of the Word. Here in this last struggle he could observe God's keeping the same distinction as He had between Abraham and the Babylonians, Isaac and Ishmael, Jacob and Esau (43:388). His conception of *Anfechtung* as a necessary ingredient of the Christian life played an essential part in justifying this struggle. To Emser's complaint that there was not a house in which Luther's doctrine had entered where tumult and division did not exist, Luther proudly claimed that it was a blessed unrest which God's Word awakes; for a right faith struggles against a false faith, and the suffering and persecution, which pertain to the proper nature of the Christian people, appear (7:280–81). There must be this struggle of two peoples over Scripture. Wherever the gospel goes, dissension and division must arise; where these features are absent, there are no Christians (24:435–36). And before eschatological images had come to assume the central place in his understanding of the present, Luther cast his judgment upon the deepening struggle and upon the nature of the Word's activity in history: what occurs quietly will fall into oblivion. But the discord within the womb of Rebecca, which the present judged unfavorably, would receive the better judgment of posterity (*WBr* 2:168).

A comparatively minor, yet interesting fact serves to demonstrate the emphatically eschatological nature of this period and of the Antichrist. Luther disagreed with Augustine on the question of Elijah's reappearance before the Last Judgment. Augustine had maintained that Elijah would return to earth in the last days, and

8. *WA* 8:475–76. On the idea of *serio ludere* as a methodical maxim, see Edgar Wind, *Pagan Mysteries in the Renaissance* (New Haven, 1958), p. 189.

9. Preuss, *Prophet*, pp. 9, 26–28.

he related the reappearance of the prophet to the task of converting the Jews.[10] Luther himself cannot accept this pious hope. In the first place he could not discover any scriptural basis for such a belief. Furthermore, it conflicted with his own understanding of the present. Luther was willing to identify Elijah with John the Baptist or with the contemporary outpouring of the Word, but he could not accept a future Elijah. The last time and the last days were now present and the Papacy with the Turk constituted the eschatological figure of the Antichrist which immediately preceded Christ's coming (10/1/1:146–48).

The spate of apocalyptic and astrological literature about the turn of the century only served to confirm Luther's basic interpretation of the period. Although at one moment he insinuated that the present tumult might be the flood which a Tübingen professor had predicted for 1524, he rejected astrology as a science.[11] Just as his theology discountenanced all astral influence upon man and particularly upon Christians, Luther rejected the Aristotelian explanations and assimilated the natural events, signs, and heavenly phenomena of his time into the prophecies of Scripture.[12] For Luther the re-emergence of the gospel had but one meaning: it signified the imminent approach of the end. While at all times the gospel had been preached in the world, never had it been so publicly preached as in this last time (14:84). No age more than his own had been so full of signs whether they were in the sky or on earth in the form of a monkish calf. But nothing attested so much to the imminence of the end as the brightness of the evangelical light (53:169; 11:380). For the preached gospel was like a light whose extinction would be preceded by a great burst of illumination. The gospel which now expanded would disappear in a puff and the Last

10. *City of God,* XX, 29. Cf. Otto of Freising, *The Two Cities,* VIII, 5.

11. *WBr* 2:248. *WA* 23:10. Cf. Koehler, *Quellen,* pp. 216–19. A. Warburg, "Heidnisch-Antike Weissagung in Wort und Bild zu Luthers Zeiten," *Gesammelte Schriften* (Leipzig and Berlin, 1932), *1,* 500, 512, 545.

12. Warburg, p. 650.

Judgment come. Similarly was it with a sick man who before death rallied, as if restored, but then expired (*TR* 5488).

Intimately associated with his awareness of the restored gospel and its eschatological significance is a continued comparison. He likens the present evangelical light to that at the time of the old Church, the primitive Church, and most particularly the Church of the apostolic period. In the greater number of instances Luther compares the present evangelical light as being similar but not quite equal to the light of the gospel during the apostolic period. While recognizing this sign of the end, he asserted with the same breath that not since the time of the apostles had there been such a light (11:208; 17/1:389). In 1520 he remarked that sacred letters had not been treated in a thousand years with such integrity and that this gift of God conformed most closely to that in the age of the apostles (*WBr* 2:149). With the return of the study of languages, Luther believed that the present period held the gospel almost as purely as the apostles but with greater purity than at the time of Augustine and Jerome (15:39).

Occasionally Luther goes beyond this proximate, yet ultimately subordinate, relationship of the present evangelical light to the apostolic light of the gospel and suggests a continuity, if not an identity. He revealed this tendency early in his career, when he expressed his admiration for thinkers toward whom he felt an affinity. His enthusiasm for Tauler caused Luther to consider this German mystic almost to be born from the age of the apostles, and in Valla he thought to perceive the remaining ember or new tinder of the primitive Church (10/2:329; 6:183). The most important example of this tendency comes from his late tract, *Against Hans Worst,* in which he argued that the present Church of the gospel was the true, old, apostolic Church. Here Luther enters into the language of his opponent, Heinrich von Wolfenbüttel, and seeks to deny any novelty or innovation that would separate his Church from the true Church. He does not understand his reformed Church as any return to, repetition, or recovery of the Church of the apostles as an historical period. He merely uses the apostolic Church as a guarantee for the integrity of the Word, sacraments, and keys, and he rests the argument for the validity of his Church upon something far more venerable than age or apostolicity, namely the eternal Word which maintains the identity of the true Church in any period. It is in this sense that the former, old Church which had been behind a cloud now shone again. The gospel's re-emergence in an apostolic Church signifies the end. In accordance with the prophecy of Daniel, this event does not look backward to a pristine past but forward to the Last Judgment (51:485–86).

For Luther, therefore, the restored light of the gospel, which had been presaged by Hus and which was now embodied in the present reformation, signified the final event in the Church's life prior to Christ's coming. Yet after the eschatological nature of this event has been emphasized, there still remain aspects in Luther's judgment of his own period which need examination. Accompanying this consciousness of the last time as the present, there moves a sense of urgency and emergency which inheres to the immediate situation but derives from God's lordship over history. By his conception of necessity and his appeal to the exigencies of the situation, Luther manifests a fearless disregard for that authority which bases itself on age, example, and precedent. Indeed he asserts the ever new, unique, and creative nature of events produced by the Word in history.

In urging the Bohemians to break with a tonsured priesthood and accept a ministry based on the Word, Luther allows his conception of emergency or necessity to participate with the Word of God in effecting the new event which pertains to the life of faith:

> They say that it is a new thing and without example to elect and create bishops. I reply: it has even been demonstrated most anciently by the examples of the apostles and their disciples, granted that by the contrary example and pestilential doctrines of the papists, it has been abolished and extinguished. There-

> fore one must strive all the more to reject this recent example of pestilence and recall the ancient and proper example. Then if it may still be particularly new, yet when the Word of God may shine and command, and necessity of souls at the same time compels, the novelty of the thing may move absolutely nothing but the majesty of the Word will. For what, I ask, is not new which faith does? Was it not a new ministry at the time of the apostles? Was it not new that Abraham offered his son? Was it not new that the children of Israel moved across the sea? Will it not be new to me when I pass through death into life? But the Word of God is seen in all these things, not novelty itself; otherwise, if novelty were sufficient to prevent [an action], none would ever believe in the Word of God.
>
> Believe, therefore, brethren, in the Word of God and the novelty in your own example will not move you. For if novelty is worth something why was it not sufficient when you Bohemians alone resisted the popes and you did all that for John Hus? Was not this a new thing and without example, even contrary to the example of the entire earth up to today, when you were not even strengthened with manifest scriptures as you are in this case? If then you alone had ventured to follow, confess, and regard the law, howsoever obsolete and extinct, when there was little or no necessity of souls, why now do you not follow, confess, and regard your abolished law, so supported with the armor and shields of the arsenal of David together with the urgency created by necessity of souls and a wretched captivity? [12:192–93]

Luther's argument from necessity, which sought to persuade the Bohemians in an immediate and practical situation, possesses important implications for the working of God and His Word in history and for the peculiar nature of the present reformation. Luther reveals his unwillingness to separate the concrete dilemma and necessity itself from the activity of God's Word. In the present instance the immediate urgency and concrete dilemma pertain to the Bohemian practice of sending across the Alps for ordination. Necessity arises from this continuation of a false priesthood and the consequent injury to consciences produced by the lack of a public ministry of the Word. Thus the Word of God creates the situation of necessity which makes the same Word of God necessary (12:170–71).

Luther had appealed earlier to necessity as a means of sanctioning a particular act and, in the same year as the tract to the Bohemians, he leaned heavily on the argument from necessity in order to promote his own conception of the ministry (6:407–08; 11:412–14). In all three instances the same question was at stake, a lapse in the administering of the sacraments and the consequent peril to souls. From canon law Luther derived the appeal to necessity in such cases, but he made the legal concept conform to the needs of the evangelical ministry and his own theology.[13] According to his conception of the public ministry only one thing was necessary—hearing the Word (cf. 12:37). Yet the charge of innovation presented a new obstacle to this mandate for reform. By binding the concrete emergency to the activity of God's Word, Luther suggested that both necessity and innovation inhere to the Word and its absolute authority. As he later explained to the ecclesiastics gathered at Augsburg in 1530, what is changed according to God's Word is no innovation, for the eternal Word is both older and newer than anything human. It changes and rules both old and new and cannot be affected by either (30/2:320–21).

13. Luther's statement reads: *Denn nott bricht alle gesetz und hatt keyn gesetze*. Although Luther evidently encountered the concept in the *Decretum*—Dist. 1, c. 11, *de cons.*—Professor Schafer Williams kindly directed my attention to its first definite appearance in the Western legal tradition—the pseudo-Isidorean decretals. Cf. P. Hinschius, *Decretales pseudo-Isidoreanae et capitula Angilramni* (Leipzig, 1863), p. 700: *necessitas legem non habet*. Gaines Post, "The Theory of Public Law and the State in the Thirteenth Century," *Seminar, 6* (1948) 56, suggests even earlier statements of this concept.

In the same year Luther had occasion to restate the intimate association of necessity with the Word. When the Elector John asked his counsel with respect to the election of Ferdinand as Roman king, Luther asserted that nothing was to be undertaken without Scripture or necessity. He observes that all histories teach us that future things do not stand in man's knowledge or power, and where God or necessity does not promote an enterprise it turns out quite differently from what one intended. The Christian, therefore, must remain with God and not without necessity proceed into the uncertainty of a future event (*WBr* 5:699). Ultimately, this necessity relates to that will of God which works immutably, yet without compulsion, and includes human action as an effective *cooperatio* (18:616–17). The outcome of man's cooperation remains with God and its success depends upon God's giving the opportune moment.

Not accidental is Luther's association of the argument from necessity with the ever new nature of acts performed in faith. The attribute of being new possesses no validity or strength in itself, yet it characterizes the life of faith. While Luther was not adverse to using antiquity as an argument, he never based the final authority for an idea or an act upon anything less venerable than the eternal Word of God. At the same time that he rejects any form of novelty in doctrine, he repeatedly emphasizes the fact that the life of the believer cannot be guided by the examples and precedents established by others. Man must face the future aware that by acting in faith he experiences a new and unique event. However numerous the examples may be, the events or instances of faith are without example because always there remain in faith new events, new objects, new persons (31/2:543–44).

Thus for understanding God's action in history, Luther's argument from necessity and his assessment of innovation represent two important aspects of the human cooperation in that divine operation which is history. And for understanding the special nature of this present period of reformation, the elements of necessity and newness play their parts. Any period and any act of history is unique and unprecedented. Particularly true is it of this last age in which God has given the appointed time by the restored light of the gospel. Furthermore, a sense of urgency and even emergency prevails in this period of reformation. For the final abomination has assumed a new and more terrible dimension in this last time, and the Word now presents Luther's own Germany with its challenge and crisis.

> Greater, however, and more difficult are our necessity and cause than ever existed at any time in the Church. For we have against us the dregs and end of the world, that final fury of the pope and Turk who want to and will devour us. [43:397]

The Signs of the End

Once Luther had articulated the Reformation as the restored light of the gospel and the course of the Word in the world, he had to cope in terms both of practical action and of his own thinking with those forces which worked to shape, alter, and even resist the impact of the Word. For the place was Germany and the time the sixteenth century, and the Word's effectiveness could not escape those other forces which existed in time and place and must now react to the Word. The problem therefore becomes one of understanding how the action of the Word relates to the diverse forces which resist it, or how Church history in the last time moves upon the broad stage of Germany in the sixteenth century. This problem centers upon a complex of ideas which associates the movement of the Word in history with contempt for this Word and God's punishment for such human ingratitude. Included in the complex are the influence of the last time and a new aspect to the final abomination. To appreciate this complex of ideas requires a brief consideration of a concept which Luther inherited from medieval historiography.

Few ideas have persisted with such tenacity in historiography as that of the *translatio imperii*. The idea of transference sought to explain the major crises of world history by which supremacy is taken from one people and given to another. This idea first appeared in Roman historiography. Through his *Chronicle* and commentary on the book of Daniel, Jerome introduced it into Christian historiography. At first the idea was used fairly indiscriminately, and it was not until the twelfth century that the number of world monarchies came to be fixed at four in accordance with Daniel's vision.[14] As it developed, the idea of transference was applied to wisdom, virtue, and other forms of human accomplishment as well as to political power. Of greater relevance for the present problem is the fact that both the Old and the New Testaments suggested an idea of *translatio religionis* which was later accepted into the *Glossa Ordinaria*. God's rejection of the Jews for the Gentiles allowed the Middle Ages to entertain an idea of the transfer of religion, grace, or the Kingdom of God.[15]

With Otto of Freising in the twelfth century, all these aspects of the idea attained coherent and definitive expression. In accordance with the book of Daniel, the number of world monarchies was clearly limited to four. Secondly, Otto followed his teacher, Hugh of St. Victor, in reintroducing a familiar medieval theme: the process of world history became a movement of all power and competence from the East to the West. Babylonia had been the mother of arts and sciences, and the transference of wisdom, which great thinkers and heroes had implemented, paralleled the transference of empire. Otto lumped spiritual and secular knowledge together and made Abraham and Moses the highest bearers of the secular wisdom. In Church history proper the East-West movement appeared in the mission of Peter and Paul which the Roman Empire had made possible. The displacement of one holy language by another revealed this same movement. Otto saw monasticism, the veritable heart of the Christian religion, moving from East to West where it was more richly fulfilled. With the completion of this movement

14. Goez, *Translatio Imperii*, pp. 31–39.
15. Ibid., pp. 378–81.

in the West, and with the decay of empire, the end was at hand.[16]

Luther's tract of 1524, *To the Burgomasters and Counsellors,* indicates a general acquaintance with the concept of transference; but whatever he accepted from the common usage of the idea, he distinctively adapted to conform with his theology. For his own conception did not involve a transference of empire or of culture but a transference of the gospel from which all other blessings derived. This course of the Word (*cursum verbi*) he conceived far less narrowly than a direct East to West movement, since he attributed to God greater freedom in controlling this movement. Furthermore, he associated the divine gift with his conception of the opportune moment, which could not be ignored with impunity. In considering the flourishing state of languages, arts, science, and learning among the Germans, he warns his countrymen that their hour, which entails responsibilities as well as benefits, has come:

> Dear Germans, take advantage, because our moment has come. Gather in, while it still shines and is good weather. Use God's grace and Word while they are present. For you should know that God's Word and grace is a traveling object that rains blessings. It does not return to where it has once been. It was with the Jews, but away it went and they now have nothing. Paul brought it into Greece. But again it went away through neglect, and Greece now has the Turks. Rome and the Latin lands have also had it, but away it goes and they now have the pope. And you Germans are not allowed to think that you will have it forever, because it cannot be retained by those who show ingratitude and contempt. Grasp it and retain it, whoever can. [15:32]

On several other occasions Luther reiterated this idea of the Word's course and in each instance the Jews, Greeks, and Romans lay as

16. Ernst Benz, "Ost und West in der christlichen Geschichtsanschauung," *Die Welt als Geschichte,* 1/1 (1935), 490–503. Goez, pp. 112–22.

shattered peoples in the wake of the Word. The Germans, the last people, faced now a similar fate (13:200; 41:196–97; *TR* 4123).

The improved condition of languages, which had been instrumental in restoring the gospel's light, served as Luther's major proof that God had bestowed on Germany its opportune moment (15:31). Luther recognizes that God has visited other lands with this gift, but to the Germans it means their opportunity to shed their reputation as beasts and acquire through the new arts and improved knowledge of languages a competence, honor, and piety both in understanding Scripture and in directing worldly authority. For the gospel has come through the medium of languages. Luther sees the Roman Empire as an instrument which disseminated the two holy languages together with the gospel. Similarly the Turks, by conquering the Greeks, have caused languages to be spread. Where the study of languages expires, the suppression of the gospel follows. With the decline of languages after the time of the apostles, the gospel and faith declined, and the abomination of the Papacy grew out of their ignorance. Through the desuetude of linguistic studies, all persons including the fathers and St. Bernard down to the present participated in that darkness of Scripture which sophists believe pertains to the nature of Scripture. Still exhorting his Germans, Luther claims that the gospel will run clearly where preachers exist who have the linguistic knowledge to expound it (15:36–42).

If Luther could consider languages together with the gospel itself as divine gifts which God transmitted by means of empires, no doubt existed either in this writing or in other statements as to the auxiliary and subordinate relationship of linguistic studies to theology. At this time of Germany's opportunity when both languages and theology flourished together, the supremacy of the latter became immediately evident and persisted in Luther's judgment. Seeking to recover a pure theology long hidden to the Germans, he unearthed treasures in the writings of Tauler, Johann von Goch, Wessel Gansfort, and the author of the *German Theology*. He sought to illuminate their endeavors. Hoping that the future belonged to them, he asserted in 1522 that if Germany ever was the scion of the Lord, it was at this moment. While he admitted that among the four Wessel could not equal Rudolf Agricola in humane letters, he considered the Dutch nominalist far superior to Agricola in purity of theology (10/2:329–30). Luther readily acknowledged, however, the debt owed to humanistic studies by the new theology and its German advocates. Writing to the humanist Eobanus Hess, he stated that languages stood to the reformation as John the Baptist to Christ (*WBr* 3:50). In his judgment of Erasmus before the final rupture he preserved this same relationship. Erasmus had done what he had to do; he called men away from sacrilegious studies and introduced languages. But the archhumanist himself would die like Moses in the plains of Moab without attaining to the better studies in piety (*WBr* 3:96–97).

Germany's hour was upon her. Very early Luther had associated the fact of the gospel's clarity with the necessity for gratitude and adherence to its message (*WBr* 2:149). But he did not have to wait long for the inevitable disappointment. In considering the Peasants' Revolt, he lamented the reception of the gospel in Germany: many persecute it, few read it, even fewer accept it, and those who do are listless, allowing schools, pastorates, and pulpits to fall into decay. Luther could hardly marvel that God punished the Germans for this contempt of the gospel. While all might not be equally responsible for the revolt, he accepted a common responsibility for the gospel's neglect (18:395–96). In 1525 Luther pressed the charge of responsibility upon an ungrateful Germany and articulated the idea that the brighter the light, the greater the punishment for not heeding it (17/1:389).

Amidst the darkening eschatological scene and the growing ingratitude of the Germans, the threat of the Turk assumed an obvious function in Luther's understanding of the last time. Long before Suleiman conquered at Mohacs and began his advance upon Vienna, Luther had adumbrated the main features of his general attitude to the Turkish danger. As early as 1518 he denied any scriptural basis for fighting the Turk. Rather than indulging in a crusade, it would be better to grapple with existing wrongs within oneself and to improve the face of the Church (*WBr* 1:282). A few years later he clearly stated that, through the Turks, God punished Germany's sins; he protested against any form of a crusade and maintained that the first task was self-improvement and the hope for a gracious God (7:443). At the end of the decade, the siege of Vienna by the Turks made necessary a clarification of this position. If Luther accented the eschatological import of the issues, he changed in no sense the main emphases of his argument. In advising his Germans on the proper attitude to adopt, his definition pursued the lines of the Regimente: as a Christian, one must be penitent and oppose the Turk with suffering and a passive martyrdom; as a loyal subject of the Emperor, one must serve and fight in an army which was distinctively imperial rather than Christian (30/2:173–80). By no means were the two responsibilities confused in a new holy war that might force the Apocalpyse.[17]

Other considerations, however, motivated the urgency of Luther's tract on the Turks. At no other time in his life was he so certain of the imminence of the end, and in the months from late 1529 to the early part of 1530 he worked feverishly to understand and incorporate the event of the Turk into the total scheme of history. Returning from the Marburg colloquy, Luther met Myconius in Eisenach and there learned of a mysterious Franciscan, John Hilten. This man had engaged in some rather unusual activities in Livonia and had been imprisoned in the Franciscan monastery at Eisenach from 1477 to 1498. He had prophesied that a man would come in 1516 who would destroy the realm of the monks and correct doctrine. But what interested Luther in this bizarre figure was the Franciscan's commentary on Daniel 7 to 9 and the last chapters of Revelation. Luther appeared to be more than usually importunate in attempting to discover from Myconius more information on

17. But cf. Harvey Buchanan, "Luther and the Turks 1519–1529," *ARG*, 47 (1956), 145–60.

Hilten's application of Daniel 7 to the Turk. Fragments of Hilten's commentary reached Wittenburg and passed through the eager hands of both Luther and Melanchthon.[18] Luther later claimed Hilten as a martyr who had died for holding views similar to his own (53:410).

At the same time, Luther's correspondence and activities indicate that he was moving toward the formulation of his own ideas on the meaning of the Turk. Eschatological images abound. The Germans are exhorted to repentance before the final wrath of God, and Christ is expected to appear and destroy Gog and Magog (*WBr* 5:166–67, 170). To Nicholas Hausmann in November, Luther made the identification of Gog with the Turk, Magog with the pope—the former being the external or worldly enemy, the latter the spiritual or ecclesiastical enemy of Christ (*WBr* 5:176; cf. 28). Working during these months in what he called Johannine haste (*WBr* 5:346), Luther pursued his investigation of the prophets Daniel and Ezekiel and began to associate the Turk and pope more closely. Scripture told of two abominable tyrants who would waste the Church before the Last Judgment. Here he still identified the Antichrist with the Papacy alone, which would work spiritually to destroy the Christian faith. The other tyrant was the Turk, which would effect its purpose physically and externally upon Christ's Kingdom. A detailed examination of Daniel 7 revealed to Luther that the little horn represented the Turk which would succeed the Roman Empire and yet not be as great (30/2:161–66). Shortly afterward in his new preface to Revelation he again associated the Turk with the Papacy and the closing scene of Armageddon. But rather than having the Turk participate in the figure of the Antichrist, Luther contended that when the Devil is unloosed from his millennium of bondage, he brings forth the Turk (*WAB* 7:414, 416).

18. On Hilten, see Otto Clemen, "Schriften und Lebensausgang des Eisenacher Franziskaners Johann Hiltens," *ZKG*, *47* (1928), 402–12. Paul Johansen, "Johann von Hilten in Livland," *ARG*, *36* (1939), 24–50. Leonhard Lemmens, "Der Franziskaner Johannes Hilten," *Römische Quartalschrift*, *37* (1929), 315–47. Cf. *WBr* 5:162, 191–92.

After the moment of extreme eschatological expectancy had passed, Luther continued to exploit this close association of Turk and pope as the respective external and internal wasting of the Church in the last time. He tentatively allowed the Turk to participate in the figure of the Antichrist. But its entirely external nature made Luther unwilling to make a firm identification of the Turk with the Antichrist. Whereas the Antichrist must sit in the temple of God, the Turk was more truly the beast because it stood outside the Church and openly persecuted Christ (42:634–35). When he reflected again upon Daniel in 1538, Luther noted the common origin of Turk and pope at the time of Phokas and found no difference between the two religions except for ceremonies (*TR* 3104b). He associated the two realms of pope and Turk on the grounds that both denied the marital state, and as the two last abominations they would share a common end (51:260; cf. 41: 114–15). When he learned of a reported treaty between the pope and the Turk, he believed that the world would not long exist after such a unique event (*WBr* 10:553). Thus, while he continually linked the Antichrist of the Papacy with the Turks as the apocalyptical people of Gog and Magog, he never fully permitted the Turk to participate in the image of the Antichrist. This double abomination of the last time, which Luther had elucidated, was to be elaborated by his successors. Melanchthon emphasized the twofold nature of the Antichrist in his negotiations with Byzantium, and later protestant polemicists distinguished two Antichrists.[19]

Although the crisis in Luther's understanding of the Turk came in 1529, the major emphasis in his argument only became apparent in his later utterances on this problem. For the Last Judgment still remained impending, and the sins of the German people increased. Consequently, there was a growing emphasis upon the Turk as God's scourge and flail for punishing this ungrateful people. By contending that Germany must expect the Turk until she repented,

19. Ernst Benz, "Melanchthon et l'église orthodoxe," *Irénikon, 29* (1956), 165–76. Polman, *L'Élément historique*, pp. 176–78.

Luther moved on the high plateau of the great prophets. The Turk was the Germans' schoolmaster and must correct and teach them to forego their present sins and security and to fear God. He urged pastors to bring their congregations to public repentance (51:594, 606). He placed little value in Ferdinand's proposed armament against the Turks; they represented God's flail and wrath, and the sins of the Germans were too great for God to grant this people a military victory (*WBr* 9:491–92). Through prayer alone might the Turk be defeated and the Last Judgment hastened (51:614).

As God's scourge for the sins of the German people, the Turk provided Luther with his instrument for attacking social injustice and religious torpor. At the outset of his career he had referred to the papists as the real Turks (6:427; cf. 5:573); now in the closing years of his life he turned the image inward upon his own Germans. Vain appeared all armaments when the true untamed Turks—the spiritual and eternal Turks of avarice, pride, luxury, usury, and contempt for the Word—existed within one's own household (*WBr* 9:548). In their own impiety and contempt for the Word, he and his fellow Germans were twice Turks (*WBr* 10:309). In his *Admonition to Prayer,* Luther's indictment of society included all estates, but he centered his attention particularly upon the tyrants, usurers, and rascals among the nobility who believed that God had given the Germans the gospel and delivered them from papal captivity for their own exploitation and gain (51:588, 623). Luther seemed to be aware of the fact that life for many peasants proved less vexatious under the Spahis than under the regular nobility.[20] In a letter of the same year as this tract, 1541, he expressed his despair over Germany, which had received the true Turks into its nobility, courts, councils, and cities. The Germans fail to pray against the real Turks in their midst but turn their prayers against the obvious enemy. Yet unless God terrifies and humbles the nobility with the tyrannies of the Turks, Germany will continue to

20. Hans Pfeffermann, *Die Zusammenarbeit des Renaissancepäpste mit den Türken* (Winterthur, 1946), p. 167. Cf. *WA* 51:624.

suffer more severely from their tyrannies than from those of the Turk. The nobility together with the princes conceive traps and chains for the peasants and civilians; they avenge the papal servitude with a new oppression of the people (*WBr* 9:547).

Luther's growing dissatisfaction with the upper classes in Germany did not always remain within the conception of the Turk as God's scourge. Luther watched with dismay and chagrin the steady aggrandizements of the princes and nobility in both Regimente and their appropriation of the Reformation to their own advantage. He remarked how the unruly princes now assumed the protection of the papal clergy only in order to intimidate and fleece them (32:487). In criticizing the new Church order of Duke Maurice, he discovered the functionaries of the court infiltrating the churches and controlling the ban. He lamented the confusion of vocations. Just as the Papacy had mixed the Church with polity, now the princes mixed polity with the Church (*WBr* 10:436). Nevertheless, in other instances he could praise the Saxon princes and discover only contempt and malevolence in the nobility, magistrates, civilians, and peasants (43:287).

Germany and the Turk, the Turk and the Antichrist, the light of the gospel and the contempt for the Word—all stand under the pressure of the last time. According to the Word which creates the Church and moves through history, the Christian people finds its locus with the Jews, the Greeks, the Romans, and now with the Germans. And just as the Church maintains and preserves the world, thus Germany must attribute whatever good she possesses to the abject and maligned Christians (44:346). But over Germany in this last time stands the thresher of God's wrath (51:623–24). Contempt always follows the Word, and after the evangelical light there comes the great darkness and then the Last Judgment. What Jerusalem had once suffered would now be Germany's fate (*TR* 5512).

Germany's ingratitude and contempt for the Word possessed another aspect which pertained more directly to the spiritual Regiment and to the life of the Church. In the same breath with which he condemned the nobility for seeking unlimited authority and lamented the lost opportunity of a dying Germany, Luther attacked the false prophets who excited heresies and contemned the Word (*WBr* 10:23). While he could define groups among the sectarians and even distinguished the six heads of the sacramentarian sect, he generally considered Sacramentarians, Anabaptists, and spiritualists as a single entity (*WBr* 4:42). In his strife with the Sacramentarians, he perceived the wrath of God which allowed the Devil to direct darkness and error upon the Germans because of their ingratitude (23:73). The reformer referred to the sacramentarian leaders as his Absoloms and shared something of David's anguish (*WBr* 4:19). It pained him to observe how the sectarian fanatics, who under the Papacy had not dared to breathe, now, when freed from this tyranny by the gospel, taught confidently and became the worst enemies of the Church (32:484; 51:587). In reflecting upon the defection of these groups, he maintained that had they cooperated with him and pressed the single article of justification, together they might have overthrown the Papacy. Instead, by impugning the sacraments, destroying images, and abrogating ceremonies, they had only served to strengthen the Papacy (40/1:354–55).

Luther's identification of the sectarians with the papists derived from a theological judgment chiefly in respect to the distinction between gospel and law and the question of revelation. He accused both of following a working rather than a justifying Christ. The Jews, papists, and sectarians represented those of all ages who, relying on their own merits, confound the corporal with spiritual blessings (40/1:389, 395). He saw the papists and Anabaptists as two wolves with their tails tied together; although they differed in outward appearance and in elected works, in spirit they were one (40/1:36, 605). The Anabaptists and sectarians were the new jurists and sophists who, by foreswearing to hold private property or public office or to defend themselves, effaced in a new way the distinction between the two Regimente (32:300–01). Lastly, the Anabaptists, Sacramentarians, and papists were alike in their abandonment of the gospel for their own special revelations (43:225; 42:112; 50:245).

In Luther's later thought there emerges at times a shadowy notion of what he calls epicureanism or skepticism, by which he understands the significance of the sectarians in the last time. The most extensive statement of this new reality appears in his commentary on the last chapter of Daniel, written at a time when he had experienced the confusion of the sacramentarian strife and when he most keenly expected the Last Judgment. To Luther the whole world seemed on the verge of succumbing to Islam or epicureanism and no more temporal events could be expected (*ARG* 23:6–7). Luther states that he does not describe those external events such as the destruction of Jerusalem and Rome but the spiritual affliction which concerns the life of the Church immediately before Christ's coming. He finds that already in Italy and Rome this last devastation has begun, for there one makes a mockery of faith in an epicurean manner. Children are no longer baptised and the people have been deprived of the Word and sacraments. The Devil now attacks in a double fashion through the Antichrist: on one side by the epicurean contempt for the sacrament and the Word; on the other by anxiety and despair of consciences (*ARG* 23:42).

The latter attack plainly refers to the papists. But if epicureanism pervades the Papacy and is thoroughly eschatological in character, it represents an essentially new, different, and final phenomenon which can only be associated and not identified with the Papacy. The epicureans present a problem, because they appear to embrace two groups: first, those persons, particularly Italians, who perhaps have been influenced by the new philosophies of the Renaissance and have become indifferent to the most fundamental aspects of the Christian faith; secondly, by emphasizing their contempt for the Word and the sacrament of the altar, Luther may mean all the sectarians, not excluding the papists, but most especially those whose views on the Eucharist differ from his own.

The rest of his commentary emphasizes this second possibility as constituting the substance of epicureanism, but he insinuates an element of atheism into the jungle of sectarians. With the restored light of the gospel, the Church not only suffers from the Antichrist but also from the schismatic spirits, heretical Sacramentarians and Anabaptists who add now to the abomination. In this last time avarice, usury, and obstinacy will have advanced so far that the gospel will be banished as with Lot at Sodom and Noah before the Flood. Claiming Lyra and other exegetes for support, Luther then states that after the fall of the Antichrist the world will live freely and assert that there is no God. The world will become so epicurean that public preaching will be silenced and the gospel will be contained within private houses as it was with the apostles before the destruction of Jerusalem. Luther completes his consideration of the last chapter of Daniel by observing that such a lamentable situation would not last for more than 1290 days, because without the pulpit faith cannot endure for long (*ARG* 23:42–48).

To appreciate the eschatological significance of the epicureans in Luther's reflections upon Daniel at this moment, it is necessary to recall some of the variants in the legend of the Antichrist. Disagreement arose as to whether Christ himself or the Archangel Michael would destroy the Antichrist. The uncertainty may have contributed to an important transformation. In Jerome's *Commentary on Daniel,* the idea appears that between the destruction of the Antichrist and the Last Judgment an interval of forty-five days would occur, which represented the difference between the 1290 and 1335 days of Daniel.[21] The existence of an interregnum proved useful to medieval millenarianism. On the other hand, Nicholas of Lyra described this period as one of forty-five years granted for repentance, but through the licentious nature of people it would become a period of *pax et securitas* comparable to that before the Flood.[22]

21. W. Bousset, *The Antichrist Legend,* trans. A. H. Keane (London, 1896), pp. 224–25; 227–29.

22. Nicholas de Lyra, *Postilla . . . super Esaiam. Hieremiam. ezechielem et danielem . . . Tercia pars* (Nuremberg, 1493), EEiii-EEiii^{v}.

Luther now applies Lyra's idea to his own purposes. By the Archangel Michael he understands Christ himself working through the power of His gospel (*ARG* 23:42). Luther writes in 1530 as though the Antichrist had fallen. Because one lives in the last time, he can now open the sealed book of Daniel and peer into those future events which have now become present (*ARG* 23:44). It is in this context that Luther sees the growth of epicureanism. After Michael there would come the growth of heretics and sects, which will silence the public gospel. These last 1335 days would not be generally understood until the Judgment Day itself. To Luther all the signs announced by Peter and Paul had been fulfilled, and in 1530 one only awaited a Noah (*ARG* 23:45–48).

In the eight years that bracket the composition of this work, Luther elaborated upon the philosophical and Italianate nature of epicureanism. In 1526 he described the epicureans as followers of Pliny because they denied that man had a natural awareness of the Deity (19:206). Later he clearly described a group which opposed the pope as well as Christ and Mohammed. While he suggested that this group could be found among the papists and particularly the Italians, he referred to them as the epicureans who believed absolutely nothing, were secure from all heresy and error, and were strong in the epicurean faith (30/2:206). In 1534, when he looked back upon the sack of Rome, Luther claimed that the returning mercenaries brought back the epicurean poison from Italy into Germany (51:236–37).

Yet the curious twofold nature of epicureanism persisted in Luther's thought. This apparent confusion by which he could lump together the entire left wing of the Reformation with the skeptical, philosophical, and even irreligious elements of the Renaissance—this herding together of diverse elements which opposed his own understanding of the Christian faith—points to a dilemma in his personal experience. For Luther found himself confronted with a new spirit which, unlike the Papacy, lay outside the world of Christian dogmatics. His designations of epicurean, skeptical, and atheist for this new phenomenon offer no indication as to its nature, since the terms have another and frequently uncertain content. The best clue seems to exist in his judgment of Erasmus which informs his notion of epicureanism.

In the new age which Luther darkly experienced as the final agony of faith, Erasmus was among the very first to receive the name of atheist; but more significant for the present argument were the accompanying appellations of Lucianist and epicurean.[23] During his controversy with Erasmus, Luther believed to discover in the humanist's use of words and in his neglect of the simple sense of Scripture a trace of skepticism and epicureanism which would consider the Word of God and the future life as pleasant fables (18: 605, 613, 626). In his final judgment of the great humanist, Luther considered him the enemy of all religions, but most particularly of the Christian, and the archetype of epicureans and Lucians (*WBr* 6:566). Erasmus' *Annotations on the New Testament* appeared to Luther as very epicurean and full of poisons, promoting the grammatical at the expense of the evangelical. He accused the humanist of being a cause of the Sacramentarians and attributed to him the rise of Zwingli and the apostasy of Egranus (*TR* 5670). Luther often related the Enthusiasts to the Arians because they both manifested the same doubt about the Eucharist (cf. 23:684–85). Now he completed the chain of relations by making Erasmus an Arian and discovering the common ground in their ambiguities and simulation. He attacks Erasmus' insidious figures and his lubricity. He is an Arian not only in his failure to abide by the simple sense but by calling Christ "man" and by remaining silent about His divine majesty. In respect to Erasmus' preface to his edition of Hilary, Luther finds him justifiably condemned as the promoter of the Arians. Erasmus mockingly tends to deny the Trinity, employs

23. *WBr* 5:28. On the significance of such terms, cf. H. Busson, "Les Noms des incrédules au XVIe siècle," *Bibliothèque d'Humanisme et Renaissance, 16* (1954), 273–83. Busson would suggest that the term "atheist" was new to the western world and first appeared around 1540, a decade after Luther's application of the term to Erasmus.

vulgar and obscene terms to describe the Incarnation, and casts uncertainty upon the most elemental doctrines (*WBr* 7:32–38; cf. *TR* 4899; 30/3:531). In this portrait of epicureanism, Luther recoiled before the devious method and unsettling results of this new spirit. His terrible indictment of the dying humanist could hardly have been intended as an epitaph. For both Luther and history itself, the future belonged to this vague, ill-defined force which eroded the foundations of established Christian belief.

The epicureans were to flourish briefly in a time pressed between the fall of the Antichrist and the impending Parousia. In his lectures on Galatians, Luther urged a comparison between his own experience and that of Paul. As with Paul and his Galatians, the fanatic spirits have arisen and would follow to destroy his work. The sectarians would pervert his own work as they had done to Paul's (40/1:263, 353, 610). When in 1537 he reviled the followers of Schwenkfeld and Enthusiasm in general, he recognized these movements as a sign of the Last Judgment's imminence. From Scripture he knew that after the revelation of the Antichrist, people would become so licentious that they would reject both Lutheran and papal doctrine and recognize no God (50:119–20). In considering his own time, he discovered further scriptural support for the idea that after the ruin of the Antichrist, the epicureans and atheists would run rampant (*WBr* 10:335).

The consequent uncertainty in Luther's view of the final events reflects the twofold struggle in which his life unfolded, and it demonstrates the projection of his own experience into his view of Church history. After 1525 the reformer found himself engaged on two major fronts. On the one hand stood the proliferating sects, the growth of religious torpor—epicureanism. When fighting on this front Luther wrote as though the Antichrist had already fallen by having been revealed and that the destruction of the epicureans constituted the final event. At moments of extreme eschatological expectation he would assert this view. On the other hand stood the Papacy, and the violence of the struggle on this front convinced him that only Christ's coming would resolve the conflict (38:251; 51:553; 50:89; 45:47). Because this view occurs in his more public and important pronouncements, it would appear to represent the main strand of his eschatological outlook. Yet he never relinquished the other view. Although both views can be included in his conviction that the Lord alone would release the hidden Church from its terrible struggle with the world of unbelief, the two strands still persist. Luther's vacillation reflected not an inconsistency in his judgment but the dilemma of his life. There could be no resolution.

Thus Luther gathered up the diverse elements in the existing eschatological scene and fused them with the abominations prophesied in Scripture. The Antichrist, the threat of the Turk, the lost opportunity of Germany, the proliferation of new sects, the increasing lack of zeal for the cause of the gospel—each contributed to the burden and disappointment of Luther's later life. Each contributed to that expectancy and longing for the blessed Day of Judgment which distinguished the eschatological mood of the Reformation from the medieval *dies irae*.[24]

At the same time, a concern for posterity accompanied his eschatological beliefs and a desire to warn future generations struggled with his sense of the imminent end. In the same breath he could even express the two conflicting attitudes (30/2:367:23–25). Moreover, he was not oblivious to the positive and enduring features of the movement which had been his task to initiate. The driving force of the gospel was never forgotten and up to the end of his life Luther demonstrated his awareness of the accomplishments wrought by the restored evangelical light. He marveled that God should have propagated the gospel beyond his wildest hopes (43:331–32). He admonished the younger generation to benefit from the present blessed time; this generation was more fortunate than his own and would never know the dangers and miseries through which their elders had lived (40/1:298; 47:582). Finally, he claimed to leave

24. Preuss, *Prophet*, p. 236. Cf. Paul Althaus, "Luthers Wort vom Ende und Ziel der Geschichte," *Luther Mitteilungen der Luthergesellschaft* (1958), pp. 98–105.

behind him not a melancholy face to the churches but a flourishing one with sound doctrine and sincere pastors which would grow in time (*WBr* 10:335). These statements, all of which derive from the last ten years of his life, cannot be overlooked in attempting to determine the historical judgment of the reformer confronted by the Absoloms of his later experience and the increasing complexity of the final abomination.

Luther and the End

The main principles of Church history as they appear in this period must once again be asserted and secured before bringing this study to its conclusion. In the last time of the Church, God rules over all events as the Lord of history whose actions can only be apprehended by faith. Man acts in the divine lordship as *cooperator Dei*. The Church lives in the world, bears the world, and involves the world's end with its own consummation. Furthermore, any concluding remarks must demonstrate the fact that Luther's view of history is neither an abstraction which exists apart from its participant nor a neat plan which claims to comprehend all acts and purposes and seeks to order events in terms of its own image. As a present divine operation history reveals no predictable pattern to Luther but only to its Lord and Author.[25] It is not an abstraction but something which he lives as a *cooperator Dei*, and lives intensely in the strained atmosphere of the last time.

These principles appear with a remarkable clarity and force in Luther's correspondence during the critical period of the Diet of Augsburg in 1530. Luther had moved down to the Coburg Castle in order to be nearer a scene of action in which he was denied participation. There on his Sinai he set up the three tabernacles to the work which he sought to accomplish: one to the Psalms, one to the prophets Jeremiah and Ezekiel, and one to the *Fables* of Aesop.

25. Cf. Georg Merz, *Glaube und Politik im Handeln Luthers* (München, 1933), pp. 43-44.

While waiting for the arrival of his writing case, he acquainted himself with his new residence—its occupants and watchmen, its towers and chambers, and his own two rooms with their northern exposure upon the Thuringian Forest (*WBr* 5:285–87).

As with his followers at Augsburg who must await the leisurely advance of the recently crowned Emperor, Luther had also to wait now for his writing case and, with greater impatience in the subsequent months, for news from the decisive scene of action. In order to dispel the thoughts which crowded through his mind, he indulged his fancies during a brief period of enforced inaction. Outside, in a thicket below his window, the daws and crows gathered and held their own diet. Day and night, incessantly, he could hear their cries which blended into a monotone. In young and old, great and small, he could observe the single black color of their bodies and the gray of their eyes. Amidst this diet of daws he noted the proud bearing of their princes and great ones and could perceive an entire nobility. In this vast gathering the emperor had not yet appeared. Luther meditated upon their molestation of the corn, barley, and wheat of the surrounding domain, and his mind turned inevitably to the papists and sophists who, chattering monotonously, abused and pillaged the goods of another kingdom. It was spring and he could rejoice in hearing the first nightingale. But to the south at Augsburg, his friend Melanchthon found himself engaged on several fronts with the medieval Church and empire—the traditional authorities of Latin Christendom. For the cause of the gospel and for the hidden Church it was a moment of grave crisis (*WBr* 5:289–95).

During the subsequent months a significant correspondence came to pass between the Coburg and Augsburg that revealed the different outlooks and temperaments of the two great leaders of the Reformation: Melanchthon—patient, careful, irenic, a giant in any age, yet dwarfed by the colossal dimensions of his colleague; Luther, who exhorted, admonished, importuned—decisive in his disapproval, swift to indignation, uncompromising in his convictions, highly critical, frequently irritable, the banner of faith. Although the latter often lashed out with impatience and dissatisfaction, the correspondence reflects a profound, mutual regard and an enduring partnership. Yet despite a curious harmony and complementing of abilities which constituted their collaboration, seldom did this partnership appear under greater strain than during these trying weeks. Melanchthon began from a natural distaste and dreadful fear of all strife and controversy. While zealous in proclaiming true evangelical doctrine, he sought the far more difficult goal of ecumenical peace and unity. Luther began with the conviction that strife and controversy were an essential feature of Church history and the life of faith. Certain of God's effecting action in history and of the world's imminent end, he found an ecumenical concord neither possible nor desirable.

When Melanchthon revealed himself to be worn with his anxieties and efforts, Luther explained to his colleague that his cares did not result from the magnitude of the cause but from the magnitude of their unbelief. It was Melanchthon's philosophy not his theology which vexed him (*WBr* 5:399–400). Then Luther confronted his friend with the God who was Lord of history and to whom man must respond in faith:

> The end and outcome of the cause torments you because you are not able to comprehend it. But if you were able to comprehend it, I would not want to have any part of this cause, much less be its author. God has placed it in a certain common place which you have neither in your rhetoric nor in your philosophy: it is called faith and includes all that man does not see or understand. If someone attempts to make it visible, apparent or comprehensible, as you do, He repays the person's labor with cares and tears as you are repaid with all of us vainly remonstrating. The Lord has declared himself to reside in thick darkness and lurk in secret places. Who wills something, God makes it otherwise. If Moses had sought to compre-

> hend the outcome as to how he would escape the army of Pharaoh, Israel might still today be in Egypt. May the Lord increase the faith in you and in all of us. [*WBr* 5:406]

Luther's complete recognition of himself as a participant in God's cause now passed from the realm of cold doctrine in his teaching on the *cooperator Dei* to a fiery assertion of his own conviction:

> He who created me will be the father of my child, the husband of my wife, my counselor, the preacher of my parish, and better than I myself—yes, even better with me dead than with me alive—I, who impede with my life His work (*illud*).
> [*WBr* 5:418]

Nor is God obligated to effect His work through the present supporters of His cause.

> If we prove unworthy, let it be done through others.
> [*WBr* 5:400]

Nor does there exist any question as to the justice of the cause. Throughout there runs the certainty that God will protect and preserve His Church and lead it out into that future kingdom:

> While you contemn your life, you fear for the public cause. As regards the public cause, I am strong and undisturbed because I know with certainty that it is just and true, even the cause of Christ and of God. . . . Thus I am almost a safe spectator and these threatening and ferocious papists do not affect me. If we fall, Christ will fall with us, indeed that ruler of the entire world. And if such were possible, still I would prefer to fall with Christ than stand with Caesar . . .
>
> But in vain do I write this because you continue to rule those

> matters rationally according to your philosophy . . . and you kill yourself. Nor do you see that the cause wishes to be acted beyond your hand and counsel, even beyond your care. May Christ prevent it from coming into your hand and counsel, although you still pertinaciously desire it; then we would all perish in one glorious holocaust. . . . I pray, have prayed, and will pray for you, nor do I doubt that I am heard, for I feel that Amen in my heart. If what we want will not be done, nevertheless what is better will be done. For although everything in the world may indicate the contrary, we expect a future kingdom. [*WBr* 5:412–13]

Behind this important collaboration and the final achievement of the Augsburg Confession lay a basic and most fateful conflict in outlooks. In this passionate correspondence Luther's statements concerning God as the Lord of history, the Church's continuity as a recognition in faith of this divine omnipotence, man's activity in history as *cooperator Dei,* and that strife which Christian faith introduces into the world—all these statements were taken seriously and projected themselves from the learned treatises into the counsels and actions of history. Melanchthon had no reason to question the fundamental principles of his friend as statements of doctrine. Yet in actual practice he operated from different assumptions and with different intentions. His humanistic training and his respect for the fathers made him more sensitive to the ancient traditions of the Church and more desirous of preserving the old polity in a modified form.[26] Melanchthon revealed an unwillingness to dissolve the bond with Rome and endanger both an ecumenical unity and European civilization. He appeared as the great representative of a historical Christendom to Luther, who rebuked his young colleague for his excessive concern for posterity and the public peace and his anxiety in attempting to fashion the future. Man could not improve upon

26. Friedrich Wilhelm Kantzenbach, *Das Ringen um die Einheit der Kirche im Jahrhundert der Reformation* (Stuttgart, 1957), pp. 111–16.

the divine Providence (*WBr* 5:417–18). Luther opposed the power of faith to his friend's historical and philosophical considerations as well as to his feeling of responsibility for the Christian unity of the West. For Luther, historical action signified an obedience to the first commandment; if one proceeded according to a preconceived historical image, one no longer obeyed. In history there existed only the commands of God, not the constructions of men.[27] Although Luther's basic principles of Church history stand forth magnificently expressed in these letters, the correspondence also reveals the significant differences between the two giants. And these differences boded ill for the future of Luther's ecclesiology and conception of history.[28]

The latter part of this correspondence illuminates another area of Luther's thought—the distinction between the Regimente and the relationship of the Regimente to the impending Judgment Day. When the negotiations at Augsburg turned to a possible reconciliation in doctrine, Luther became increasingly restless and urged the necessity of discontinuing them. Employing the imagery of Greek drama, he believed to see the epitasis or paroxysm of the Diet in this last theater of history (*WBr* 5:500; cf. 416, 458, 471, 472). Luther enjoined his followers at Augsburg not to seek a doctrinal compromise or concord, for Christ and Belial could not be united. Dogmatic unity was plainly impossible unless the pope wished to abolish his Papacy. On the other hand, he expressed the hope that political concord and peace might be achieved. The duty and the achievement of the evangelicals existed first in making their public confession and secondly in seeking peace (*WBr* 5:458–59, 470, 577–78). But when it appeared that important concessions might

27. Merz, pp. 41–44.

28. These lines were written before the important work by Peter Fraenkel, *Testimonia Patrum* (Genève, 1961), came to the author's attention. Fraenkel clarifies the critical attitude of Melanchthon in his appeal to the fathers and his refusal to consider any period of the past as normative for the Church. The study sketches Melanchthon's view of Church history, which, if it differs significantly in some of its emphases, agrees in its main outlines with that of Luther.

be made for the sake of peace, Luther warned that more was to be feared from his own party than from his adversaries. It was not for man to divine future wars but to believe and to confess (*WBr* 5: 628–29).

Apart from the doctrinal dissension which would persist to the end, Luther's explicit hope for peace and political agreement is significant both for the distinction between and the coordination of the two Regimente. It reflects his definite conservatism in matters relating to the worldly Regiment—a conservatism which derived directly from his imminent eschatology. In all his actions and thoughts Luther attempted to prepare men for the coming Kingdom of God which would consummate history on the Judgment Day. Any form of disorder, war, or anarchy disturbed the world by making it difficult for God to build His kingdom. God's impending solution to all human problems made it impossible for Luther to support any radical reform in the worldly Regiment or to follow the revolutionary minds and visionaries of his day. The imminence of his eschatology has well been designated as the limiting principle to all his pronouncements and actions in the worldly Regiment.[29]

For the Church, however, its struggle in the world and against the world must go on to the end. Unlike her two previous temptations or persecutions, the Church could expect no relief or solution from any emperor or temporal ruler in this final temptation of the Antichrist. Only the Lord's return would destroy the *Endechrists Regiment*. The very fact that the Antichrist had been revealed attested to the imminence of Christ's reappearance. Until that moment the Church as a poor little band must remain, strengthened by prayer, doctrine, and admonition. Until the end the Lord would disturb the Antichrist and all his papal following, which continued to include the greater numbers and power (45:47). The abomination must remain in the holy Church up to the Judgment Day and the

29. Merz, p. 17. George W. Forell, *Faith Active in Love* (New York, 1954), pp. 156–60, 175.

Church must guard itself from corruption till the moment of Christ's return (51:553).

In his unique propensity for merging his own personality with the biblical figures whom he described, Luther identified himself more closely with Noah than with any other person. In Noah he early discovered that strength of conviction which enabled one man to stand against a licentious, ungrateful world and through faith endure the terrible temptations, the haunting doubts: Are you alone wise? Are you alone pleasing to God? Is it that only you are not mistaken? Do you really consider all the fathers to have erred (42:300; cf. 14:189; 24:173)? The situation of a single man, who was confronted by the unbelief of all the world and had nothing but the Word of God to rely upon, captured his imagination and understanding. He could even suggest in 1541 that just as one hundred twenty-six years elapsed between Adam's death and Noah's birth, similarly the same number separated Hus from Luther (53:40).

Toward the end of his career these references became less personal and more general in their significance; the emphasis moved from the person of Noah to the time of Noah. In the twilight of his life and in the darkening shadows of an age which drained rapidly under an eschatological pressure toward its prophesied end, Luther returned often to Christ's prediction that the last days would be like those of Noah before the Flood. The world strained toward an age comparable to Noah's (42:320–21, 288). He continued to make this observation in the letters of his final years (*WBr* 10:309, 335, 370). To him nothing save the contempt of the world before the Flood could adequately express this present incredible neglect of the Word. When some calamity was impending God sent the Word beforehand, almost as an announcement, inviting the impious to repentance and the pious to patience. It had been this way with Noah before the Flood, with Christ and the apostles before the destruction of Jerusalem, and now in the present age God imparted the pure gospel before the advent of the Turk and the terrible day of judgment upon Germany (25:357–58). But the world, not knowing and not desiring to know anything about Christ, was world and would continue to be world. As it had been before the Flood, before the overthrow of Sodom, before the Babylonian Captivity, the destruction of Jerusalem, the sack of Rome, the misery of Hungary and Greece, so it now occurred before the destruction of Germany (*WBr* 10:442–43). The opposition between the Church of the Word and the unbelief of the world could only be resolved by the final conflagration of Christ's coming.

Shortly before his death, Luther wrote to a friend concerning the present evangelical light and the apparent insignificance, yet all-encompassing meaning, of its few adherents—this small group, this hidden Church, engaged in its last and most terrible struggle with a world of unbelief:

> I believe that we are the last trumpet which prepares for and precedes the advent of Christ. Therefore, although indeed we are infirm and scarcely do we sound in the presence of the world, yet we sound greatly in the assembly of the heavenly angels who will follow us and our horn and thus make the end. [*WBr* 11:59]

EPILOGUE

THE PRESENT STUDY began with the admission that Luther was not a Church historian. Nevertheless, it proceeded in the conviction that there existed in his thought a definite, if implicit, view of Church history. It ends with the assertion that this view represents a major expression of the Christian interpretation of history.

In its broadest implications, Church history for Luther revealed that view of history which arises from the acceptance of Jesus Christ and the doctrine of the Atonement. Augustine had given to this understanding of history its definitive pattern, and from him Luther adopted some distinctive features. One of the most important was that of the idea of two communities or kingdoms differing in their origins, orientations, and ends and opposing each other throughout all time. The persisting difficulty in understanding the precise meaning of Augustine's *civitates* has its counterpart later in a similar confusion concerning Luther's intention in the Regimente and the kingdoms. For both Augustine and Luther struggled to express a common mystery and truth: that the meaning of history lies hidden with God's redemptive purpose, which, working in the world, creates a holy people; and that this people must remain historically bound to the divinely created orders, scattered and unidentified in a *corpus permixtum* until released and brought together in that future Kingdom of God at the end of the *procursus* or historical course.[1]

Luther shared with Augustine many of the ideas common to the Christian understanding of history: God as Lord of history, the central and eschatological event of Jesus Christ, and the one-directional movement of history toward that consummation which ever remains with God. Yet important differences distinguished the two men. Only the most salient may be noted here. Unlike Augustine, Luther lived and thought in the shadow of the impending end of this historical course; his eschatology reflected that of the New Testament. Secondly, the themes of this history for Luther were faith and unbelief. These themes do not pertain to Augustine in the same way. While the latter occasionally employed the terms, they could never claim to be the controlling principles of his theology and ecclesiology as they were for the German reformer. *Amor sui* and *amor Dei* remain the constitutive principles of Augustine's historical view. To attribute to him faith and unbelief as definitive principles is to perpetuate an imprecision and to distort his theology.[2] Finally, the Church was fully and really present for Luther from the beginning of time and was not prefigured before Christ's birth. Much as he owed to the great African doctor, Luther's view of history was biblical rather than Augustinian; in every feature it imparted its scriptural origins, and in the reformer's doctrine of the Word of God it rested upon the substance of Scripture.

It is easy to magnify and exaggerate the differences between Luther's view of Church history and that of the fathers. The twentieth century is the heir to only fragments of the Christian

1. On the significance of *procursus*, see Theodor Mommsen, "St. Augustine and the Christian Idea of Progress," *Journal of the History of Ideas*, *12* (1951), 370–72.

2. See the otherwise superb study of Heinrich Scholz, *Glaube und Unglaube in der Weltgeschichte*. Karl Löwith, *Meaning in History* (Chicago, 1957), p. 170, follows Scholz.

world of thought. To a person standing within this intelligible structure and observing its intellectual proponents, the differences appear to be greater and more momentous than for one who observes these same distinctions from the outside. Indeed one must be satisfied with shades of differences and new emphases. Augustine's Church did begin with Adam, yet it never had the concrete reality that Luther gives it in his treatment of the patriarchs. On the other hand, the pedagogical element—the sense of growth and development—is present in Luther, but it never achieves the emphasis which it enjoyed with the fathers. For Augustine as well as for all the fathers and the Scholastics, the Church was a *congregatio fidelium*, yet faith did not have the constitutive force which it possessed with Luther. The German reformer shares with his predecessors all the elements of a Christian understanding of history but in different proportions. The centrality of faith inevitably produces an emphasis upon the identity of the Church at all times and the existential reality of personal commitment; it tends to undermine typology and allegory and to obscure the sense of growth, learning, and accumulation.

In estimating the influence of Luther upon historiography, one cannot treat an implicit view of Church history as a factor. One can only refer to the impact of Luther's thought upon the historical understanding of the sixteenth century. In general, the Reformation re-established the transcendental perspective of God upon history.[3] On the one hand, the presence of God's judgment upon history reasserted the essentially inward nature of the Christian Church while endangering its visible, external universality. On the other hand, the presence of Christ at all moments of time emphasized the importance of personal experience and, through the immediacy of the divine relationship, gave a deeper meaning to the individual events and persons of history. This new meaning and its significance for historical thought can best be seen in Luther's treatment of typology.

3. Karl Holl, "Die Kulturbedeutung der Reformation" in *Ges. Auf.*, *1*, 523.

The relation between type and antitype is figural rather than causal; both historical events obtain their meaning from a divine plan which stands above and outside of history. Although Luther had recourse to typology, his belief in Christ's abiding presence at all moments of history serves to spring the typological system of two polar events. To the Christian believer in any period, the fulfillment of the promise is present behind all the figures and words of the prophets. Luther allows the events of the Old Testament to assume their own worth outside of a typological system. The result was not a simple replacement of a figural with a causal view of history. Nevertheless, the new depth and meaning given to temporal events and persons as bearers of God's activity enhanced the worth of the individual historical factor and signified an important departure from medieval forms of thought.[4]

The effect of Luther upon historical thought is readily perceptible in other areas. Protestantism perpetuated Luther's attitude toward the Papacy as the Antichrist and continued to employ many of the historical arguments which the reformer had incorporated into his polemic.[5] Of greater significance, however, was the struggle over the sources and validity of theological doctrines which had begun at Leipzig. The controversy raged throughout the century and prepared the ground for the scientific history of Christian doctrine.

In respect to the *Magdeburg Centuries* of Flacius Illyricus, the influence of Luther produced a decisive shift in the understanding of Church history. Flacius consciously broke with Eusebius and his school and made doctrine rather than the narration of persons and events the main theme of Church history.[6] The subsequent emphasis upon pure doctrine demonstrates how Luther's successors struggled to continue the individual elements of their great predecessor's

4. On this idea, see the perceptive article by Hans Martin Müller, "Die Figuraldeutung und die Anfänge der Geschichtstheologie Luthers," *Kerygma und Dogma,* 7 (1961), 221–37.

5. On this point, see Preuss, *Antichrist,* pp. 183–274.

6. Polman, *L'Élément historique,* p. 216.

theology but allowed its richness, breadth, and import to elude them. As representative of the Melanchthonian school, Veit Dietrich felt the necessity of supplying the present pure doctrine with a definite form in order that the fate of the primitive Church might not be repeated. The future of the Church remained secure; a renewed fall became impossible if true doctrine succeeded to posterity. This attitude betrayed an anxiety before the historical development and before history itself.[7] Such an anxiety was quite alien to Luther with his fearless rejection of all historical absolutes.

Luther's view of Church history depended upon his doctrine of the Word for its persistence. But, with remarkable rapidity, the traditional forces moved in to obscure and extinguish the evangelical and kerygmatic quality of theology for which the reformer had worked during his lifetime. In his effort to oppose the Melanchthonian interpretation of justification, Osiander sought to maintain Luther's doctrine on this crucial point. In effect, however, he undermined the evangelical conception of the Atonement and Luther's understanding of the Word as the divine announcement and imparting. Osiander separated Scripture and Word and left the door open for the theory of a verbal inspiration. On the other hand, Bucer separated Word and Spirit and moved nearer to a verbal and mechanical inspiration of the Bible. The reintroduction of Aristotle and philosophy into theology served to bury Luther's conception of the Word of God. With the Melanchthonian school and Lutheranism, the Word of God was no longer understood as the proclamation of God but as doctrine. Luther's unity of outer and inner Word dissolved before individual proofs and arguments.[8]

The recovery of the kerygmatic quality of Scripture in modern theology has, in many respects, brought Luther closer to the twentieth century than he ever was to his contemporaries. With this

7. Meinhold, *Die Genesisvorlesung,* pp. 93–94.

8. On the collapse of Luther's doctrine of the Word, see Bornkamm, *Wort,* pp. 46–55; Gustaf Aulén, *Christus Victor,* trans. A. G. Herbert (New York, 1957), pp. 123–28; Jaroslav Pelikan, *From Luther to Kierkegaard* (St. Louis, 1950), pp. 24–48.

new appreciation of Luther's work and particularly of his doctrine of the Word, ecclesiology and the understanding of Church history have been affected. For each there exists the possibility of losing its narrow doctrinal shackles and of reinterpreting itself in the light of the Word of God. The view of Church history implicit in Luther's works continues to provide the fundamental assumptions underlying one of the main types of Church history. The history of the Church appears as the history of the proclamation of the Word of God and its effects upon the world.[9]

Luther's view of Church history persists. It persists, however, not as something *sui generis* but as derivative from the great reformer's theology and as expressing the central themes of the biblical understanding of history. The strictly historical elements of this view disappear; the Papacy as the Antichrist, the imminence of the end, the polemical context—these fall away. What remain are the permanent features of any Christian understanding of history, raised now to a new level by that distinctively Lutheran factor, the redemptive activity of Christ which impinges upon every moment of time. Thus emerges a Christian view of history: God transcendent as Lord of history, the Church as a poor remnant, the centrality of faith, the continuing fact of apostasy, the struggle with the world, the hope for the future kingdom. And active throughout the entire *procursus*—distinguishing, redeeming, and maintaining the faithful—moves the Christ who is present.

9. For contemporary statements of this view, see Heinrich Bornkamm, *Grundriss zum Studium des Kirchengeschichte* (Gütersloh, 1949), p. 17; and particularly Gerhard Ebeling, "Kirchengeschichte als Geschichte der Auslegung des Heiligen Schriften," *Sammlung Gemeinverständlicher Vorträge und Schriften aus dem Gebiet der Theologie und Religionsgeschichte, 189* (Tübingen, 1947).

BIBLIOGRAPHY

Althaus, Paul, *Communio Sanctorum: Die Gemeinde im lutherischen Kirchengedanken, I Luther,* München, 1929.

—— "Luthers Gedanken über die letzten Dinge," *Luther-Jahrbuch, 23* (1941), 9–34.

—— "Luthers Wort vom Ende und Ziel der Geschichte," *Luther: Mitteilungen der Luthergesellschaft, 3* (1958), 98–105.

Arquillière, H. -X., *L'Augustinisme politique,* Paris, 1934.

Auerbach, Erich, *Scenes from the Drama of European Literature,* New York, 1959.

Aulén, Gustaf, *Christus Victor: An Historical Study of the Three Main Types of the Idea of Atonement,* trans. A. G. Herbert, New York, 1957.

Bakhuizen van den Brink, J. N., "La Tradition dans l'église primitive et au XVIe siècle," *RHPR, 36* (1956), 271–81.

—— "Traditio in de Reformatie en het Katholicisme in de zestiende eeuw," *Mededelingen der Koninklijke Nederlandse Akademie van Wetenschappen, 15* (Amsterdam, 1952), 27–71.

Bauer, Karl, *Die Wittenberger Universitätstheologie und die Anfänge der deutschen Reformation,* Tübingen, 1928.

Baumgartner, Ch., "Tradition et magistère," *RSR, 41* (1953), 161–87.

Benz, Ernst, "Die Geschichtstheologie der Franziskanerspiritualen des 13. und 14. Jahrhunderts nach neuen Quellen," *ZKG, 52* (1933), 90–121.

—— "Luther et l'église orthodoxe," *Irénikon, 28* (1955).

—— "Melanchthon et l'église orthodoxe," *Irénikon, 29* (1956), 165–76.

——— "Ost und West in der christlichen Geschichtsanschauung," *Die Welt als Geschichte, 1* (1935), 488–513.

BERGER, HEINRICH, *Calvins Geschichtsauffassung,* Zurich, 1955.

BEYER, HERMANN WOLFGANG, "Gott und die Geschichte nach Luthers Auslegung des Magnificat," *Luther-Jahrbuch, 21* (1939), 110–34.

BIZER, ERNST, *Fides ex Auditu,* Neukirchen Kreis Moers, 1958.

BLANKE, FRITZ, "Miszellen zu Luther," *Zeitschrift für systematische Theologie, 4* (1926), 235–39.

BOAS, GEORGE, *Essays on Primitivism and Related Ideas in the Middle Ages,* Baltimore, 1948.

BOEHMER, HEINRICH, *Martin Luther: Road to Reformation,* trans. John W. Doberstein and Theodore G. Tappert, New York, 1957.

BORNKAMM, HEINRICH, *Grundriss zum Studium der Kirchengeschichte,* Gütersloh, 1949.

——— *Luther und das Alte Testament,* Tübingen, 1948.

——— *Luthers geistige Welt,* Lüneburg, 1947.

——— *Das Wort Gottes bei Luther,* München, 1933.

BOUSSET, W., *The Antichrist Legend,* London, 1896.

BOUWSMA, WILLIAM J., *Concordia Mundi: The Career and Thought of Guillaume Postel 1510–1581,* Cambridge, Mass., 1957.

BUCHANAN, HARVEY, "Luther and the Turks 1519–1529," *ARG, 47* (1956), 145–60.

BUSSON, H., "Les Noms des incrédules au XVIe siècle," *Bibliothèque d'Humanisme et Renaissance, 16* (1954), 273–83.

CAMPENHAUSEN, HANS FREIHERR VON, "Reformatorisches Selbstbewusstsein und reformatorisches Geschichtsbewusstsein bei Luther 1517–1522," *ARG, 37* (1940), 128–49.

CARION, JOHAN, *Chronica,* Wittenburg, 1532.

CHENU, M. D., " 'Authentica' et 'Magistralia': Deux lieux théologiques aux XIIe–XIIIe siècles," *Divus Thomus: Commentarium de philosophia et theologia,* Piacenza, 3e série, *2* (1925), 257–85.

COHN, NORMAN, *The Pursuit of the Millennium,* London, 1957.

COLLINGWOOD, R. G., *The Idea of History,* Oxford, 1946.

CONGAR, YVES, "Ecclesia ab Abel," *Abhandlungen über Theologie und Kirche: Festschrift für Karl Adam,* ed. Marcel Reding (Dusseldorf, 1952), pp. 79–108.

COURCELLE, P., "Luther interprète des Confessions de Saint Augustin," *RHPR, 39* (1959), 235–50.

COURVOISIER, JACQUES, "De la Réforme comme principe critique du protestantisme," *Verbum Caro, 7* (1953), 11–24.

CRANZ, F. EDWARD, *An Essay on the Development of Luther's Thought on Justice, Law, and Society,* Harvard Theological Studies, 19, Cambridge, Mass., 1959.

CULLMANN, OSCAR, *Christ and Time,* trans. Floyd V. Filson, Philadelphia, 1950.

——— *The Early Church,* trans. A. J. B. Higgins and S. Godman, Philadelphia, 1956.

CUSHMAN, ROBERT E., "Greek and Christian Views of Time," *Journal of Religion, 33* (1953), 254–65.

DANIÉLOU, JEAN, *The Lord of History,* London, 1958.

——— "Déluge, baptême, jugement," *Dieu vivant, 8* (1947), 97–112.

——— "Saint Irénée et les origines de la thélogie de l'histoire," *RSR, 34* (1947), 227–31.

——— "La typologie millenariste de la semaine dans le christianisme primitif," *Vigiliae Christianae, 2* (1948), 1–16.

DANNENFELDT, KARL H., "Some Observations of Luther on Ancient Pre-Greek History," *ARG, 42* (1951), 49–63.

DE GHELLINCK, JOSEPH, *Le Mouvement théologique du XIIe siècle,* Bruges, 1948.

——— " 'Pagina' et 'Sacra Pagina': Histoire d'un mot et transformation de l'objet primitivement désigné," *Mélanges Auguste Pelzer* (Louvain, 1947), pp. 23–59.

——— "Patristique et argument de tradition au bas moyen âge," *Aus der Geisteswelt des Mittelalters: Studien und Texte Martin Grabmann . . . gewidmet* (Münster, 1935), *1,* 403–26.

——— "Pour l'Histoire du mot 'revelare'," *RSR, 6* (1916), 151–57.

DEMPF, ALOIS, *Sacrum Imperium,* München und Berlin, 1929.

DENEFFE, AUGUST, *Der Traditionsbegriff,* Münsterische Beiträge zur Theologie, *18,* Münster, 1931.

DILLENBERGER, JOHN, *God Hidden and Revealed,* Philadelphia, 1953.

EBELING, GERHARD, *Evangelische Evangelienauslegung: Eine Untersuchung zu Luthers Hermeneutik,* München, 1942.

——— *Kirchengeschichte als Geschichte der Auslegung der Heiligen Schriften,* Sammlung Gemeinverständlicher Vorträge und Schriften aus dem Gebiet der Theologie und Religionsgeschichte, *189,* Tübingen, 1947.

——— "Die Anfänge von Luthers Hermeneutik," *ZTK, 48* (1951), 172–230.

——— "Die Bedeutung der historisch-kritischen Methode für die protestantische Theologie und Kirche," *ZTK, 47* (1950), *1,* 1–47.

Elert, Werner, *Morphologie des Luthertums, 1,* München, 1931.

Fausel, H., "Luther und Melanchthon während des Augsburger Reichstags," *Theologische Aufsätze: Karl Barth zum 50. Geburtstag* (München, 1936), pp. 405–16.

Fenton, Joseph Clifford, "Scholastic Definitions of the Catholic Church," *American Ecclesiastical Review, 111* (1944), 59–69.

Flesseman-Van Leer, E., *Tradition and Scripture in the Early Church,* Assen, 1954.

Florovsky, G. V., "Sobornost: The Catholicity of the Church," *The Church of God: an Anglo-Russian Symposium,* ed. E. L. Mascall (London, 1934), pp. 51–74.

Forell, George Wolfgang, *Faith Active in Love,* New York, 1954.

——— "Luther and the War against the Turks," *Church History, 14* (1945), 256–71.

——— "Luther's View Concerning the Imperial Foreign Policy," *The Lutheran Quarterly, 4* (1952), 153–69.

Fournier, Paul, "Les Collections canoniques romaines de l'époque de Grégoire VII," *Memoires de l'Académie des Inscriptions et Belles-Lettres, 41* (1918), 271–395.

——— "Un Tournant de l'histoire du droit 1060–1140," *Nouvelle Revue historique de droit français et étranger, 41* (1917), 129–69.

Fraenkel, Peter, *Testimonia Patrum: The Function of the Patristic Argument in the Theology of Philip Melanchthon,* Travaux d'humanisme et renaissance, 46, Genève, 1961.

Franck, Sebastian, *Chronica, Zeÿtbuch und Geschÿchtbibel,* Strassburg, 1531.

Geiselmann, R. J., "Das Konzil von Trent über das Verhältnis der Heiligen Schrift und der nicht geschriebenen Traditionen," *Die Mündliche Überlieferung,* ed. Michael Schmaus (München, 1957), pp. 123–206.

GERDES, HAYO, *Luthers Streit mit den Schwärmern um das rechte Verständnis des Gesetzen Mose,* Göttingen, 1955.

GERRISH, B. A., "Biblical Authority and the Continental Reformation," *Scottish Journal of Theology, 10* (1957), 337–60.

GILLMANN, F., "Romanus Pontifex iura omnia in scrinio pectoris sui censetur habere," *Archiv für Katholisches Kirchenrecht, 92* (1912), 3–17.

GILSON, E., "Église et cité de Dieu chez Saint Augustin," *Archives d'histoire doctrinale et littéraire du moyen âge, 28* (1953), 5–23.

GLOEGE, GERHARD, "Offenbarung und Überlieferung," *Theologische Literaturzeitung, 79* (1954), 214–35.

GOEZ, WERNER, *Translatio Imperii,* Tübingen, 1958.

GOGARTEN, FRIEDRICH, *Demythologizing and History,* trans. Neville Horton Smith, London, 1955.

GRANT, ROBERT M., *The Bible in the Church,* New York, 1948.

GRAVIER, MAURICE, *Luther et l'opinion publique,* Paris, [1942].

GREEN, WILLIAM M., "Augustine on the Teaching of History," *University of California Publications in Classical Philology, 12,* 313–32.

GRIMM, HAROLD J., "Luther, Luther's Critics, and the Peasant Revolt," *The Lutheran Church Quarterly, 19* (1946), 115–32.

GRISAR, HARTMANN, and FRANZ HEEGE, *Luthers Kampfbilder: 3, Der Bilderkampf in der Schriften von 1523 bis 1545,* Freiburg im Breisgau, 1923.

GRUNDMANN, HERBERT, *Studien über Joachim von Floris,* Leipzig and Berlin, 1927.

——— "Die Grundzüge der mittelalterlichen Geschichtsanschauung," *Archiv für Kulturgeschichte, 24* (1934).

HÄGGLUND, BENGT, *Theologie und Philosophie bei Luther und in der occamistischen Tradition,* Lund, 1955.

HALL, GEORGE F., "Luther's Eschatology," *The Augustana Quarterly, 23* (1944), 13–21.

HECKEL, JOHANNES, "Initia iuris ecclesiastici Protestantium," *Sitzungsberichte der Bayerischen Akademie der Wissenschaften: Phil-hist. Klasse,* Jahrgang 1949, 5, München, 1950.

HERDING, OTTO, "Geschichtsschreibung und Geschichtsdenken im Mittelalter," *Theologische Quartalschrift, 130* (1950), 129–44.

HILLERDAL, GUNNAR, "Luthers Geschichtsverfassung," *Studia Theologica, 7* (1953), 28–53.

——— "Prophetische Züge in Luthers Geschichtsdeutung," *Studia Theologica, 7* (1953), 105–24.

HOLL, KARL, *Gesammelte Aufsätze zur Kirchengeschichte, 1,* Tübingen, 1923.

——— "Der Streit zwischen Petrus und Paulus zu Antiochen in seiner Bedeutung für Luthers innere Entwicklung," *ZKG, 38* (1920), 22–40.

HOLSTEN, WALTER, "Reformation und Mission," *ARG, 44* (1953), 1–32.

JEDIN, HUBERT, "Kirchengeschichte als Heilsgeschichte," *Saeculum, 5* (1954), 119–28.

JENKINS, DANIEL, *Tradition, Freedom and the Spirit,* Philadelphia, 1952.

JOACHIMSEN, PAUL, "Der Humanismus und die Entwicklung des deutschen Geist," *Deutsche Vierteljahrschrift für Literaturwissenschaft und Geistesgeschichte, 8* (1930), 419–80.

JOURNET, CHARLES, *The Church of the Word Incarnate,* trans. A. H. C. Downes, New York and London, 1954.

KAMLAH, WILHELM, *Apokalypse und Geschichtstheologie,* Berlin, 1935.

KANTOROWICZ, ERNST H., *The King's Two Bodies,* Princeton, 1957.

KANTZENBACH, FRIEDRICH WILHELM, *Das Ringen um die Einheit der Kirche im Jahrhundert der Reformation,* Stuttgart, 1957.

KELLY, J. N. D., *Early Christian Creeds,* London, 1952.

——— *Early Christian Doctrines,* New York, 1958.

KESTENBERG-GLADSTEIN, RUTH, "The 'Third Reich,' " *Journal of the Warburg and Courtauld Institutes, 18* (1955), 245–95.

KINDER, ERNST, "Gottesreich und Weltreich, bei Augustin und Luther," *Gedenkschrift für D. Werner Elert* (Berlin), 1955, 24–42.

——— "Die Verborgenheit der Kirche nach Luther," *Festgabe Joseph Lortz,* ed. Erwin Iserloh and Peter Manns: *1, Reformation Schicksal und Auftrag* (Baden-Baden, 1958), 173–93.

KITTEL, GERHARD, *Theologisches Wörterbuch zum Neuen Testament, 3,* Stuttgart, 1933.

KOEHLER, WALTHER E., *Die Quellen zu Luthers Schrift "An den christlichen Adel deutschen Nation,"* Halle a. S., 1895.

——— *Dogmengeschichte als Geschichte des christlichen Selbstbewusstseins: 2, Das Zeitalter der Reformation,* Zurich, 1951.

——— *Historie und Metahistorie in der Kirchengeschichte,* Tübingen, 1930.

——— *Luther und die Kirchengeschichte nach seinen Schriften, zunächst bis 1521,* Erlangen, 1900.

KOHLMEYER, ERNST, "Die Geschichtsbetrachtung Luthers," *ARG, 37* (1940), 150–70.

——— "Zu Luthers Anschauungen vom Antichrist und von weltlicher Obrigkeit," *ARG, 24* (1927), 142–50.

KRUGER, GERHARD, "Geschichte und Tradition," *Lebendige Wissenschaft, 12,* Stuttgart, 1948.

KRUMWIEDE, HANS WALTER, *Geschichte in der Theologie Luthers,* Göttingen, 1952.

KURZE, D., "Prophecy and History," *Journal of the Warburg and Courtauld Institutes, 21* (1958), 63–85.

LACKMANN, MAX, "Thesaurus Sanctorum: Ein vergessener Beitrag Luthers zur Hagiologie," *Festgabe Joseph Lortz, 1,* ed. Iserloh and Manns, (Baden-Baden, 1958), 135–71.

LADNER, GERHART B., *The Idea of Reform: Its Impact on Christian Thought and Action in the Age of the Fathers,* Cambridge, Mass., 1960.

LANDGRAF, A., "Sünde und Trennung von der Kirche in der Frühscholastik," *Scholastik,* 5 (1930), 210–47.

LAU, FRANZ, *Luthers Lehre von den beiden Reichen,* Berlin, 1953.

LE BRAS, GABRIEL, "Les Écritures dans le Décret de Gratien," *Zeitschrift der Savigny-Stiftung für Rechtsgeschichte,* Kanonistische Abteilung, *27* (1938), 47–80.

LEVISON, WILHELM, "Bede as Historian," *Bede: His Life, Times, and Writings,* ed. A. Hamilton Thompson (Oxford, 1935), pp. 111–51.

LILJE, HANNS, *Luthers Geschichtsanschauung,* Berlin, 1932.

LITTELL, FRANKLIN HAMLIN, *The Anabaptist View of the Church,* Boston, 1958.

LOCHER, G. W., "Das Geschichtsbild Huldrych Zwinglis," *Theologische Zeitschrift, 9* (1953), 275–302.

LOEWENICH, WALTHER VON, *Augustin und das christliche Geschichtsdenken,* München, 1947.

——— *Luthers Theologia Crucis,* München, 1929.

——— *Von Augustin zu Luther: Beiträge zur Kirchengeschichte,* Witten, 1959.

LÖWITH, KARL, *Meaning in History,* Chicago, 1957.

LOHSE, BERNHARD, "Reason and Revelation in Luther," *Scottish Journal of Theology, 13* (1960), 337–65.

LOVEJOY, ARTHUR O. and GEORGE BOAS, *Primitivism and Related Ideas in Antiquity,* Baltimore, 1935.

LUBAC, HENRI DE, *Catholicism,* trans. Lancelot C. Sheppard, New York, 1958.

LYRA, NICHOLAS DE, *Biblia latina: Postilla fratris Nicolai de lyra super Esaiam. Hieremiam. ezechielem et danielem . . . Tercia pars,* Nuremberg, 1493.

MAURER, WILHELM, "Die Anfänge von Luthers Theologie," *Theologische Literaturzeitung,* 77 (1952), 1–12.

——— "Freiheit zur Reformation der Kirche," *Lutherische Rundschau, 7* (1957), 137–50.

——— "Humanismus und Reformation," *Theologische Rundschau, 3* (1931), 49–74; 104–45.

——— "Melanchthon as Author of the Augsburg Confession," *Lutheran World, 7* (1960), 153–67.

——— "Was verstand Luther unter der Reformation der Kirche?" *Luther: Mitteilungen der Luthergesellschaft, 2* (1957), 49–62.

MCGIFFERT, A. C., *The Apostles' Creed,* New York, 1902.

MEINHOLD, PETER, *Die Genesisvorlesung Luthers und ihre Herausgeber,* Forschungen zur Kirchen- und Geistesgeschichte, *8,* Stuttgart, 1936.

——— "Luthers philosophische und geschichtstheologische Gedanken," *Blätter für Deutsche Philosophie, 10* (1937), 56–73.

MENKE-GLÜCKERT, EMIL, *Die Geschichtsschreibung der Reformation und Gegenreformation,* Leipzig, 1912.

MERZ, GEORG, *Glaube und Politik im Handeln Luthers,* München, 1933.

——— "Das Problem der Tradition in der reformatorischen Theologie und in der protestantischen Kirche der Gegenwart," *Kirche und Kosmos, 1* (1950), 64–76.

MOLDAENKE, GÜNTHER, *Schriftverständnis und Schriftdeutung im Zeitalter der Reformation: 1, Matthias Flacius Illyricus,* Stuttgart, 1936.

MOLLAND, EINAR, "Le Développement de l'idée de succession apostolique," *RHPR, 34* (1954), 1–29.

MOMMSEN, THEODOR E., "St. Augustine and the Christian Idea of Progress," *Journal of the History of Ideas, 12* (1951), 346–74.

Müller, Hans Martin, "Die Figuraldeutung und die Anfänge der Geschichtstheologie Luthers," *Kerygma und Dogma, 7* (1961), 221–37.

Muller (-Bardorff), Johannes, *Geschichte und Kreuz bei Luther,* Schriftenreihe der Luther-Gesellschaft, *2,* Weimar, 1938.

Nigg, W., *Die Kirchengeschichtsschreibung,* München, 1934.

Otto, Bishop of Freising, *The Two Cities,* trans. Charles Christopher Mierow, New York, 1928.

Outler, Albert C., *The Christian Tradition and the Unity We Seek,* New York, 1957.

Palmer, R. R., *Catholics and Unbelievers in Eighteenth Century France,* Princeton, 1939.

Pauck, Wilhelm, *The Heritage of the Reformation,* Boston, 1950.

Pauck, Wilhelm, ed., *Luther: Lectures on Romans,* Library of Christian Classics, *15,* Philadelphia, 1961.

——— "The Idea of the Church in Christian History," *Church History, 21* (1952), 191–214.

Pedersen, E. Thestrup, "Schöpfung und Geschichte bei Luther," *Studia Theologica, 3* (1949), 5–33.

Pelikan, Jaroslav, *From Luther to Kierkegaard,* St. Louis, 1950.

——— *Luther the Expositor: Introduction to the Reformer's Exegetical Writings* (*Luther's Works,* Companion Volume), St. Louis, 1959.

——— "Cosmos and Creation: Science and Theology in Reformation Thought," *Proceedings of the American Philosophical Society, 105* (1961), 464–69.

——— "Church and Church History in the Confessions," *Concordia Theological Monthly, 22* (1951), 305–20.

——— "Luther's Attitude towards John Hus," *Concordia Theological Monthly, 19* (1948), 747–63.

Pfeffermann, Hans, *Die Zusammenarbeit der Renaissancepäpste mit den Türken,* Winterthur, 1946.

Pfister, Rudolf, "Reformation, Türken und Islam," *Zwingliana, 10* (1956), 345–75.

Pflanz, Hans-Henning, "Geschichte und Eschatologie bei Martin Luther," *Deutsche Theologie, 5* (1938), 246–90.

PIEPER, JOSEF, "The Concept of Tradition," *The Review of Politics, 20* (1938), 465–91.

POLMAN, PONTIEN, *L'Élément historique dans la controverse religieuse de XVIe siècle,* Gembloux, 1932.

——— "Flacius Illyricus, historien de l'église," *Revue d'histoire ecclesiastique, 27* (1931), 27–73.

POST, GAINES, "The Theory of Public Law and the State in the Thirteenth Century," *Seminar, 6* (1948), 42–59.

PRENTER, REGIN, *Spiritus Creator,* trans. John M. Jensen, Philadelphia, 1953.

PREUSS, HANS, *Martin Luther: Der Prophet,* Gütersloh, 1933.

——— *Die Vorstellungen vom Antichrist im späteren Mittelalter, bei Luther und in der Konfessionallen Polemik,* Leipzig, 1906.

——— "Was bedeutet die Formel 'Convictus testimoniis scripturarum aut ratione evidente' in Luthers ungehörnter Antwort zu Worms," *Theologische Studien und Kritiken, 81* (1908), 62–83.

REU, M., *Luther and the Scriptures,* Columbus, Ohio, 1944.

RIETSCHEL, ERNST, *Das Problem der unsichtbar-sichtbaren Kirche bei Luther: Darstellung und Versuch,* Schriften des Vereins für Reformationsgeschichte, *50,* 1932.

RITSCHL, OTTO, *Dogmengeschichte des Protestantismus, 1,* Leipzig, 1908.

RITTER, MORIZ, "Studien über die Entwicklung der Geschichtswissenschaft," *Historische Zeitschrift, 109* (1912), 261–341.

RIVIÈRE, JEAN, "Cajétan défenseur de la Papauté contre Luther," *Revue Thomiste, 17* (1934–35), 246–65.

ROUSSEAU, OLIVIER, O. S. B., "La Typologie augustinienne de l'Hexaemeron et la théologie du temps," *Festgabe Joseph Lortz, 2* (Baden-Baden, 1958), 47–58.

RÜCKERT, HANNS, "Die geistesgeschichtliche Einordnung der Reformation," *ZTK, 52* (1955), 43–64.

——— "Schrift, Tradition und Kirche," *Vorträge: Aus der Arbeit des Evangelischen Bundes,* Lüneburg, 1951.

RUPP, GORDON, *The Righteousness of God,* London, 1953.

——— "Luther and the Doctrine of the Church," *Scottish Journal of Theology, 9* (1956), 384–92.

SAARNIVAARA, UURAS, *Luther Discovers the Gospel,* St. Louis, 1951.

——— "The Church of Christ according to Luther," *Lutheran Quarterly, 5* (1953), 134–54.

Saint Augustine, *The City of God,* trans. Marcus Dods, New York, 1948.

Schäfer, Ernst, *Luther als Kirchenhistoriker,* Gütersloh, 1897.

Schmidt, Roderick, "Aetates mundi: Die Weltalter als Gliederungsprinzip der Geschichte," *ZKG, 67* (1955–56), 288–318.

Scholz, Heinrich, *Glaube und Unglaube in der Weltgeschichte: Ein Kommentar zu Augustins De Civitate Dei,* Leipzig, 1911.

Schürer, Emil, *Geschichte des jüdischen Volkes im Zeitalter Jesu Christi,* Leipzig, 1886.

Schwarz, W., *Principles and Problems of Biblical Translation,* Cambridge, Eng., 1955.

Seeberg, Erich, *Gottfried Arnold: Die Wissenschaft und die Mystik seiner Zeit,* Meerane i. Sa., 1923.

——— *Luthers Theologie, 2,* Stuttgart, 1937.

——— *Luthers Theologie in ihren Grundzügen,* Stuttgart, 1950.

——— *Studien zu Luthers Genesisvorlesung,* Gütersloh, 1932.

Skysgaard, Kristen Ejner, "Schrift und Tradition," *Kerygma und Dogma, I* (1955), 161–79.

Smalley, Beryl, *The Study of the Bible in the Middle Ages,* Oxford, 1941.

Spitz, Lewis W., "History as a Weapon in Controversy," *Concordia Theological Monthly, 18* (1947), 747–62.

——— "Veit Ludwig von Seckendorf and the Historia Lutheranismi," *Journal of Religion, 25* (1945), 33–44.

Stange, Carl, "Luther und das Konzil zu Pisa von 1511," *Zeitschrift für systematische Theologie, 10* (1933), 680–710.

Stupperich, Robert, "Die Reformatoren und das Tridentinum," *ARG, 47* (1956), 20–63.

Tavard, George H., *Holy Writ or Holy Church,* London, 1959.

Tierney, Brian, *Foundations of the Conciliar Theory,* Cambridge, Eng., 1955.

Törnvall, Gustaf, *Geistliches und weltliches Regiment bei Luther,* München, 1947.

Torrance, T. F., *Kingdom and Church,* Fair Lawn, N.J., 1956.

Tuveson, Ernest Lee, *Millennium and Utopia,* Berkeley and Los Angeles, 1949.

VASILIEV, A. A., "Medieval Ideas of the End of the World: West and East," *Byzantion, 16* (1942–43), 462–502.

VOLZ, HANS, *Die Lutherpredigten des Johannes Mathesius,* Leipzig, 1930.

VOSSBERG, HERBERT, *Luthers Kritik aller Religion,* Leipzig, 1922.

WARBURG, A., "Heidnisch-Antike Weissagung in Wort und Bild zu Luthers Zeiten," *Gesammelte Schriften, 2,* Leipzig and Berlin, 1932.

WATSON, PHILIP S., *Let God Be God!,* London, 1954.

——— "Luther's Doctrine of Vocation," *Scottish Journal of Theology,* 2 (1949), 364–77.

WINGREN, GUSTAF, *Luther on Vocation,* trans. Carl C. Rasmussen, Philadelphia, 1957.

——— "Justification by Faith in Protestant Theology," *Scottish Journal of Theology, 9* (1956), 374–83.

WOLF, ERNST, "Leviathan: Eine patristische Notiz zu Luthers Kritik des Papsthums," *Peregrinatio: Studien zur reformatorischen Theologie und zum Kirchenproblem* (München, 1954), pp. 135–45.

ZAHRNT, HEINZ, *Luther deutet Geschichte,* München, 1952.

REGISTER

The following register includes all Luther's tracts, prefaces, sermons, and exegetical works used in this study; it does not include the correspondence, *Table Talk,* or *German Bible.* The register has been arranged according to the volume and page in the Weimar edition, with a brief title to identify each work, and the date of composition.

WA	TITLE	DATE
1:154–220	Die sieben Busspsalmen	1517
1:350–74	Disputatio Heidelbergae	1518
1:375–79	Vorrede . . . der "deutschen Theologie"	1518
1:394–521	Decem Praecepta Wittenbergensi	1518
1:522–628	Resolutiones . . . de indulgentiarum virtute	1518
1:644–86	Ad dialogum Silvestri Prieratis	1518
2:1–26	Acta Augustana	1518
2:153–61	Disputatio . . . adversus criminationes . . . Eccii	1519
2:180–240	Resolutio . . . super propositione sua decima tertia	1519
2:250–383	Disputatio . . . Lipsiae	1519
2:388–435	Resolutiones Lutherianae	1519
2:436–618	In epistolam Pauli ad Galatas . . . Commentarius	1519
2:621–54	Contra malignum . . . Eccii iudicium	1519
3:1–652	Dictata super Psalterium	1513–15
4:1–462	Dictata super Psalterium	1513–15
5:1–673	Operationes in Psalmos	1519–21

6:99–134	Tessaradecas consolatoria	1520
6:170–95	Condemnatio doctrinalis—Responsio	1520
6:196–276	Von den guten Werken	1520
6:277–324	Von dem Papstthum zu Rom	1520
6:349–78	Ein Sermon von dem neuen Testament	1520
6:381–469	An den christlichen Adel	1520
6:484–573	De captivitate Babylonica	1520
7:12–38	Von der Freiheit eines Christenmenschen	1520
7:91–151	Assertio omnium articulorum M. Lutheri	1520
7:152–86	Warum . . . Bücher von D. Martin Luther verbrannt sind	1520
7:237–45	Sermon gepredigt . . . von dem Reich Christi	1521
7:259–65	An den Bock zu Leipzig	1521
7:266–83	Auf des Bocks zu Leipzig Antwort	1521
7:299–457	Grund und Ursach aller Artikel	1521
7:538–604	Das Magnificat	1521
7:605–13	Martini Lutheri Responsio extemporaria ad articulos . . . Wormatiam	1521
7:614–88	Auf das . . . Buch Bocks Emsers zu Leipzig Antwort	1521
7:698–778	Ad librum . . . Ambrosii Catharini . . . responsio	1521
8:4–35	Deutsche Auslegung des 67 (68) Psalmes	1521
8:210–40	Der 36 (37) Psalm Davids	1521
8:398–476	De abroganda missa privata . . . sententia	1521
8:477–563	Vom Missbrauch der Messe	1521
8:564–669	De votis monasticis . . . iudicium	1521
10/1/1:1–728	Kirchenpostille 1522	1522
10/1/2:1–208	Adventspostille 1522	1522
10/2:175–222	Contra Henricum Regem Angliae	1522
10/2:311–17	Vorwort zu Wesseli epistolae	1522
10/2:327–30	Vorrede zu Gochii fragmenta	1522
10/3:13–20	Predigten des Jahres 1522. Nr. 2	1522
10/3:65–68	Predigten des Jahres 1522. Nr. 11	1522
10/3:72–80	Predigten des Jahres 1522. Nr. 13	1522
10/3:170–75	Predigten des Jahres 1522. Nr. 30	1522
10/3:371–79	Predigten des Jahres 1522. Nr. 54	1522

32:238–46	Predigten des Jahres 1530. Nr. 28	1530
32:299–544	Wochenpredigten über Matt. 5–7	1530/32
34/1:369–78	Predigten des Jahres 1531. Nr. 39	1531
34/2:360–406	Predigten des Jahres 1531. Nr. 97	1531
34/2:537–46	Predigten des Jahres 1531. Nr. 112	1531
36:219–23	Predigten des Jahres 1532. Nr. 30	1532
37:134–36	Predigten des Jahres 1533. Nr. 33	1533
37:304–07	Predigten des Jahres 1534. Nr. 14	1534
38:171–256	Von der Winkelmesse und Pfaffenweihe	1533
38:257–72	Ein Brief . . . von seinem Buch der Winkelmessen	1534
38:273–79	Vorrede zu Antonius Corvinus	1534
39/1:134–73	Die Disputation contra missam privatum	1536
39/1:181–97	Die Disputation de potestate concilii	1536
39/2:34–91	Die Zirkulardisputation über Matt. 19:21	1539
39/2:145–84	Die Promotionsdisputation von . . . Scotus	1542
39/2:284–336	Die Promotionsdisputation von Georg Major . . .	1544
40/1:1–688	In epistolam S. Pauli ad Galatas Commentarius	1531 (1535)
40/2:1–184	In epistolam S. Pauli ad Galatas Commentarius	1531 (1535)
40/3:476–594	Enarratio Psalm 90	1534/35
41:79–121	Predigten des Jahres 1535. Nr. 13	1535
41:182–203	Predigten des Jahres 1535. Nr. 17	1535
41:239–42	Predigten des Jahres 1535. Nr. 21	1535
42:1–673	Vorlesungen über 1. Mose	1535–45
43:1–695	Vorlesungen über 1. Mose	1535–45
44:1–825	Vorlesungen über 1. Mose	1535–45
45:25–48	Predigten des Jahres 1537. Nr. 5	1537
45:465–733	Das XIV. und XV. Capitel S. Johannis	1538, 1537
47:232–627	Matthaus Kapitel 18–24 . . . ausgelegt	1537–40
49:570–87	Predigten des Jahres 1544. Nr. 34	1544
50:1–5	Vorrede zu R. Barns	1536
50:16–33	Vorrede zu Tres epistolae Ioannis Hussii	1536
50:34–39	Nachwort zu . . . Übersetzung	1537
50:65–89	Donatio Constantini	1537
50:96–105	Ioannis Nannis . . . disputatio mit Luthers Postfatio	1537

INDEX

Date Due

Apr. 2. 64			
APR 14 '64			
JAN 16 '68			
FEB 4 '71			
DEC 16 '74			
OCT 18 '79			
MAR 7 '80			
NOV 18 '80			
OCT 27 '82			